Parenting
with the
Ex Factor

How to raise children in a Complex Family.

Jill Darcey

Although you may find the practices, disciplines, and understandings in this book to be useful, they are made available with the understanding that neither the author nor the publisher are engaged in presenting specific medical, psychological, emotional, sexual, or spiritual advice. Nor is anything in this book intended to be a diagnosis, prescription, recommendation, or cure for any specific kind of medical, psychological, emotional, sexual, or spiritual problem. Each person has unique needs and this book cannot take these individual differences into account.

Copyright © Jill Darcey, 2010

The moral right of the author has been asserted.

No part of this book may be used or reproduced in any manner whatsoever without written permission from Jill Darcey except in the case of brief quotations embodied in critical articles or reviews.

ISBN 978-0-473-16207-8

Published by Complex Family Foundation.
www.ComplexFamily.com

A CIP catalogue record for this book is available from the New Zealand Library.

Edited by Judith Sanssweet; www.ProofreadNZ.co.nz
Cover Design by Lorraine Bailey; www.AsOne.co.nz
Printed and Bound by Astra Print; www.Astra.co.nz
Back Photo by Lester de Vere; www.Lester.co.nz

Every effort has been made to ensure that this book is free from error or omissions. However, the publisher, the author, the editor, or their respective employees or agents, shall not accept responsibility for injury, loss or damage occasioned to any person acting or refraining from action as a result of material in this book whether or not such injury, loss or damage in any way due to any negligent act or omission, breach of duty or default on the part of the publisher, the author, the editor, or their respective employees or agents.

To

my three children

Acknowledgements

My heartfelt thanks to ...

My beloved, Simon, for being beside me. I treasure and passionately embrace the intimacy of our relationship. I admire and respect who you are and your amazing contribution to my life and our family — thank you. Always all ways.

My three children for the privilege of being your mother — you delight, inspire and refresh my world daily. Thank you for all your support and encouragement. I am grateful for our cherished years so far and look forward to our lifetimes together.

My parents; you gave me the best to start my journey of life. I caught energy, creativity and spontaneity. You taught me how to value character, how to see through the issue to the hidden principle, and how to give without trading. Most of all, you impressed upon me the importance of living an authentic spiritual connection.

My friends and family who have believed in me, shown me who I am, and encouraged me when I could no longer hear my heart sing. There are so many to whom I owe gratitude; in naming a few I trust I do not diminish each encouraging word or gesture that cheered me on — thank you to you all! Of specific mention is Fiona - for seeing what I couldn't, and ensuring I didn't sell myself short by taking a normal job; Lynn-Marie - for holding presence when I needed it held; Ann - who has enthusiastically taught me to hear what my beloved feels; Sonya - for friendship; explaining the opposite to me, and how we genuinely celebrate our steps along the way. Christophe and Dana - for the gift of enlightenment, education and love.

My editor, Judi, who turned my text and verbose explanations into a coherent written manuscript. Thank you for 'getting it' and sharing your personal experiences and delights; it all added to the complete enjoyment I felt through the editing process.

My quiet contributors: Helen and Greg, who challenged and chiseled the scope; Robbie, who generously mentored while daring me to do better; Stephen, who saw I had a message to be delivered; Anton, who got me thinking with structure; Lorraine, who calmed nerves and created symbolic brilliance; Lezette, who kept my energy flowing; and Sharon, for your kindness, advice, and support during some harder years.

My clients who have intimately shared their life stories with me over the years, enabling me to continue my education through gaining privileged knowledge and witnessing real results.

Finally, but not least — my Ex and his wife, the children's stepmother. For without you both, I would not have had the opportunity to gain such experience and attain the wisdom. Thank you for sharing in the raising of our three fantastic children.

Table of Contents

Introduction	3
Life Changes	1
Leaver and Leavee	11
Natural vs. Normal	21
Focusing on Yourself	22
Focusing on the Children	27
Inside the Mind Of ...	37
Inside the Mind of the Leavee	38
Inside the Mind of the Leaver	47
Inside the Minds of the Children	54
Natural vs. Normal	57
Focusing on Yourself	60
Focusing on the Children	62
Ages and Stages	71
Stage 1 :: Womb – 12 months	76
Stage 2 :: 6 – 24 months	82
Stage 3 :: 18 months – 4 years	88
Stage 4 :: 4 – 7 years	94
Stage 5 :: 7 – 12 years	101
Stage 6 :: Teen years	107
Stage 7 :: Young Adulthood	115
Beyond ...	120
Concerning the Children	121
Breaking the News	123
Day-to-Day Care	134
Routines	147
Friends & Family	163
Work	171
School	176
Pets	185
Mobile Phones, iPods, Laptops	187

Changing Tack in Parenting	199
Discipline	207
Sibling Rivalry	229
Sexuality	236
The Super Parent	249
Special Events	257
Stepparents	261
Inside the Mind of Your Partner	267
Inviting the Stepparent	276
How To; When Your Partner is Stepparent	278
How To; When Your Ex's Partner is Stepparent	300
The Blended Family	309
Matrimonial Home	309
Legal Matters	313
The Law	313
The Messages	317
The Alternative	325
The Courts	336
Money Matters	339
Income	342
Possessions	348
Working It Out	351
How To Move Forward	356
Refinement	367
Beyond Leavee and Leaver	368
How To Heal Your Ache	370
Five Principles	373
Four Tools	381
Three Attitudes	388
Graduation	395
Getting it Working Well	397
Because They are Children	403
Complex Family Foundation	409
Epilogue	411

Introduction

"Your kids are so well adjusted, Jill, it's great to see — especially after what you've all been through." That was intended to be a compliment, one I had come to accept through hearing it so often, yet it was one that left me somewhat dissatisfied with myself, both as a mother and as a person. The well-meaning praise seemed to carry a judgement with it — that my children were unfortunate and disadvantaged because their parents were no longer married. They were sentenced to live their formative years with a certain disability; they were relegated to a position where they would have to accept second-rate opportunities, development, and goodness from life.

In the early days, I struggled to embrace the heartbreak, distress, and overwhelming sense of failure that came with the divorce. I also found it challenging to entertain even the possibility that some good could come from such devastation and dysfunction. On the surface, my duty-bound sense of goodness and responsibility kept me functioning admirably, but I carried an inner heaviness, an unshakable sense of my children's misfortune at having to live with disruption and the new influences on our daily living. I categorised my divorce as an experience my children had not deserved, and put myself on a never-ending treadmill to make it all better. I constantly worked to fix it, to make it whole, and to compensate for their loss; it was not their doing, they were innocent bystanders caught in the adult drama of their parents' world; they deserved something better.

My story is no different from tens of thousands of others every year; the uniqueness comes from my choice of attitudes and pathways as we moved through the divorce and into our subsequent lives. I soon realised I had chosen a path less travelled, as in looking for resources and guidance, I was astonished by quantities of assistance and support available to those seeking retribution or revenge, but found little available to support a journey of relative harmony and cooperation. I walked a lonely path and experienced how true the saying is, "It is never crowded along the extra mile."

While I can say I have neither the clarity nor knowledge of a sage, it is from a place of inner peace that I have been carried and mercifully granted wisdom beyond my years. It is my intention to pass on a portion of what I have come to value.

I have endeavoured to refrain from the temptation to 'tidy things up' that faces authors who include personal aspects of their life's journey, and hope I haven't strayed too far, or embellished circumstances or events, to present a favourable image of myself while diminishing another.

My family has been gracious in allowing our lives to become a little more widely known than might otherwise have been. They have entrusted me to convey our moments of triumph and gently share our despair as accurately as possible — and I have chosen to give you the normal rather than just the best and the worst.

While the temptation is to highlight those irregular moments of highs and lows in an attempt to present a more dramatic story, that is not the point of this writing. Although this book may entertain a little, that is not its primary intention; rather, its purpose is to share the normality of our daily lives and reflect the significant changes that are a result of the transition in family dynamics. It is intended to impart the practical approaches, yet offer depth, compassion, and understanding for you as you grow forward while you hold the blessings contained in your divorced life.

As I write, I do so with respect and honour for my Ex who shared in giving life to our family. He is a man who, through the bond of creating life, will forever be part of my life — regardless of the choices, circumstances, and differences we live with today.

At times our path has been bumpy, it has felt very broken (shattered really) and beyond split (more like severance), yet we have taken the best and worst, the normal and not so normal, the advantages and disadvantages, and made our family whole again. I wish I could say it has been easy, but that would be nothing short of a lie. It has taken every bit of courage and strength I could muster, while I experimented, learned, practiced, and grew along the way. As I look back today, the journey has definitely been worth it; and I trust this book and all it contains will improve your journey as well.

Chapter One
Life Changes

There's camaraderie even between strangers when you mention "The Ex." Without another word said, there's a tone, a movement of the eyes, and a certain tilt of the head that says, "I know what you mean." There's a recognition that we have walked through uncharted terrain and survived — even if we do carry our battle scars.

Although yelling matches, flying objects, packed suitcases, threats, bribes, lies, courtrooms, lawyers' offices, financial loss, shattered dreams, and children left in tatters are normal, it doesn't have to be this way. It is possible to adopt other strategies, make other choices, break free from the hopeless statistics, and have both parents and family thrive. Successful *parenting*, once you move beyond the relationship your children were born into, has more to do with your attitudes and choices than it does with luck. As difficult as it is to believe, it even has little to do with your Ex or the situations that cross your paths. What it does have to do with are your own attitudes and choices, and those people you allow to influence you. There are no magic wands to wave or quick fixes to take to guarantee smooth sailing ahead, but there are some real principles, tools, and tips 'n tricks that will make the path considerably more gentle and worthwhile for everyone.

Traditional mindset would have us believe marriage is the most significant decision we will make in our lives; while current events show this is no longer the case. The contract made with the person with whom one chooses to have a child (or children) is possibly the most significant personal contract we will ever make. While we frequently outlive our marriages, the children will carry the genes of their other parent throughout their lives. The link is forever — regardless of one's willingness to foster or hinder that relationship.

Complex Family

Broken Homes and Split Families are the accepted phrases to describe a family structure where the parents are no longer living together. While these are the usual terms, if children constantly hear or say they are from a *broken home* or *split family*, the implication and the effect for them is that something is wrong, needs to be fixed, or put back together. Issues do exist — without a doubt they do — and sometimes the family can feel very broken, but when parenting is done well inside any structure, everyone can thrive.

The objective here is to shift our thinking, and the thoughts of our children, by using different words. Altering terminology may seem trivial, but I've come to appreciate the subtle power that phraseology has over our thinking as adults, to say nothing of the effect it has on the minds of our children. As we restate or *reframe* our perspective, we are able to leave the grey cloud that shadows our family's psyche to make us believe we are disadvantaged, and step out into the warm sunlight as we embrace a new way of being a whole family.

This new term is neither good nor bad, advantaged nor disadvantaged, split nor whole, broken nor together, right nor wrong. It casts no judgement; it only describes what is. The new family is a *Complex Family*.

So what is this? In broad terms, it is a family that has been touched by separation, divorce or some form of family breakdown. The family portrait no longer sits comfortably within a traditional photo frame. Many parenting techniques, books, and courses no longer seem practical, or even sensible, because things have simply changed. Regardless of the circumstances surrounding the separation, there is one thing we all have in common — things have become just a tad more complex.

Complexities range from family relationships, friendships, geographical issues, income changes, cultural environments, schedules, discipline, rules, traditions, religious beliefs, expectations, holidays, celebrations, pets, dietary preferences, schooling . . . you name it — it's no longer simple.

> *The Complex Family is a family touched by separation, divorce or some form of family breakdown.*

When you are able to operate successfully as a Complex Family, you will find a greater sense of 'wholeness', a state of being that will surpass both your current expectations and experiences. From my own journey, and from those with whom I've worked whether in friendship, coaching, or counselling, I've learned that it is possible, even probable, to raise marvellous, healthy, happy children, free from the statistically prophesied doom, while living within a Complex Family environment.

Throughout this book, we will take this Complex Family and make it simply *family*. In bite-size pieces, we will work our way through many normal issues and give you real answers that work. Depending on the ages and stages of your family at this moment, you may find particular portions more relevant than others; in spite of that, I suggest you read the whole book, and then put it aside until the moment strikes when you remember, "Ah, I read about that." Take it from the bookshelf and remind yourself of the principles and processes that have worked well for so many.

Each chapter contains insights, issues, and learnings from the parents', and sometimes the children's, perspective. You will be able to read real case studies (names altered for privacy) to deepen your understanding and find specific *How To's* to work with and practice. I have included a sample of Frequently Asked Questions (FAQs) that have come up over the years and some exercises to help bring the learnings into your own personal situation in a practical day-to-day way.

The Children

> *"If you bungle raising your children,*
> *I don't think whatever else you do well matters very much."*
> ...... Jacqueline Kennedy.

Most of us recognise that famous quote from a member of a family struggling with its own issues in the face of public scrutiny and devastating heartbreak. In our culture, where extended family bonds are diminishing, we live with a strange combination of increased globalisation and growing attitudes of isolation. We have been seduced by the power of money, and have even come to believe it can help us achieve good parenting. In lifestyles of ever-increasing consumption — that we believe to be essential — we have lost, or forgotten, the importance of creating intimate relationships with our children.

As parents within a Complex Family, we are given one of the greatest opportunities to succeed in raising our children as we come to understand that they are the innocent bystanders in an adult drama. Do you remember being a new parent with your newborn in your arms? You were so full of hopes and dreams that one day your precious little bundle would realise their innate potential and touch the good fortune of love, health, and wealth?

Now, here you are divorced or separated, and alarmed by the statistics; how quickly the words like *broken home* or *split family* take on a momentum all of their own. The statistics tell us children from such families are five times more likely to be poor. They are more likely to drop out of school early; they are more likely to be in trouble with the law; and they are also more likely to become teen parents. They are more likely to become divorced; and finally, as a result of all this, they are more likely to die before the average age from ill health. These are the *facts*; they are part of the emotional agony and guilt you feel. The combination of facts and emotions can add further fuel to the *Great Divide* (the gap between Mum and Dad), as they feed your senses of justified blame, hatred, and resentments that can last a lifetime.

However, as part of a Complex Family, you don't have to give up on those early dreams; while the statistics are there, and you may watch others around you in wreckage, or you may even have experienced your own parents' divorce, your children can have a different kind of life — with happier outcomes. To become a healthy family with a new form of wholeness, you must first change your perspective, and become a Complex Family instead.

Much like a blank canvas, children come into this world with every bit of potential to become a masterpiece. As we create a Complex Family, we add a bold mark to that canvas. The question we then need to ask is not whether the separation should or should not have occurred, but rather, has the divorce taken our children's canvas and touched it with a flame to burn centre-stage? Or, has it slashed the canvas with a knife, cutting so completely that a part is lost? With either scenario or any other, our children will be the ones who ultimately choose; our job is to develop their reservoir of security, creativity, and knowledge, so they can bring forth their own masterpiece.

> Develop their reservoir of security, creativity, and knowledge so your children can bring forth their own masterpiece.

Life Has Changed

Although the previous relationships are changed, they will be with you forever. Regardless of circumstance, it is now your choice how your new relationships will be formed. It is a wise person who can recognise the opportunities disguised within these circumstances.

The objective of this book is to help you gain the wisdom and the skills required to develop your ability to see the great gift that lies hidden within the wrapping paper of problems; this will give you the courage to begin afresh.

For starters, the relationship between the parents needs to be a new one. It has to be. What happened between you must become part of your history — as painful, disappointing, or reckless as it may have been. If you focus on the previous circumstances as fuel for your justifications or blame, you will only increase the existing shortcomings. Now that you are separated, your issues may not have gone away, but they will be out of immediate sight. Having said this, you would ignore the obvious, and be rather naïve to believe that your Ex will no longer annoy you or cause you hurt; as many people post-marriage have discovered, it's no easier *out* than *in*; it just changes.

As you enter this new relationship, it is studded with obstacles; first, you now have a precedent for irreconcilable differences, and second, the subject of future interactions will be about the children. This second factor is particularly unique to the Complex Family; it instantly reaches deep into your heart and emotions, and constantly stirs the cauldron of reaction.

Recognising life has changed is a good first step; understanding the significance of these changes is the journey ahead. For most, the first year or two are definitely the hardest, but many couples prolong this chaos, and still pay lawyers and see the insides of court rooms for years. There are the couples who, a decade or two down the road, are still battling it out every time family occasions force Mum and Dad to attend, with complicated seating arrangements and constant avoidance games being played. However, more find a year or so later, a new sense of normality is established; it may vary in pleasantness, but life tends to settle into the new pattern.

If there is Ex tension, the beauty the new start was meant to provide could suffer; on the other hand, the separation could have brought welcomed relief and new prosperity for both parties. Yet still for the majority of divorcees, some time later what we really find is a resigned tolerance, an acceptance of the inevitable exchange of pleasantries. The sad part is, these two teams have not necessarily forgiven or even accepted what life has thrown their way; this relief seems to come as more of a wearing-down, or fed-up with the irritation the Ex constantly seems to provide, so each person involved seeks solace in ignorance and invisibleness from the other, and it is in this that normality is welcomed back to their otherwise chaotic life.

I can assure you, divorce is not a life sentence to parental failure. Be encouraged — it can be the beginning of a foundation firmly based on the concepts of living a more authentic and meaningful life with your children. As many of us have experienced post-divorce, fathers become Dads, often far exceeding what they would otherwise have been. Mothers become Mums who find joy in being the mum, rather than someone who struggles to live up to traditional expectations.

> Divorce is not a sentence to parental failure … it can be a more authentic and meaningful life with your children.

There is a newness and freshness to being a parent when you work constructively with your Ex to provide the *best of both worlds*, as my children frequently describe their lives.

Cultural Changes

Expectations from life evolve, and generational changes happen more rapidly these days than in previous centuries. As modern technology stimulates communication and cultural exposure, the masses are slowly awakening to previously stored secrets. Freedom of speech along with an increased focus on human rights has liberated our choices, and affected our willingness to surrender our lives to both religious and cultural expectations.

As did many in our generation and those before us, we entered into marriage with high expectations. Young and unprepared, we complied with the required cultural containment when hormones and inexperience combined and needed to find a way to be acceptably expressed. It wasn't that we necessarily wanted to *marry*, it was expected of us — and we quietly obliged. This left little room for a wise choice of partner, and many young couples as they have matured feel they were compelled to make a lifelong commitment they might not otherwise have undertaken if they had been free from cultural patterns and presumptions.

My mother, married at the tender age of 19, had already been given the most unflattering title of *spinster* on her marriage certificate. My father, however, only two years her senior, carried the rather heroic title of *bachelor*, that even today embodies the ultimate freedom men supposedly desire. While the roles of man and woman have come a long way since those days, our acceptance of the fallout from this cultural change is far from complete. Divorcees for decades have carried an aura of shame and judgement, been considered unworthy parents, and labelled as selfish individuals who know little of love and commitment. In our slow moving culture, this contradiction adds to an individual's inner confusion. On one hand we pioneer freedom, and on the other, we continue to judge the very choice this freedom offers.

Following generations have moved away from young marriages, and babies after the acceptable two-to-five-year period; instead, they opt for adventures upon foreign shores, higher education, and career advantages before they 'settle down' with lifelong commitments to marriage and family.

Culturally we are changing, albeit slowly. Although the generational uniqueness is still an influence, as parents, we are wise to consider empowering the decisions that our children will make, rather than dictate or forbid when it come to their relationships. As we support their move towards constructive relationships irrespective of label, it will help to remove the poison divorce has historically created and give the opportunity for wisdom to grow and develop when learning about relationships. This is not to encourage or validate divorce as the better option, but neither is it to invalidate our choice when we see the madness some former beliefs have produced in life-altering decisions whilst many are so ill-prepared.

Choosing Your Sport

Deciding to make a fresh start does not for a moment belittle the consequences of the decisions you've made, or those that have been made for you; it means you will begin to walk a new path and, as parents, build something new. It's neither starting again, nor going over old ground; to borrow a phrase, sometimes there is just too much water gone under the bridge. This time, you will turn your attention forward and focus on the continuing roles you have as parents. This is about recognising the new game — Parenting — and becoming excellent at it.

Since the divorce or separation, what has occurred is a major reshuffle of teams and players. When you were both on the same team, you wore the same colours and you shared joint strategies, spoken or not. But now, your Ex is following different tactics, talking to different coaches, learning unfamiliar maneuvers, and it all feels a tad unnerving. In the shift to two teams what you start to feel is the constant pressure of an opposing team instead of the unity of a single team. This change has you easily fooled into believing their strategies and strength require you to call in an umpire or referee to take control — but this is a different game. What you are now playing is *parenting with an Ex*; as with other sports, you can choose how you want to play it.

Some sports are *competitive* and have teams that grind it out against the opposition, as they work to reach the other end of a field or court. The direction of play is opposing and produces tackles, bumps and bruises, with tactics that work to trick, overcome, and conquer as happens in rugby, football, basketball, and so on.

Even in sports like athletics, kayaking, swimming, sailing, gymnastics, and skiing, where the players focus on their own tactics, strategies, and skill, they still compete with the one who offers the challenge. This sportsperson still feel aches and pains after a good workout, but that is because they have pushed themselves instead of being subjected to another's force.

It is your choice to make your parenting similar to that of kayaking or rugby. This will be determined by whether you want to learn and refine your life as a parent with another's force against you or do you want it to come from your own desire for excellence? Although the choice may not seem to be within your control, by the time you progress through these pages, I'm sure you'll see the choice belongs to you and not to another — and this includes your Ex.

Sporting teams become finely tuned, highly skilled, and fit for purpose when they have another team to play alongside and continuously challenge them. Likewise, in the game of Complex Family parenting, if you can learn to develop a new game plan, you can become great parents. Now you have become two teams in one game with a field of possibilities.

Cooperation Not Competition

Another aspect of sportsmanship is *cooperation*; this does not diminish the desire for excellence that comes from competition, it focuses on the manner in which the result is achieved. Instead of looking for winners and losers, teams work together cooperatively to create the desired result.

Take kayaking as an example: you are parents on Time River as it carries your family downstream with its current. You continue to raise your children, but the manner in which your family journeys down the river is your choice. This journey continues whether you proactively choose your style or simply react to the flowing current.

Before your separation, parenting was kayaking in a two-seater and juggling the children onboard; now you separated, you are in separate kayaks practicing singles.

You can make this hard work if you want to try paddling upstream, or wish for what could have been, or if you try do it all alone and refuse to acknowledge the substantial load you have on board the smaller kayak. It's not easy to have children in a single, emphasising the lack of stability, space, and restricted power.

The smart thing to do in your altered situation is to accept the problem and look for a way to solve it. Find a way that you can each remain in your own kayak and yet cooperatively build a structure between the two that keeps your children safe, protected, and nurtured, while you both paddle giving strength, stability, and support for all. This level of cooperation still allows for independence and difference, but it keeps the focus on raising your fantastic family.

> You have become two teams, in one game, with a field of possibilities.

Leaver and Leavee

Although many couples are known to have an amicable first conversation when deciding divorce is an option, few remain in this space. The leap between logic, heart, emotions, and practical changes are enormous; the first flicker of new hope that one day you may discover your much fantasized soul-mate is quickly snuffed by the realities your new state forces upon your life — and the lives of your children. Your spouse has failed to meet your expectations, and perhaps you have failed to meet theirs; yet your pointing finger quickly becomes cemented in a blaming position as you build a justifiable story to defend your side of the situation.

Much of our western culture permits No Fault Separation where neither party is blamed for the demise of the relationship; this could also be called No Responsibility Divorce. It fails to recognise the uniqueness in the choices, responses, and ongoing consequences for both parties. From my personal experience, followed by study and years of counselling and coaching others, the two positions are fundamentally different. By recognising these differences and identifying the two opposing perspectives, you will be able to more easily transition through the limitations of either.

If we were to have an objective here, an overall goal, it would be to assist all divorcees (with children) to move towards a central point where their positions become neutral. This means it simply becomes an event that has occurred. If you view it similar to an educational experience, it helps you in life; you learn a lot from it; you even grow from it; eventually it is no longer inflamed by wretched memories, hateful stories, and resentful attitudes. That is to say, while the divorce or separation is a fact in your life history, you will choose to become free from the story surrounding it: a story that is full of emotions, excuses, or blame, and one that ultimately limits your life and the lives of your children.

To help explain the difference between the two perspectives, I will use an analogy: in the same way children are born into this world, some come through a C-Section and others, by natural childbirth; whichever method is endured, the baby is born. In the instance of the natural birth, labour may be experienced with unbelievable pain; but it is pain that stops once the baby is delivered. The relief is almost instantaneous; and even if we need a little time to heal, the excruciating pain is generally over. However, with a C-Section delivery, the birthing experience is generally pain-free; that is until the anaesthetic wears off — remember that burning sensation when you tried to get up and walk for the first time? It quickly reminds you that you didn't get off easily at all. These are two sides of one birthing coin. In a similar way, divorce is like another coin; each person experiences their side in a way that may starkly contrast with the other. To identify and continue to work with either side, I have simple terms to keep it easy:

Leaver - the one who leaves the relationship.

Leavee - the one who is left.

These two terms, Leaver and Leavee, can at times be a little blurred by circumstances, but characteristically they are not. (I'm aware of the contradictions such a simplistic model provides, but my belief is that the merits outweigh any disadvantages.) In the case of affairs or abandonment, the Leaver will inevitably be the one who appears to shun the prior covenant and decides to build a life elsewhere. Let's take a wife who finds out her husband is with someone else, and then chooses to terminate the marriage. While, circumstantially, it could be argued she is the Leaver, as she is the one to initiate the marriage ending, her feelings and emotions could sometimes be those of a Leavee, not a Leaver. Another more subtle and blurry situation is a couple who parade themselves as having had an amicable conclusion. In all the years of working with those separating or separated, I have yet to meet a couple who, in the first instance, are truly free of the characteristics of either the Leaver or Leavee.

We will now take a closer look at both the Leavee and Leaver, identifying some of the key differences and what these translate to during and after the change in relationship. In either case, we look at the extremes, and realise that along any continuum, there are shades.

The Leavee

... experiences a devastating life blow that they find incomprehensible because their beliefs and 'preconceived notions' defy their ability to accept the event. The Leavee is the one whose entire belief-system, values, and judgements exist around the notion that *marriage is for life*. It is unquestionable; they struggle to understand how another can see it as permissible to think otherwise. The very thought of leaving a marriage is an idea blocked before it is given a chance to penetrate the sacred walls of the institution. The conversations that concern disagreements between husband and wife only serve to reinforce the lack of choice one has once married — especially in a marriage that has children.

> The Leavee's ... belief-system, values and judgements exist ... that marriage is for life.

> I was the Leavee.
>
> A reasonably cool moonless night brought darkness everywhere; there was only the streetlight that cast its warm glow onto our white concrete drive. Its luminescence subtly highlighted the row of blue and yellow

pansies delicately bordering the stone's harshness and welcomed all who came to our front door. Inside, we'd just completed the routine with our three precious children: bedtime stories, brushing teeth, filling hot-water bottles, and other rituals before giving them butterfly kisses and hugs goodnight, and wishing them peaceful sleep.

Downstairs, leaving our three kids to rest, the familiar sense of relief that all parents know, was topped off that night by a little sigh and the thought, "Ah, the evening is now ours. It's our time to relax and spend some time together."

Comfortably taking our favourite spots on the couch, those famous words "We need to talk" came from my husband's lips.

I instantly felt a grip around my heart. What have I done? What have I forgotten? Did I screw up? Is this good news or bad? What now? A hundred questions passed through my mind within a split-second, as I tried to think, I wracked my brains in a frenzied panic, while a bold and cheerful "Sure, about what?" came from me — I was amazed at the calm and strength I heard in my reply. My uneasiness did not subside, and no reassuring smile or gesture came from him.

There was a look of intense seriousness and a deep awkwardness that taunted an otherwise handsome face as the words just fell out from him. "It's over — and I've decided I no longer want to be married to you."

That cold steely grip I'd felt only a few seconds earlier had done little to prepare me for this gob-smacking sentence. The sensation around my heart instantaneously moved downward; a churning stomach, swirling head, and a feeling that my entire body wanted to perform some sort of miracle to awaken me from this immediate nightmare. Every part of me wanted to be able to scream, "Cut! Wrong script!"

Rewind to only a few minutes earlier, as we had tucked our children into bed and kissed them good night; we were a couple, a couple with a great future ahead of us, and as far as my understanding went, this inner desire was a shared belief — a belief that our married life was forever. In one statement, he'd taken the picture titled Our Lives Together Forever off the wall and put his fist right through it, shattering the glass, frame, and photo.

Catching my breath, I eventually repeated "You no longer want to be married — and it's over?" making sure I'd heard straight. We had both been blessed with solid skills in communication, so I knew there had to be more to this subject than one sentence. He, of course, said, "Yes, that's what I said" and with that, the floodgates opened and released what, to my thinking, was a rather poor explanation.

Regardless of all that was said that night — reasons, excuses, or reassurances — there was one essential piece of information that changed my life forever — "It's Over." That was as pivotal a moment in my life as the discovery that the earth was not the centre of the universe was for science. It changed everything I'd previously understood, believed in, or thought I knew.

There was something about the marriage contract that I'd been totally blind to before. It took two of us to walk down the aisle; it took two of us to commit to each other for life; we both promised to always be there as a witness to each other's life. It took two of us to trust each other with our dreams and hopes. But it only took one of us to decide it was not going to be like that anymore — and choose to walk away. It took two to build, one to destroy.

From my perspective, I'd married, had three children in less than three years with my husband, and had lived a good life. A decade later, my husband told me he'd met someone else, fallen in love, and our marriage was over. These rather basic facts are not unique; however, my choice to move beyond being a Leavee is.

To do this, I first had to learn to live the wisdom from St Augustine:

"Resentment is like drinking poison and hoping the other person dies."

When I knew my marriage was ending, the most important choice I made was not who got what or where the children would go, it was which path I would choose for myself? Would I drink 'poison' and ask others around me to do the same, or would I learn to walk an alternative path? Once the defining decision was made, the choices amongst the myriad of options ahead became relatively simple.

As challenging as it has been for over a decade now, I have lived as an example for my family; I've endeavoured to help them learn to embrace and accept differences. I have assisted in the creation of a family culture where personal grievances are dealt with, the primary focus remains on raising our children, and we do our best to follow the principle of The Highest Good for All. It hasn't always been easy, many times quite the opposite, but it has always been as simple as making a great choice, one step at a time.

The Leaver

. . . may not articulate it, but they live a version of their understanding of the following principle; I am responsible for my life and happiness therefore *betrayal of myself to not betray another is still betrayal; it is the highest betrayal of all*. They believe others can also make the choice to live by this principle, and there is often an element of dismissive blame should someone choose not to.

> The Leaver ... I am responsible for my life and happiness ... betrayal of myself ... is betryal.

As a Leaver, one may grieve the loss of the relationship well before confronting the spouse. They may have agonised over it, felt an inner hollowness or deadening numbness that steals their zest for life; however, they have decided to refuse to settle for the status quo and turned to divorce as their way forward — sometimes, it seems to offer the only option for personal survival. For others, a catalyst appears and ignites the hope for a better life; this helps the complexities of divorce to pale into insignificance when compared to the potential of what life has on offer ahead.

In Leavees, the focus is on broadening their perspective and developing their wisdom — in effect, bringing about a paradigm shift; but even before that, we must give them hope. We dare them to hope again, to believe their lives can be rebuilt and that their children will not become statistical delinquents or suffer as a result of the parental separation.

For Leavers however, while attaining wisdom is a consistent theme, the development of hope is not necessary. Leavers already have the hope of a better life, as this is usually the driving force behind their decision. What they do need however, is the courage to handle the situation well.

> At the time of our divorce, we met in corporate offices where I was presented with The Papers; I was asked to have a quick read and then sign them. It was straight down to business. I found it ironic that the pomp and ceremony surrounding the signature on the piece of paper that bound us in marriage was in such contrast to the corporate coolness for the one that severed us.
>
> As part of the form-filling process, we were asked to state our irreconcilable difference — this highlights the biggest difference between the Leavee and the Leaver's world — and it took me until this moment to get it. I calmly said, "We don't have one. We don't argue; we don't fight; we have a great family; we care about each other; we don't really have any reason for this to happen; it just has." In my mind it was very simple, we didn't have an irreconcilable difference that I could put down on paper — we could work through anything, and I had been willing to do so.
>
> His look said it all; but being gifted with words, he verbalised his thoughts all the same. He adjusted his look just a little as if to suggest I was really stupid, and with a slightly quizzical brow, he said, "Yes we do, I don't want to be married to you."
>
> That was the moment it actually struck me. It was just that simple — he wanted out. It was two years since he'd moved out, and all that time, I'd been looking for some big, complex reason to explain why all this had happened — and it just wasn't there — it was purely a matter of his

choice. Our's had been a teen relationship that progressed into a marriage; it was not the heady falling-in-love choice. Now, he was in love; there was no guarantee he'd get more out of life once divorced, but he knew it would be his choice, and that was reason enough.

Another Leaver ...

Cathy had been married six years and had a two-year-old boy. She believed she'd given Brian every opportunity to change his addictive behaviours and deceit. They increasingly damaged Cathy's expectations of life as she knew it could be, and eventually she faced the possibility of divorce.

Brian was unable to hold long-term jobs and to earn a stable income; in her view, he was irresponsibly forfeiting time and focus as an at-home-dad in favour of his addiction to computer gaming. Cathy would come home from her demanding job or on-call weekends, to a house of chaos and apathy, with the simplest of daily tasks not completed. Intimacy had escaped long ago, and any feeling of partnership had been shattered; Cathy felt that she alone had to drag her husband and son through life. Unable to carry this burden, she sought relief by becoming a Leaver.

Another ...

A whirlwind romance peaked with a tropical wedding before being topped off with a honeymoon pregnancy: this was the beginning of life for Elizabeth and Stephen as a couple. Stephen, at the milestone of 40 years, was happy to have a baby; and Elizabeth, in her late 20's, was pleased with the security of marriage as she embarked upon this next chapter of her life.

Within three months of married life, Elizabeth's intuition was ringing alarm bells, and before the pregnancy was over, Stephen had succumbed to the common temptation that has seen many great men fall. Stephen, being the Leaver, left Elizabeth's family dream shattered before it even began.

And one more ...

Twenty years of marriage and three children later, Michelle felt every part of her creativity and spark had died. Unsure of going anywhere or making a single decision without Graham's voice inside her head, approving or disapproving her every move, Michelle's self-worth was at an all-time low.

Being a part-time working mother, Michelle found favour in the eyes of a gentleman she met through work, and before long, her life with Graham became a painful detention centre from which she longed to escape. The psychological handcuffs and heart-numbing routine of her marriage compelled her towards gaining her freedom and independence; albeit her actions would be judged as an irrational surge of impulse. Michelle believed she would live a healthier example for her daughters, and followed her heart in newfound love. She secretly dreamt, hoped for, and planned her escape for years before D-day finally arrived.

As a Leaver, before moving into the life ahead, it is vital to be sure you have arrived at divorce as a *last resort*, and not as a convenient alternative. This means you have explored all avenues carefully, taken into account the consequences, and still hold the belief that this is the best choice you can make. If you have not thoroughly explored these avenues, your belief in the freedom of choice may well lead you, as a Leaver, into a chasm of denial, doubt, regret, confusion, guilt, or some other equally destructive behaviour that can lead you down the road to inner personal numbness.

Alternatively, if you have received help, counselling, and guidance, and have seriously practiced the art of relationships, and face *Irreconcilable Differences* as the inescapable outcome, your path ahead may well be relatively free from the turmoil of guilt, emotional manipulation, and destruction. In its place, a sense of relief will become your new normality.

The following Check List is for anyone considering such a pivotal decision. It should be worked through thoroughly:

- Have you been wise and careful with who you talk to about your relationship issues?
    Talking to someone who supports your point of view is not the best option; instead, find a neutral party, someone who is committed to finding solutions, whatever they may be.

- Have you sought professional help together both as a couple, and separately?
    If not, continue to develop your relationship.

- If your heart is drawn to someone else, would you be prepared to leave the marriage knowing this other person was not going to be there?
    If not, continue to develop your relationship.

- Can you identify the current relationship issues and have you been working on these?
    If not, continue to develop your relationship.

- If the current issue was fixed, would you consider staying in the relationship?
    If yes, continue to develop your relationship.

- Is there a spark of willingness and commitment for change in the relationship from both of you?
    If yes, continue in your relationship.

- Are you absolutely convinced your soon-to-be-Ex cannot, and does not want to change?
    If yes, accept that they are unwilling or unable. If not, continue to develop your relationship.

- Are you willing to accept that life may become very complicated for a time, with financial constraints, time pressures and emotional support?
    Are you convinced of your decision? We are not talking about trial separations; this is the end. Trial separations are discouraged as they inevitably fail to achieve constructive results, create more pain, and leave larger scars.

Natural vs. Normal

Many things that happen to us during our daily lives are *normal*, but this doesn't mean they are at all *natural*. It is normal for us to speed around in cars while strapped to our seats, talk on a mobile phone, listen to the radio, and drink our coffee while on our way to work, but none of this is natural. The difference between these two powerful words will grow in clarity as we begin to make parenting choices as part of a Complex Family. What we regard as commonplace, everyday occurrences, are not necessarily parts of the path we ought to travel. To highlight the difference between the alternative choices ahead, I will use two terms:

Natural = something that exists in or is caused by nature.

Normal = an attitude or behaviour that conforms to a standard: usual, typical, or expected.

As we parent with an Ex, whether during the separation period or in the years following, we will experience a range of emotional responses: some are *natural*, but most are, regrettably, *normal*. If we continue to react in a normal manner, we will perpetuate the current dysfunction that exists in families around the world. If, instead, we begin to focus on raising great children within the Complex Family environment, we will begin to understand what our natural choices truly offer.

Normal places children in roles as supporting characters within the life drama; they are there, but only serve to highlight the causes and effects. Natural removes children from being involved in the drama, and allows them to hold the leading role in their own lives. Normal will usually make things worse; Natural may sometimes include an apparent temporary worsening, but it enables greatness to arise. In some ways, this is like a caterpillar that needs to decompose before emerging as a butterfly.

The following are examples of *natural vs. normal*:

- When making decisions, to feel confused at times is *natural*.
- Having made a decision, to feel guilty is *normal*.

- To feel confident in our choices is *natural*.
- To feel judgement from others is *normal*.
- Responding to change is *natural*.
- Reacting to change is *normal*.

Throughout this writing, I will continue to draw the comparisons between what would be *natural* and *normal*, and highlight the need to make these choices simply, one step at a time, to effect real change for yourself and your children.

Focusing on Yourself

The single biggest factor in parenting is *Leading by Being*. Rather than the more familiar phrase of *leading by example*, *leading by being* encompasses the more crucial aspects of who one is as represented by their attitudes and beliefs, and focuses less on what one is doing. In a Complex Family, this factor becomes more important than ever. While this may be the most important facet of parenting, you cannot automatically assume you know what messages your children absorb from the person you are *being*. These aspects are invisible and are only demonstrated through your daily manner. To ask your children to be, or to behave better than you do yourself, is doomed to failure; however, if you can build constructive consistency into your beliefs, actions, and voice, you will grow a strong, healthy family, regardless of its structure.

> *"Who you are speaks so loudly, I cannot hear what you are saying."*
> .... Ralph Waldo Emerson.

Each chapter of this book will give practical How To's for you to work through. To get the greatest benefit from these, as you read, take time to consider how you feel about what you're reading and make some notes for yourself — don't wait to come back to it later. Your family is unique, and whilst many circumstances are painfully repetitive, you need to bring these suggestions into your unique environment for them to become meaningful. I encourage you to listen to the little voice inside as you read. It is the one that at this moment says, "I don't have a voice." That's it — start listening!

This little voice will be the most powerful asset you carry through your years of parenting. In the times you feel confused about what you ought to listen too, this particular little voice can be powerful; it has some unchanging characteristics that are worth noting as it can be confusing to hear voices, and one can be accused of being a little mad. Sadly, it is also true that some people have undertaken hideous crimes, and then claimed to have heard a voice telling them what to do; therefore, it's important to make sure you are listening to one that will constructively add to your life. A commonsense reality check needs to be run before you obey; some characteristics to check for are:

> Leading by Being. To ask your children to be, or to behave better than you do yourself, is doomed to failure.

- The voice is always quiet, strong, calm, and seeks to do no harm.
- As you invite it to speak, this voice will grow in clarity and give you peace, but it will always await an invitation.

As this may sound a little fluffy and far out in these early stages, let's change gears. This path is not for the faint-hearted or reckless; it takes courage, strength, and stamina, but it inspires greatness. A simple way to demonstrate the voice that is going to add to your life is to practice this exercise. While reading the words in the next few lines, be aware of how you feel:

- *Expansion . . . opening up . . . sends out . . . stays . . . revealing . . . sharing . . . healing . . . giving . . . holding dear . . . letting go . . . soothes . . . amends.*

How do you feel? Do the words make you feel lighter? Is there a sense of possibilities and a better future? If you can feel this subtle change, remember it; this is the feeling that will always guide you. When your little voice is in line with these concepts, you can confidently follow it.

Now, read the following words and see if you notice a subtle change.

- *Constricts . . . contracts . . . closes down . . . draws in . . . runs . . . hides . . . hoards . . . harms . . . clings to . . . clutches . . . holds close . . . grasps . . . attacks.*

Now how do you feel? This has been a demonstration I've used with many clients over the years, and the results have been unanimous.

As you continue to read this book, grab a highlighter and start marking the phrases that give you a *light-bulb moment*, a moment where you go, "A-Ah! I got that". That way, you can easily return to them when you receive an undesirable e-mail or phone call, or when you feel completely rung out and want to fight back. Pick up this book and reread something that previously gave you a helpful insight and you'll find the encouragement you need to continue.

Facing Reality

Facing reality means you have a realistic and accurate view of your current situation, rather than just an overlay with a picture of a possible future — whether it's one you're dreaming of or dreading. Ask the question: *where am I currently?* In answering this, you need to stick with the facts, not the story that surrounds it. Here's an example of the difference:

The story would be something like this ...

> I am doomed: my husband has just left, and I've got three kids to look after. There's a huge mortgage, and now I'm going to lose the house because I haven't got a job and I know I can't find a job quickly enough, so the bank will take the house from me and my life is ruined. Furthermore, no one understands me; nor are they helping as much as I want them to.

Facts:

> I am separating from my spouse. I have three children. I currently live in the matrimonial home that has a large mortgage.

> I have no means of income. I am hurt and angry, and feel scared when I think about my future.

Give this step a go; you may find it easier to do with someone you can trust to make you stick to the facts, not help you create the story. Remember, while you are hurting, it is very normal to feel temporary relief, and an easing of pain, when you surround yourself with those who help to create better stories; however, this does little to assist in the long-term. What is natural, however, is to feel a mixture of emotions, and there are always some raw facts; so focus on those.

As an early step in this journey, you need to develop an acceptance for your present state, wherever you are; however, before you can begin to do this, you need to know where that is. When you can accurately see your current position, it will give you the power to make the choices that will constructively help you, and your children, to move forward. The alternative will cause you to stagnate, and eventually spin in small circles of endless, repetitive cycles.

Dealing with Failure

To begin to create a Complex Family, you first have to eliminate the feelings of *doom* you have — a belief that you and your children are jeopardised because you have experienced divorce, separation, or some other form of family breakdown. To do this, you must first deal with the sense of failure.

If you are comparing your separated life to your original life plan — meaning living with the same person *until death do us part* — irrespective of life's twists and turns, then you will believe you failed.

However, if you compare it to providing a healthy home environment, full of learning, consistency, love, and the development necessary for you and your children to handle what life sends as your challenges, this is not a failure.

To do this there are five steps to work through. These will allow you to examine your beliefs surrounding your new position, and then walk through a process that will allow you to identify the aspects you can change and those you cannot — to make choices that will enable you to grow beyond the feelings of doom and failure and into a stronger commitment to live in greater freedom.

1. Write down the areas of parenting in that you now feel disadvantaged. Beside each area write the words *compared to*. Through this process, you will begin to reveal some beliefs you hold. If they encourage great parenting, work out how these beliefs can be expanded to allow even greater parenting — and transform any perceived disadvantage to an advantage. It could be something like this:

   > I feel that my family is disadvantaged because we're separated and failed. We haven't made the marriage work and now our children will suffer like so many the other kids have because of it. This is compared to — a family that hasn't split up.

2. Ask yourself, "Is this True?" Write down your answer.

   > Partly. But now I'm forced to add — some children don't suffer. Maybe the children will only suffer if we continue fighting and bickering at one another.

3. Ask yourself, "What do I believe is my parenting ideal?"

   > I believe children suffer when parents fight; it is negative for them to be in hostile homes. My parenting ideal is to have a friendly, warm and encouraging home for my children, while I open many opportunities for them to develop.

4. Write down how you are willing to change your perspective so that you no longer believe you or your children are disadvantaged. Ask yourself, "What can I do to turn this to an advantage?"

   > I can learn how to have better conversations with my Ex. I can move into a house that will provide a safe and fun-loving space for us to live. I can do the things with the children I have wanted to do but previously felt I wasn't at liberty to do so — like music.

5. Finally, write a new statement confirming your new perspective. Suggestion: write in a little notebook or on a small card that you carry with you throughout the day so every time you feel a pang of being disadvantaged, you can remind yourself of your new perspective and choices. Carry this until you no longer need the reminder.

> My family can become a happy and healthy Complex Family through living free from constant anger and hostility in our former family structure.
>
> It is important for me to create a fun-loving, warm and open home for my children to grow up in, while I continue to create opportunities for them to be stimulated and encouraged during their developmental years, regardless of the structure.

Focusing on the Children

Creating the Environment

Every home, group, organisation, workplace, city, or country has an environment or culture. Our environment is made up of the unspoken rules and unwritten codes that exist and shape our behaviours, reactions, and choices. Our homes have an environment that will influence the way we interpret events that occur; hence, we can have the same event occur in two different homes, and produce extremely different outcomes. To understand the environment we are working to create as part of parenting inside a Complex Family, it helps to identify two forms of environment that exist with the strategies that cohesively add to reinforce them. Keeping this broader perspective will allow you to make great choices, rather than random reactions that reflect your mood or preferences at the time.

To make this a little easier to understand, let's name the two environments Performance and Learning.

- **Performance Environments** require a person to seek external rewards for good behaviour, and expect punishment when their performance fails to meet the expectations. Performance environments are where external factors dictate and determine success.
- **Learning Environments** turn attention inwards; it focuses on inner choices and consequences. The focus moves to the individual's actions and attitudes being the best they know given their ages and stages of development.

Inside a Learning environment personal responsibility and commitment towards excellence become the pivotal elements; they are used with the overriding motivation to take learning from each experience and opportunity, and regard the unsuccessful outcomes as neither failure nor mistake. In this environment we encourage everyone to give things a go; a non-success is not failure; instead, it is recognised by the individual as one way that did not work given the initial intention. This does not create a standard of mediocrity; it focuses on the creation of true personal excellence, free from competitive entanglement.

> Punishment is the result in a Performance Environment.
>
> Natural consequence is the result in a Learning Environment.

To expand on this momentarily, and further explain how this will practically affect the choices you make as you raise your children, this is most dramatically displayed with alternative methods of practicing discipline. When you allow your children to make their own choices, and then experience the natural consequences as a result, rather than apply external punishment, you encourage natural learning paths to develop. The difference between discipline and punishment can easily be established: punishment is the result in an environment of performance; natural consequences are the results in an environment of learning.

As we progress through the chapters ahead, I will outline the How To's as you grow with your children. The differences between these two environments will become the dominant theme — with a particular focus on how you confidently make your choices. It may, at times, feel like you have taken a longer path, but it is one that will enable your children to become adults with a strong inner code; it will define who they are, and the life choices they make. Instead of being dominated by peer-pressure or apathy in the years following dependency, they will function with a strong sense of confidence, independence, and self-worth.

Two Paradigms to Shift

There are many phrases and words we use daily in our family interactions that help to create our beliefs and view of the world. As you begin parenting with an Ex, there are two primary concepts that require adjustment: *Right and Wrong* and *Better and Worse*.

Both are based within the Performance environment, and are heavily loaded with judgement and preconceived ideas that are a challenge to question. Typically, we are comfortable with our judgements as they provide the safe zone and comfortable space we live in. To be asked to question what it is that we judge as *right and wrong* or *better and worse* can leave us floundering and insecure, even defensive or aggressive. This doubtful and wobbly feeling we experience as adults is what children feel each time we say (or infer) a contradiction or negative comment about their other parent.

Many of you have experienced the attitudes of defensiveness and aggression from your children, (especially teens) if you place them into a situation that calls for divided loyalties. When this happens frequently, it is nearly impossible for your children to develop their own healthy life views. They tend to deal with these contradictions, the situations, as pointless or unsafe because it's constantly challenged through the parental conflict.

Does this lack of *right and wrong* mean we always need to agree with our Ex? No, not at all; that would hardly be natural. Fire and water are natural and also opposites, neither right nor wrong in themselves.

Likewise, it is sometimes beneficial for children to have parents who are confident to provide experiences and discussions of beliefs, ideals, principles, and ways of doing things that contradict each other. If this is done in a respectful, safe, and harmonious manner, it can add enormous value to a well-stimulated developing mind.

Beyond Right and Wrong

Unwrapping *right and wrong* will bring a mature security and strength to your family. Perhaps in your family it is *wrong* to eat some type of food, use certain words, or wear a particular piece of clothing. It is *right* to speak this way, drive that type of car, or go to a particular school, marry this race, or hold this position in a job. With these judgements, you continually shape your children's thinking concerning what is acceptable and what is not.

To a young mind within a traditional family structure, any contradiction to the home environment's thinking is met with little questioning; instead, it is usually reinforced by the statement, "In our family it's this way": safe, secure, known, and valid. To a teen's mind, as they begin the journey of evaluating the essence of these judgements, they sift through each one to ascertain if they believe the same as you do; if this process is not understood and supported by you as parents, substantial conflict can occur.

> Every time you contradict the views held by your Ex … your children will begin to feel they have to choose.

Inside the Complex Family, every time you hold something as *right or wrong* that is in contradiction to the views held by your Ex, you open the door for doubtful and wobbly feelings to enter your children's world. They may display this in a wide range of behaviour, perhaps by becoming defensive or aggressive; without a doubt though, constant contradiction will confuse them. Your children will begin to feel they have to choose; for many of them this is too difficult, and as a result, they become apathetic or dull about expressing personal opinions. This can lead to a personality that lacks conviction and life-sustaining passion.

To move away from a *Right and Wrong* mentality, we reframe situations as being **appropriate or inappropriate**. This is where our Learning environment has the opportunity to grow.

Free from judgement about events being right or wrong, basically *Events* are held as neutral — they just happen — but it is our assessment of the event (usually in context) that gives it a label of being right or wrong. What we do with that judgement is our response and a matter of *Choice*; we can either be reactive or proactive. This is to say that we either consciously choose our response or we unconsciously react from previous experiences. This will then determine the next *Outcome*.

> To move beyond right and wrong, reframe situations as being appropriate or inappropriate.

Event + Choice = Outcome

This means we cease to judge the event, and instead, observe the outcome in context of whether they are *appropriate or inappropriate* in achieving the initial intension. As you come to understand the reasons for removing *right and wrong* from your conversations, you'll learn that — regardless of the temptation to do so — using your Ex as an example of what your children should, or should not do, is not only ineffective, it's inappropriate. It sends powerful, yet silent messages that infiltrate their thinking — messages that your children will find challenging to undo in the years to come. Discussion and examination of actions as either appropriate or inappropriate, provided we are constructive, presents a great opportunity to learn. Here is a case study of this in action:

> Peter is a particularly neat and tidy sort of person who spent several years in the armed forces and learned discipline and duty. He believes his boys should mimic this orderly behaviour in their bedrooms as a basic household standard. Kim is quite the opposite. She's a happy-go-lucky woman who is far more focused on providing a homely feel to the house, so having stuff left lying around isn't of any great consequence to her.

While Peter and Kim were together, their opposing views (while they caused tension) contributed a certain balance to the home. Now that they live apart, this difference has become very apparent. During the routine pick-ups and drop-offs, Peter can't help but notice the chaos. Unable to contain his growing concern about what he believes is a poor parenting standard for his boys, when he gets them into the car he tells them how bad it is that they live in a pigsty. "That's not how it's meant to be. Your rooms should be tidy, clothes put away, and everything cleaned at least once a week."

Of course the boys already know this because that's how it is in Dad's house and has been for quite some time.

What Peter has actually told his children is very different from what he thinks he has told them. He has said *"Mum is wrong; I am right."*

While there may be great merit in orderliness in your children's bedrooms — goodness, we all wish for that — unfortunately, Peter's desire for orderliness is lost through the tone of *right and wrong* in his delivery. Can you see that his conversation is targeting the circumstantial layer, while the message that is silently sent to his children hits at their belief layer instead? It may affect the situation in Peter's favour in the short-term, but it profoundly affects the children's beliefs for years to come.

By keeping your discussions within the context of *appropriate or inappropriate*, with a little practice, you can send messages that consistently build constructive beliefs, and still attend to the needs of the moment.

Alternative Appropriate Path

1. Seek clarification:

    The boys are in the car and Peter starts the conversation by seeking clarification about his concerns. In this instance he asks, "Is it normal for your bedrooms to be in a mess, or have you just run short on time lately?"

Even if it's obvious, it's worth asking. If you remember to use a question, it gives the children an easy way out. Peter's intention here is not to "win" or to catch them out or put them into a corner; instead he facilitates an open and meaningful conversation. When you allow your children to maintain their dignity and sense of loyalty, without feeling defensive, it will allow your valuable point to get across and deliver a strong, loving, harmonious message of support.

2. Express the concern and explain why:

> Peter can express his concern in the context of making appropriate choices given a desired outcome. "Hmm, it concerns me that your rooms are so messy, and I'm wondering if you are forming poor habits that may not be good for you in the years to come. These habits can be very hard to break."

Peter is not saying they're wrong; he is using words like 'concerned' and 'wondering'. These will help to stimulate your children to think and to start forming their own opinions, instead of subjecting them to another lecture from a nagging parent.

3. Discuss differences in the context of comparing outcomes given particular choices:

> The conversation can now lead to a discussion of the differences the children feel inside either place. Peter can talk about the pleasure of arriving in a room that is welcoming, one where you can see the carpet — and at a real stretch, how good it feels to get into a made-up bed. Perhaps he could point out the natural benefits of being able to find things more easily inside a tidy room instead of the last minute panic as they rush out the door . . . or rummaging through the piles of junk scattered over the floor, bed, and desk as they search for a favourite jacket. There are multitudes of reasons to favour clean and tidy bedrooms — and all hold validity when delivered in the context of appropriate or inappropriate.

This now becomes an opportunity for Peter to have a healthy

conversation with his boys about what he believes to be appropriate bedroom orderliness; there is no need to bring their mother into it. The requirement for judgement to prove a point disappears when the intention remains focused on delivering the *key message* rather than engaging in resentful finger-pointing and laying of blame.

4. Let it go:

> Once you have said your piece — nothing more needs to be added.
>
> Tip: If you can be constructive in your tone, you will be surprised at how much faster learning occurs — especially when your children are relaxed and having some fun.

By approaching the relationship with your children's other parent from this new perspective, you can strip away the rights and wrongs of situations, and get to the core of great parenting.

Beyond Better and Worse

Let's unwrap *better and worse* and find a suitable alternative so that your children can be given true freedom of choice. The issues of superiority and arrogance have intimidated humanity throughout mankind's marred history. They have given rise to slavery and torture, and millions of lives have been cut short through a belief in *better* — as in *"my way is better than yours."* To hold this attitude within your own family fuels rifts and prejudicial thinking in your children's minds. The following is a case study; it falls short of bloodshed, but is still a damaging family division.

> Mike and Sue practiced their religious beliefs together with the family while they were married; however, once the marriage ended, Mike decided to move away from the church entirely. Four children were involved, aged 15 to four. The weekends spent with Mike meant they didn't attend church; consequently, Sue felt it would be in the best interests of the children if they were to spend more time with her so she could make sure they continued to attend the services. Mike would not compromise on his valuable time with them, and arguments followed.

Over the weeks that followed, Sue's position unintentionally sent mixed signals; her words and manner of approach inferred to both Mike and the children that it was better for them to go to church than to spend time with their father. Sue expressed this with all the ammo she could muster, and found plenty of others willing to support her cause.

The underlying issue here was really not whether the children should or should not attend church; it was Sue's belief that her way was *better*. Her passion for what she believes invalidates Mike's freedom of choice that is an expression of his reasons and personal experience.

By her words, Sue says she understands everything Mike thinks and feels; she says she has a handle on all the circumstances that led him to this point — and worse yet — that her views are better than Mike's views. Her air of superiority and arrogance, obviously, would cause Mike to react as he did.

> To unwrap better or worse ... move to different.

While Sue directed her criticism and arguments towards Mike, her children were left in a position of having to choose: either they agree with Mum which discredits or ignores their Dad's experience and preferences, and lose valuable time with him, or they disagree with Mum and thereby feel confused and compromised because they are not following her *better* way. The children are truly left in a position of 'damned if they do, damned if they don't.'

To resolve this situation, we need to change the focus. We take Sue's very staunch view of better, and move it to **different.** That doesn't mean she believes in her faith any the less; it actually gave her an opportunity to live her faith more demonstratively. Sue learns to develop her children's ideas and beliefs, not to dictate them. She starts to talk with them more, and takes the time to explain that Dad's view is not better or worse; it is just different and is based on what he believes and has experienced. While Sue openly expresses her personal preference, she is able to embrace Mike's freedom of choice, and ultimately live her faith while she gives Mike the time to be Dad, and thereby sets a true example of unity within diversity.

As Sue embraces *different*, all four children are given the opportunity to support both parents in their individual choices. They are able to move beyond split loyalties, fighting parents, and defensive behaviours; they can start to evaluate for themselves and determine what they personally believe. This will prepare them to make strong choices for themselves in the years to come.

Children need to accept and fully embrace both parents, irrespective of their personal beliefs. To give them this opportunity is to truly embody what is meant by, *"For the good of the kids."* As a parent within a Complex Family, your challenge is often to recognise the difference between the circumstances, your beliefs, and those powerful messages you send.

Chapter Two
Inside the Mind Of ...

Alternative Perspectives

It almost seems pointless to try to understand your Ex once you've parted; indeed, not having to constantly think about their interpretations or opinions may be part of the upside of no longer being together. However, your belief that since you lived together you know them adequately is where many of you start to stumble. The certainty with which you hold onto your prior impressions and notions is very destructive when it comes time to resolve issues that will inevitably arise between you.

Once you've separated, there is a great shift in the relationship dynamics: some may be very surprised to find themselves single; others may rejoice that they finally had the courage to break free. So, while I appreciate that now it might be inconvenient to have to consider your Ex's reactions or thoughts on *any* matter, it is wise to pay a little attention.

Reflecting on the reason you actually have an Ex, the majority of divorcee's acknowledge that if they'd been able to fully connect and communicate with their partner, they would probably still be together. If they understood them, and their behaviour, they might have had a harmonious home — although that's not always the case. Remembering this, the objective here is to take some time to walk in another's shoes and view the world through a fresh set of eyes.

A famed phrase that's poorly practiced is **"Seek to understand before being understood."** This sums it up; it's a timely reminder that asks you to consider another perspective first, not second; it says take heed of the importance to listen before you speak.

It's helpful to start to understand what is inside both the Leaver's and Leavee's minds. It is from the advantageous perspective of that other viewpoint, you can gain insights to behaviours that might otherwise be difficult to comprehend. As your relationship deteriorates over time, the person you married and vowed to love forever, can become someone you hardly recognise — and understand even less. Many sleepless nights can be spent in an attempt to work out this curious maze, and all you end up gaining is bleary, bloodshot, puffy eyes and frazzled nerves. If, only for a moment, you can glimpse what the Ex and/or your children may think or feel, you can dramatically improve your chances to make more constructive choices in the days ahead.

Inside the Mind of the Leavee

The cruelest thing about being stripped of everything you thought was so important is that the stripped heart, is still beating. Should someone really be allowed to take another breath when your heart has been broken in an instant of critical pain? Is this not such a blow to life that your own willingness to feel the pain should be enough to also free you from it?

With the hopes for your future shattered, you can become like a rudderless yacht, drifting powerlessly, even if you are able to find your compass or bearings. Stripped of choice, you are left dangling to work with the remaining options. Rejection, betrayal, and blame become a new all-consuming torment, with the potential to be miserable in every waking moment.

A Leavee deals with a disintegrated belief in their hopes for their future life. Where previously they had taken comfort in the surrounding obviousness of their relationship, even though it was a struggle, they always believed that change for the better was soon to be upon them; now this potential has suddenly disappeared. All prior conversations with someone who had been considered a supportive friend, and with whom the forbidden chest that held possible departure was never opened, are over. There remains a wish for it to be that simple again, where comfort could be taken, and a new perspective could get the marriage back on track . . . even if the price meant further numbing their sensitivities.

To have one's life's plans and dreams devastated is bad enough, but to be stripped of the hope for future betterment is what is really at the core of the pain. This is a pain that the Leavee often never fully looses; to make it even worse, this is an almost unfathomable consequence for the Leaver to comprehend.

As a Leavee, you grieve the loss of your relationship publicly, in the face of personal trauma. Unable to be afforded the dignity of choice, you grapple with an overwhelming sense of powerless anguish; you feel your heart has been stolen, your hope and future life taken — with no possible opportunity for it to be returned. To have your soon-to-be-Ex's demolition ball arrive without consent and knock out the foundations of your family with a full-forced blow seems incomprehensible to a Leavee. You may demand that their demolition ball go elsewhere, but to little avail; it has done its work and leaves you in an alarming state of panic.

Overwhelmed with life and the disintegration of your relationship, you do your best to cope, and plunge headfirst into survival mode. You begin a search for places to ease your hurting heart, and quickly find there is no shortage of those willing to offer a sympathetic ear. The soothing of the pain is powerfully addictive; it creates a new dependence upon others as you seek to avoid the frightening silence.

Coming with this form of rapid pain-relief is questioning, conflicting advice, and judgement by those on the fringe of happenings. You can then find yourself fluctuating between defending and loathing; in one moment you hold on to your belief that the good moments of the life you shared were indeed real; but then you look at the present situation, and recoil; you finally choose to avoid the agony and bewilderment this dichotomy presents. We spend countless hours pouring over every detail of what we missed, or what they did, hoping hindsight will mercifully be able to provide a new perspective.

As a Leavee, one encounters the manifestation of a belief-system, a set of values and judgements that exist to support the historical meaning of 'marriage is for life.' This is an unquestionable state for which the Leavee will compromise their own personal happiness, attainment of dreams, and even their sense-of-self. It comes from a core belief that commitment comes through cost; for without this, when is it we can truly know we are capable of commitment? The contract we entered into on our wedding day may well fall short of being honoured; indeed, there is a prediction it will; but the very thought of divorce is a horror story that belongs elsewhere.

> A core belief that commitment comes through cost ... the contract may well fall short of being honoured ... there is a prediction it will.

With such immense commitment, it is still prudent to ask the question, "To what are we committed?" In the case of the Leavee, the usual response is quick definitive rhetoric, almost as if there is a need to defend an inner contradiction. It's normal to hear appeasing replies of "my marriage" or "my family" as two of the myriad alternatives. Upon closer inspection of such an automated response, one may be surprised to discover they have become more committed to the Institution in which they believe, than to their unconditional loyalties for their loved one. All too often, the reasons for commitment have become justified and purpose-driven; sight of the beauty and simplicity it provides is lost because life no longer holds youthful simplicity. As youth fades, we grow up, and normally, with this increase in age comes increased complications. When faced with an undeniable lack of choice, there is a tendency to build a fort to protect the exposed vulnerability within.

The Leavee is not better or worse for possessing such belief in commitment, it is worthy of admiration to hold such a value, but when separation comes, it cuts to the core. The very foundation on which life has been built is shattered, and flaws, insincerity, and falseness are exposed. The sudden awareness that one's commitment has not been shared is intrinsically devastating.

The anger, blame, resentment, and judgement becomes easy to feed and can become an all-consuming pastime that permeates every sense. The source of feelings of discontent within the relationship have conveniently vanished from memory, and it is easy to focus on faults, and shortcomings, regardless of one's hand in their creation.

It is not uncommon to become irrational and unpredictable in such times of great devastation. Emotions can behave like a roller-coaster with its loops, slow climbs, stomach drops, and the contagious squeals of delight. One moment we believe we can survive anything, we feel 10 feet tall and bulletproof; a fleeting second passes, and we remember a moment, feel isolated, receive an e-mail, or become overwhelmed by something the children do, and we plummet into sobs of sorrow. If this ride is not brought to a conclusion, the Blame Game will be played to its fullest extent and result in savage victimhood.

> The Blame Game will be played to its fullest extent and result in savage victimhood.

You can become consumed by the inclination to compare your situation to what you presume to be your Ex's world as you try to gain your bearings and justify your actions. You can wear an aloof, non-interested disguise and harbour an inner longing to see cracks in their new life, in an attempt to ease what you perceive as your own sad miserable plight. Because you want to see the score evened, you will do your best to get front row seats for the sneak previews of justifiable disaster, and as there is no better way to get inside the walls of your Ex's new world than through the ever-so-sincere mouths of your children, you will use manipulative tactics to learn all you can about the goings on in the forbidden zone.

It is here, at this point, that the focus turns — enter the children.

There is a good reason why it takes two people to create babies; it's the forerunner to the understanding that it takes so many more to raise them. The responsibility for creating your children was a shared experience, and it was something you entered into together — as a couple — yet now through the actions and choices of one, the Leavee is left to struggle with the lack of choice in becoming a solo parent. You feel resentful of both your added burden and the compromised world your children must now live within; you know this was never part of the initial agreement.

> You feel resentful ... this was never part of the initial agreement.

In an unspoken shift, barely recognisable as anything but normal, the majority of Leavees assume that your Ex wants to change the core agreement of childcare, and by default, will relinquish their right to full parenting. To you this is completely obvious. If they really cared that much about the family, they'd stay put — otherwise, suffer the consequences. If they move away from the matrimonial home, that's their issue — they can deal with it. These simple, obvious, and rather basic facts are what they should have thought through before destroying your family.

When you look at your children, you become angry at what has been inflicted on them; hence the Ex is to be blamed. This blame is not only for your current circumstances, but also for all future repercussions arising from their decision. You desperately want to ensure your children can still have the dreams you first held for them, so you begin to claw at all chances for your Ex to continue to pay — to pay financially, emotionally, in time, and in any other form you feel might help your children or get back at your Ex — it doesn't matter how.

Within this powerless space, you rummage around looking for a single handhold to grip. You realise the power your children have on your Ex's emotions and decisions, and you are tempted to use your common bond in the ugliest and cruelest of parental powers. Through withholding or manipulation (conversations or otherwise), you find it almost permissible to transfer your pain onto the children so they can pay the Ex back. In effect, you hand out flasks of poison and feel justified in doing so out of a state of blind selfishness.

> You hand out flasks of poison and feel justified in doing so out of a state of blind selfishness.

You warn them of their other parent's shortcomings, you are desperate to expose the betrayals in the hope that your pain will be recognised. You also do this to justify your shortcomings as a parent, and delude yourself into believing you can win favour and sympathy from your children. Even in your desperate state, you are haunted by the guilt of these vulgar actions towards your children because you know this is not how it is meant to be, yet you justify it in your head to make up for your broken heart. It's in this way that your children truly become the innocent victims in an adult drama, and there is a part of you that watches, cringing at the feelings of guilt, as you heap more onto them than they should ever have to carry. This horror is rife; but it does not need to be this way. As you come to understand how powerless you actually are in a marriage when only one party wants to be there, the opportunity for a greater life is born.

> I watched a decade of my life, my marriage, all my hopes and dreams for our future and the beauty of my perfect family unit melt away. His heart had left mine and he was now beyond the marriage regardless of my desire for it to be otherwise. At the very core of my being I felt rejected, betrayed, overwhelmed, and out of control. I oscillated between hopes of

revenge and the feelings of self-pity and helplessness; I found myself on an emotional roller coaster, in completely foreign territory.

My days were spent disguising the grief and sadness so as not to affect too greatly upon the children's fragile world, while managing new employment. My nights were my time to begin to understand what to do next. In the silence and without distraction, I began to take down the walls of parental duty and corporate expectations and started to feel what was really going on inside, in an effort to work out the shambles of my current life.

I would often slip out of bed, wrap up warm in my gown, slippers and a blanket, and head downstairs where I would sit with my much-loved cat on my knee and be still in the perfect darkness and solitude. If the anxiety or worry had grown out of control, I'd sit at the computer and tap away on its keys in an attempt to gain some sense of direction and personal power; otherwise, it was just silence. It felt like I was using just the weakest of beams from a penlight to illuminate the path ahead. I longed for light from a car's high-beam headlights, or perhaps the luxury of waiting until the morning when the sun would rise, but I had to do all I could with what I knew now, and if all it provided was weak penlight beams, at least it wasn't pitch black on a moonless night.

During these nightly rituals I would become angry one moment and then plummet into sobs of heartache the next. I sometimes felt as though I was sliding headfirst toward my own doom, yet with every new question or issue I confronted, I would return to the beauty of this form of nighttime writing. It saved me from being lost within overwhelming panic attacks, and it gave me some time where I could be truly alone with my pain and quiet suffering.

This is where my divorced life could have stayed — I could have chosen to be a victim of my circumstances, yet another statistic and another broken home for the media to report on as they sensationalised how bad that year was compared to previous ones. I had seen first hand the effects of resentment and bitterness take over people's lives; I could only hope to spare myself and my children the damaging path those resentful choices would otherwise lead us to.

It was my tenacious and courageous spirit however that pulled me to continue writing. As I wrote, often unaware of the heartache that poured onto the paper, I would not stop until I came to that peaceful place out the other side — and it could be hours. That peaceful place never failed me — not once, although sometimes it took longer than others to finally open, but it always kept its promise. It was in this peace I found the path to transition to a state of mind beyond the Leavee.

It took a long time for me to unravel the chaos and fallout from this time; I found valuable lessons as I sought wisdom from all corners of the globe. Everything I had always believed to be true and right had been left in ashes, and I needed to rebuild.

As I went forward from that point, my decisions were fully based on my interpretation of the Highest Good of All; in this, protecting my children and holding a family together at the pinnacle superseded all personal grievances. I had to learn to think outside the literal, structured concepts of a black and white world, add in a little grey, and maybe, one day eventually, colour would come.

Leavee Capsules:

- *Lifelong*: We pick our battles to win the war: this means that often we will choose to overlook issues in order to stay married as we believe that is our only option. Marriage is for life; however, now that it's ended, we go to the other extreme and fight about everything because the *good person* being tolerant has failed us.

- *Responsibility*: Our Ex, because of their first choice — they left — continues to be wrong irrespective of how logical or right they may be. All further decisions are based on the premise: *They left, that's their problem and therefore theirs to solve.*

- *Judgement*: This incomprehensible decision forced upon us is *wrong*; therefore, to make sense of it, we find fault in our Ex. Because we believe strongly in *right and wrong*, we believe we are right and, therefore, they must be wrong. This is extended to include everything they say and do, because our level of confusion in our beliefs drives this hurt deep within.

- *Rejection*: *I was faulty, flawed, and obviously no longer good enough for him/her.* While trying to prove that we are still worthy, we may rebound into the arms of another; or, become reclusive and avoid intimate relationships for a very long time — maybe forever.

- *Betrayal*: They have broken our lifelong trust, shattered our hopes and dreams, and therefore, they have become our enemy.

- *Blame*: They are at fault; therefore, they are blamed for all situations ahead. Our attitude rules our thinking as we become obsessed with blame, and turn ourselves into the victim and the Ex becomes the villain.

- *Anger*: We have lost control; our Ex has made a decision that we cannot change and we feel helpless, hopeless, and powerless to do anything about it. We become so consumed by this out-of-control state that anger rages as we attempt to relieve our inner despair, or at least gain a momentary sense of control.

- *Resentment*: The ongoing, festering emotions then destructively taint our relationship with the Ex, with the children, and sadly often unknowingly, with all others.

Inside the Mind of the Leaver

Inside the mind of a Leaver, it would be easy to assume this character to be the opposite of the Leavee, but to assume this would be to diminish the Leaver in both essence and substance. Meeting the Leaver, we see someone who embodies *freedom of choice*. A Leaver believes that if something is not working, it needs to be fixed; hence, they are often those who have strong feelings about phrases like *'master of my own destiny'*, or *'life is short, make the most of it.'* With such beliefs, it is extremely challenging for a Leaver to continue with an unsatisfactory status quo. Inevitably, they will take proactive steps to change the areas of discontent, and although these may be regrettable in the current circumstances, the consideration of life beyond the moment is the point of focus. Since the marriage contract has fallen short of expectations and requirements, it therefore becomes equally valid to consider the balancing option on the marriage continuum — Divorce.

> If marriage has fallen short of expectations ... it is equally valid to consider divorce.

Our Leaver is not better or worse for having a natural compulsion towards betterment; for many of us, those feelings of being imprisoned by invisible bars, of being forced to continue to live out a life of mediocrity and compromise, is ultimately repelling. As a Leaver, you have grieved over the anticipated relationship that failed to materalise with the confines of the marriage, and have, sometimes for years, considered separation in quiet desperation.

It's fair to say, the Leaver without children is blessed with an easier path. He or she can consider their actions in private should they wish to do so, without the daily ramifications as a constant reminder. However, with children, regardless of their ages, one can be haunted by questions of why, what if, and what now?

Often, the Leaver is in the empowered position of making choices and acting upon them. Regardless of your thoughtfulness, or sadly, perhaps the lack of it, you are willing to be judged and labelled right or wrong to break free from the chains that hold you back from the experience of life as you believe it should be. You usually possess a sense of resolve that enables you to face few short-term circumstantial complications in exchange for the gain of a better future.

More often than not, with the end of a relationship, you will feel a great sense of relief and joy as hope returns, and a lightness replaces the burden of dissatisfaction you carried. This relief is quickly followed by equal doses of guilt as you then consider the effects on the one you publicly promised you would love forever, and the lifelong implications for your children. As you oscillate between this guilt and joy, relief and sadness, freedom and isolation, you remind yourself of why you left.

As a Leaver, you are often judged for your apparent lack of tenderness and sensitivity, and for your disregard for what you have caused. When this happens, you can often find consolation in being misunderstood. It is almost as if your thoughts help you to understand that you are not answerable to the opinions of those willing to judge; it reinforces your belief in personal ownership and accountability for one's life choices. In this semidetached trance, you begin your path to survival as you try to figure out how to walk the new road.

We have all seen Leavers who go through surprising personality transplants, as they project more glamourous images and pursue outrageous (occasionally even deluded) pastimes. These seldom deliver the desired outcomes as, in reality, they are done more for shock-value than to achieve a desirable lifestyle, and are best observed from this perspective.

As the Leaver, while you may appear to be in control, your inner compass sometimes spins uncontrollably. You can feel trapped, as you try to keep up appearances: you feel you have to look good to others while inside you are dealing with conflicting states of guilt, confusion, and sense of failure, combined with the realities of your new life that may not immediately live up to your expectations and leave you feeling empty and isolated.

For most, it's a real struggle to keep up a brave face while your self-esteem plummets, and in response to the continual innuendos and judgement of others, you begin to doubt the sensibility of your own choices as you quietly ask, "Is it easier out than in?" For most Leavers, the answer is an immediate, definite yes, even though it's not necessarily that the day-to-day routines are easier, but rather that they have at least gained hope — they have regained the magic that *choice* affords.

> **Leavers have gained hope ... regained the magic that choice affords.**

There is one thing Leavers are very clear on: their desire to be with and responsible for their children has not been eliminated by their choice to divorce. The certainty of this idea comes from the distinction between being in a relationship with the child's other parent and the position you hold in raising your children. It is clear these two jobs can be mutually exclusive, although historically, this has not been the case; you believe the responsibility for parenting can rightfully continue, albeit scheduled and prioritised around new life commitments.

This kind of belief sees the dissolution of the marital relationship as more of a bizarre study in cause and effect than a rejection of parental duties or desires. The marriage has outlived its value and had issues for which a solution was obviously needed. Although prior promises were made with the best information and knowledge available at the time — time has moved on, and with this movement, alternatives have become the better choice.

While you would definitely prefer to have your choices understood by your children, it is considered a bonus. You will opt to continue to take the punishment, hurt, and soreness of heart their rejection or absence will inflict, in favour of attaining the freedom life has on offer outside the marital relationship.

Emotions central to the Leaver are in stark contrast to those of the Leavee; so much so, they are perplexed by their Ex's recalcitrant behaviour, and unable to fathom their ongoing hostility after what is considered a reasonable period of adjustment by them. While these misunderstandings can cause toxic reactions and devastating isolation (that may see the Leaver recoil), this outlook stops well short of frivolous, as often Leavers are not in search of fastidious perfection. They simply believe life is theirs to create, and accept fully their responsibility to do so. Sometimes the freedom experienced can beckon them into stimulating action, and they can regain a once lost position inside the family. Dads often learn more about being great fathers than they ever thought possible; and mothers often gain a refreshing enthusiasm for life and start laughing again. As a Leaver, they begin to redefine who they are and how they choose to live their lives.

There are, of course, those who have been caught dipping in some forbidden ink pot and awaken to regretfully acknowledge their own sense of loss as they realise the havoc they have brought to a family they still desire to be an intimate member of. It is these couples who have enough love and tolerance to bridge the chasm a lack of judgement carved that often see the successful outcomes counselling can offer. In other cases, the extra-marital relationship was an action symbolic of the marriage's inner demise.

Contrary to common belief and judgements, Leavers are not found lacking in a sense of commitment; it is only upon closer observation that we find Leavers to be highly committed individuals indeed. The question is not the level of commitment, but rather to what they are committed. In contrast to a Leavee, their promise is to their own life first, and strongly maintains the separation between marital status and their child-raising responsibilities and duties.

> I remember clearly the year I turned 40, sitting up in bed one day, turning to my husband and hearing these words fly out of my mouth, "I want to leave … I don't love you any more." It didn't come as a great shock to either of us. It was as if we almost naïvely agreed, we both felt our marriage was heading on a slow train to nowhere — an empty, hollow and pointless

existence, coming as a silent thief robbing us of our hopes of future greatness.

Sadly though, after that fateful night, it turned nasty. Valiant efforts of counselling and time saw me, as both the decision-maker and mother, watch helplessly as my husband turned septic. Uncomfortably, I had the catalyst of a new love in the background that drove my reluctance to maintain the compromised status quo any longer; so our devastation unfolded much like any classic drama witnessed in a movie. The lies, deceit, threats, tears, and finally my Ex clutching at the only power he could grab, the underhanded orchestration of him telling the kids.

I moved out, leaving my children with their father. It was horrible! In the face of family and friends' equal disbelief, I was left feeling responsible for leaving my family in tatters. The intense animosity and resentment towards me was so great that I eventually moved with my new love to rebuild my life upon foreign shores. The ensuing years of interaction were mostly restricted to fighting through the legal processes, while he attempted to remove all aspects of motherhood from me.

Repairing the damage from that single decision became a mission that has continued beyond the years of child-raising, mine and those of my new love. Forever branded as the scarlet woman, the adulterer, and with a family who had disowned me and friends who had abandoned me — my children were left confused as they bore both broken hearts and a broken home. I was alone, with the soulmate I had dreamt would make this all worthwhile, and life had to continue. Would we do things differently? Indeed, with constructive support and guidance, much of our ugly path did not need to be repeated. The journey has been worth it for me personally, but the causalities are sincerely regrettable. Now remarried, and with grandchildren, both respective Ex's continue to dampen the excitement of occasions such as 21st birthdays, Weddings, new births, and Christmas.

While we deeply regret the pain it has caused, we relish finding each other and following our hearts. Our hope for all our children, and our children's children, is that they will have this kind of love in their own relationships and our example will turn from what has been a burden, to a point of freedom. In years to come, perhaps they may explore what we have learned.

Another ...

I don't know if I can say anything was particularly wrong with my marriage, but after 20 years I felt compelled to leave. I knew I wanted more from life and staying married wasn't an option I saw. For the hurt and chaos I caused to my family, I felt guilt and anxiety when I saw them, yet when alone, a deep longing for something more from life, enticed me to keep searching.

To handle the fallout of the divorce, I focused on my career, developing myself to the peaks of what I knew I wanted to achieve. Watching my children's confusion grow added to my disillusionment, and although I continued to be in their lives and supportive of my Ex, I found it hard to explain what was happening to me as I didn't know.

The aftermath continued for years beyond my initial expectations and many ask, "Am I better off now?" It is hard to say: in some ways yes, and in others, perhaps not. I am not prone to regret, but I can say I do not know if I would walk this path again, but having learned so much from walking alone, maybe I would.

Leaver Capsules:

- *Lifelong except*: Although we like the idea of marriage as being lifelong, we are not held by the chains of the institution of marriage. We carry an inner belief that embodies our commitment to the *person* we are married to, not to the marriage itself.

- *Blame*: If our Ex has emotional, physical, or substance abuse issues, we blame the addictive behaviour, and therefore, move away to be free from the destruction. It becomes their issue and therefore theirs to solve without us.

- *Failure*: There is usually a residual emotion of failure; however, this is quickly justified by the rational mind as we understand we must learn from what may otherwise appear to be mistakes. We take the feeling of failure, and turn it into a *learning opportunity*.

- *Superiority*: A common trait where we feel our Ex has diminished our ability to fulfil our potential by failing to live up to the expectations we (rightly or wrongly) held for them. With this attitude, it is very easy to lose compassion for a struggling Ex.

- *Guilt*: When we inflict hurt upon another, especially someone we care about, it hurts us too. The guilt we feel is often camouflaged through an increase in blame for the shortcomings within the relationship. Irreconcilable guilt is often due to our failure to recognise the real reasons we made the decision.

- *Relief*: The sense of inner doom has lifted and we tentatively begin to move from our dreamy hopeful state to a belief that life can now improve. We start to stretch our wings, try new things, meet new people, and rediscover forgotten passions. There is a shift from *hope* to *belief*.

- *Freedom*: We are finally free to live life the way we believe it was intended to be. We are momentarily free to act upon our beliefs, to find what had previously been missing. Often great euphoria is experienced as we turn the belief into knowing. Our experience confirms it.

- *Empowered*: We made the decision; therefore, maintain our control within the relationship and this gives us an empowered mindset. We believe we are the master of our own destiny and therefore all issues can now be resolved.

Inside the Minds of the Children

It can be a challenge to understand the children because, as adults, as much as we sometimes fail to acknowledge it, we are a distance away from remembering what life was like at their age. Although divorce and separation are adult events, this event affects the children at the very core of their existence; there is more than just their home, friends, routines, care, houses, cars, pets, rules, discipline, money, siblings, and special events like Christmas, that are affected; it also has an impact on their beliefs and perspective on life.

Children feel the effects and form their own opinions; however, these are less often heard, understood, or even considered when parenting with an Ex. To begin to understand your children is to begin to leave your judgemental stance behind you and focus on being quality parents.

Influencing Factors

So many influencing factors come into play when we talk about what goes on in the minds of children; one of the most significant factors is their age and stage of development. Due to the importance of this, I have dedicated an entire chapter to understanding the effects and offer some simple techniques to assist children in each phase; it is covered in Chapter 3 – Ages and Stages.

Another influencing factor is the type of relationship the children have been living with. If your home has been violent or abusive, a great sense of relief will most likely carry both you and your children through the initial stages of change. However, if your home has been relatively calm, your children often find it difficult to comprehend why you have uprooted their lives so dramatically, why you have not kept the status quo. If your circumstances are such that neither of you need to change the situation of your employment, and the effects upon the family's daily routines are relatively insignificant, the negative fallout from the split may be minimised. However, for those who have been at home with their children and now must go out to work, this affect is substantial and is often intensely reacted to by the children. The discomforts felt in such a case can trigger emotions that few young children can acknowledge, let alone verbalise, and unfortunately, these tend to go largely unnoticed until years later when a deep seething anger emerges.

If the catalyst for the separation involves adding a new member to your family, these circumstances affect the thoughts and judgements of your children dramatically. It is for you, as parents, to handle this with great wisdom. While you need to be authentic, you also need to be mindful of the new relationship's fragile foundation upon which you are heaping a huge load of responsibility.

If you can understand that your children will experience divorce through their own filters of circumstance, age, relationship normality, and the changes that will occur to them personally, you will have a greater opportunity to minimise the negative effects and increase the benefits they will experience. In this way, the strength of being a parent during such times of change opens the doorway to living one of your greatest personal achievements in a lifetime — successfully leading your children through divorce.

> Successfully leading your children through divorce ... is one of your greatest personal achievements in a lifetime.

Emotions

The raft of emotions your children will experience is greatly influenced by your choices as parents. If you are consumed with self-indulgent anger or hostility, your children will be forced into positions of divided loyalties, where suddenly one parent needs to be made wrong to justify the other's position and interpretation of the events unfolding.

If you become preoccupied with your career or a new love, you diminish your children's sense of their own importance, and they either build walls of staunch protection to avoid feeling the hurt, or they struggle with a sense of lack of worth that forces them into withdrawal and affects their beliefs about meaningful relationships. Your children can feel confusion, anger, judgement, fear, anxiety, relief, grief, hate, and so on, and they will always want the answer to one simple question: Why? The answer will vary depending on your relationship, their age, and your choices; you would do well to have an answer ready.

Children are like snowflakes — unique — but they feel their family has become painfully normal. They may no longer believe in fairy-tales for their family, however, they may still want to for themselves. Although you can say your children shouldn't believe in tales of happily ever-after because it's simply not reality, there is a piece of this childhood fantasy that remains deep within us; otherwise, we would not be so compelled to continue our personal quests for love, peace, and happiness, extending from our homes to our global village.

It is not that any of us, parent or child, are 'unrealistic' in our pursuit; it is this hope of goodness that drives us towards betterment. Without hope, we perish; hence, the reason our current teen/young adult generation has been labelled the Lost Generation. It is because they have sadly lost hope for their futures; the consequences of this have seen the highest rates of teen suicide ever recorded.

If your children are to be free from judging either parent right or wrong, you need to be willing to continue to protect them and nurture their youth, knowing adulthood will come soon enough.

> A Parenting Team where your children do not think something is wrong with their family ... is to embody the Complex Family in essence.

Although you can accept that you need to move beyond the prison of staying together for the sake of the children, if once free of the bonds of marriage, you can apply such dedication and commitment to yourself as a parent, you would still serve all well. To build a Parenting Team where your children do not think something is wrong with their family but rather their family has increased in experiences, lifestyles, and people, is to embody the Complex Family in essence.

Three small children, all under 5 years of age, knew little of the story or facts behind the new friend coming into our home. To them, she was warm, inviting, and beautiful — the antithesis of the imagery our fairy stories have us believe stepmothers to be.

Free to form their own relationship with her, a very proud Dad would encourage laughter and fun every time they would come into our home or when routine called for them to leave and be in their other home. They experienced both the excitement and the reluctance of parting company, but nothing more than natural apprehension or tiredness, constantly free from emotional betrayal.

The hugs and kisses that started all those years ago, haven't stopped to this day, although the conversations shared have altered somewhat. The respect shown, authority granted, and love expressed has taken time, but in the children's minds, it has always been totally natural.

Our children, now teens, have begun to understand some choices their parents made in early years, while we continue to protect them; remaining free to truly love.

Natural vs. Normal

The Leavee and Leaver have much in common, both *natural* and *normal*, as inside these supposed opposite minds, we see equal human frailty. Each person has struggled with their own sense of loss, anger at being betrayed, humiliation of misunderstandings, and adding to the complex entanglement of dependencies that eventually results in the painful pulling away towards independence. Between these two people, regardless of their current standings, we know hearts have been hurt and some are hoping to be healed.

A Moment of Truth

Ultimately, when relationships have been dysfunctional and damaging, it is very normal for many secrets to be found in the darkest corners of both the Leaver and Leavee's mind. Inside the harsh confines No Choice provides, there exists the undisclosed longing for an 'Act of God' to change the circumstances and save us from our torment. It is not unusual to find either a Leaver or Leavee, who will later confess to nights spent wishing for a fateful call to end their painful hell. Naturally, the horror of such notions forces them into silence, guilty at the mere thought without entertaining further the slightest of murmurs.

As unpalatable as this may sound, it is more common than we want to acknowledge; as there is bravery and liberty on the canvas the Leaver paints, the Leavee recoils. The Leaver's actions highlight the hypocrisy of commitment, and strangely it becomes almost an enviable position to the Leavee, albeit condemned in principle.

> To whom or what are we committed?

Indeed, in either position we find a clue to the answer to an important *natural* question, one that will provide the clue to living our most authentic life possible. *"To whom or what are we committed?"*

Short-Term Power

Although it is easy for us to judge and cast our vote, there are children (young and old) who need to be given the opportunity to love both parents regardless of how good, freeing, flawed, hopeless, or wrong their parents first appear. The responsibility to build harmony inside the developing Parenting Team rests with both parents. It is fair to say, however, the larger influencing factor in the level of devastation our children experience more often comes through the Leavee, rather than the Leaver. To create a healthy parenting relationship, the Leavee's reactions present the largest hurdle to transcend. This is not to blame the Leavee for all the bitter Ex's stories, but it is to acknowledge the extent of bewilderment divorce confronts us with.

Whilst inside a marriage, behavioural expectations are tolerated so the Leaver has been able to regulate their reactions having been granted the benefit of time, privacy, and control to grieve their loss before it is made public. However, once outside this safety-zone, belittlement, conflict, resentment, and poor behaviour is not only permitted but expected, causing increasing levels of destruction for all involved.

Although difficult for Leavee's to hear or acknowledge — given their beliefs about being wronged that justify their actions — it is paramount your children are left with the genuine opportunity to love both parents equally. When you choose this path, you as the Leavee, do not diminish their love for you by allowing them to love their Leaver parent, you increase it and will experience (and teach) the fact that love always expands to make sure there is enough to share.

In cases where parental responsibilities are abandoned, and one parent is left to continue, it helps to focus on the fact that solo parents are very capable of raising stunning young adults; raising happy, successful children does not depend on having both parents present.

The greater damage occurs where the ongoing toxic examples being lived by parents are ignored, and there is a failure to deal with issues and anger. Regardless how meandering your course has been to reach the point of having an Ex and children, there is the opportunity for you and your children to benefit. You can all excel in your futures as you find that authenticity and prosperity depend on your choices. The belief that you, or your children, are sentenced to a life of doomed relationships, as former generations have lead us to believe, is simply a limiting belief. Today, there is greater knowledge of transformation available than ever before, and you can lead your children into constructive, ongoing, developing relationships naturally.

For you to have your divorce give birth to splendid families, you are wise to consider what great parenting involves; in this way you can become strong as you lead your family into this promised greatness.

Focusing on Yourself

Frequently, our focus as parents turns to those outside of ourselves, and we forget that the greatest parenting of all starts within. It is not about providing the best physical world, nor about doing all the right things all the time, it is about who we are *Being* while we are parenting that is so important.

Once inside the Complex Family, we can become sidetracked by heartbreak, inconvenience, and constant annoyance, and forget to focus on who we are being. It is normal for us to look to our Ex, our children, or to those who are causing the chaos, and believe we must find the answers to our problem — that is to say we need to fix them — so that our life can continue as it ought to. While logically this may make sense, life seldom presents an absence of problems, but instead, urges us to continue to develop our perspective, to grow and shape our character.

> We do not need agreement to have a healthy Complex Family Parenting Team ... we need to be aware of who we are being.

As a droplet falling into the water causes a ripple that creates one ring at a time, our focus must be on ourselves first. It is natural for us to disagree with our Ex and, in fact, we do not need agreement to have a healthy Complex Family Parenting Team; rather, what we do need is to be aware of who we are being while parenting. The more we realise our state of being while carrying out our actions, the less focus we have on our Ex and the power we believe they hold over our family's happiness and future.

Identity of Parenting

The typical tears we shed as our little one starts their first day of school show the normal tendency for us, as parents, to become so identified with parenting we believe it makes us who we are. While it is part of what we do, who we are is not a parent; this is a title we carry; it is a job we do — a function we fulfil. If we believe our identity is that of a parent, we will struggle to allow our children to develop healthy independence.

If we are able to enjoy each phase our children develop through, and love the opportunities they provide, we are less likely to lose ourselves within the title. In this way, we become the parent we seek to be.

> For many years, I introduced myself as a mother of three children. Entirely the focus of my life was my mothering, ruling my every decision, and I did my best to always ensure it was to the highest of what I knew. Tired and rung out by this constant doing, my anxiety and stress was unknowingly passed onto the kids. It has only been through the development of peacefulness within that I am now the parent I was previously striving to be.

To develop a state of contentment within the mundane daily routine of parenthood while holding peace for our children to experience and learn, is to *master parenthood*. It is not about the circumstances of our separation, the irritation of our Ex, or the constant striving towards some other achievement that defines our parenting. It is purely who we are being whilst in the midst of the normality parenting provides that allows us to live each moment without complaining or nagging, and provide opportunities for each to choose their own path and understand the consequences of those choices. In this way, we develop wisdom. The state of *being* takes the focus away from expectations and turns us gently, inviting us to look at who we are, so we can infuse the life of others with greatness.

> Master parenting; develop contentment in the mundane ... hold peace for your child to learn and experience.

To move into great parenting irrespective of our family structure, we need to display acceptance, respect, and the daily lifestyle of personal power defined by boundaries. If we cannot be this with our Ex, our children will have no shortage of opportunities to question the validity of our own parenting style, with none more ready to do so than our critical teens who are searching for their own identity while evaluating what they believe the purpose of life to be.

To live aware of who we are *being* is challenging. This is the very essence of fulfilment when parenting. It is when we take our eyes off the Ex, and turn a deaf ear to those around us who want to bag and belittle, that we focus ourselves on who we are being within every interaction. We cannot change our Ex to suit our choices, lifestyle, or desires; we separated because it did not work the first time around, so the time has come to look in another direction.

Focusing on the Children

I believe most of us have what it takes to be genuinely great parents; more often than not, it is through ignorance rather than mindful choice that we neglect some of the most crucial aspects of parenting.

Beyond the basic requirements of love, nurturing, food, clothing, shelter, and education, the next layer involves four key elements. Let's go through each of these in more detail to understand how they affect the developmental years, and expose some common-day misconceptions.

These four key elements are: Time, Structure, Stimulation, and Protection

Time

There is a debate amongst those who facilitate parental education that has raged for years — Quantity vs. Quality. These two opinions have been frequently flaunted by those on either side of Mothers Working Outside of the Home argument. The purest believe that children need their mother at home and that the quantity of time spent with them is of paramount importance. The progressive attitudes in defense of the working mother, place weight on the quality of time. Free from judgement either way (as I have done both), I have come to satisfy my requirement for an answer through what I believe is more important than both;

> **"Wherever You Are, Be There."**

Today, more than any time previously known in our history, distraction is our new norm. We will answer phone calls, return text messages, or read a magazine or newspaper while we wait for our coffee to be brought to our table, whilst our child sits alongside, regardless of what side of the Quantity/Quality argument we believe we belong on. Between mobile phones, iPods, and all other forms of screen-based entertainment, we have our attention more focused on those absent, than with those in front of us. To give our children Time is to be Present. It is to value the interaction regardless of how ordinary it may appear.

> Wherever you are,
> Be there!

> John is a well-paid senior executive who can provide every new toy imaginable for his kids — and he does. They have the latest and greatest technology money can buy, ranging from personal iPods to full in-home theatre. He is not unlike many diligent, hardworking, and intelligent men; he possess a fatherly desire to be at as many kid's events as his work allows.
>
> Rushing from the office to make the 7:00 p.m. parent-teacher interviews, he greets his boy with a quick hug, asks about his day for a gratuitous 30 seconds, and as he does, automatically reaches into his pocket for his new phone. Proudly giving facts and figures as to its brilliance, how he can now access his work inbox from anywhere, anytime. "Ding." His concentration snaps elsewhere, he immediately texts, and laughs audibly at a reply while sadly his attention has moved to another, and away from his son sitting quietly beside him.
>
> John is perplexed at the teacher's concern for his boy's lack of concentration.

This is alarmingly common; and let's not pretend we don't do it ourselves. Many women enjoy believing they can multitask and therefore excuse themselves, but I beg to offer an alternative opinion. We are no more able to focus on texting and at the same time hold a meaningful conversation with someone in front of us than men are. And our children feel it. Quietly, distraction robs us of opportunities that our present moment offers. Whether we are doing the washing, taxiing kids, writing a thesis, having dinner, or going shopping, *be there*. Pay attention to whatever it is you are doing and absorb the uniqueness within each instance. When you do this, you will excel in all your doings.

For our children to feel they are valued and important, loved and worthwhile, a simple priority of focus is pivotal. If we are miles away in thought while with our children, the time with them is of little consequence and can be fulfiled by anyone. Have you heard yourself ask the question "How's your day been?", and then be unable to recall the answer. We may even ask it again before we get pulled up by our child for having just told us. How many of us know our children's friends' names? What about what they look like? Would you be able to spot them around the local shops, especially out of school uniform? Have we taken the time to understand what is happening inside their friends' families? The next time you are ready to scold your teen for their dismissive glance towards your friend, ask yourself, do you know theirs?

Our children (especially teens) need our support, wisdom, and guidance as we move through this change in family structure; perhaps they felt too much distance when it didn't really matter to believe we will truly be there for them now that it does. *Being There* is about focus, attention, and intention.

The debate about *quantity* and *quality* cannot be settled outside of circumstantial factors, this can only be done at the core of Being Present.

Structure

Structure gives strength, sturdiness, security and soundness to our family life. It creates the safety-zone for growth and healthy development. If we provide structure, we provide the framework for our children's masterpiece. Providing this much-needed structure is achieved through boundaries, routines, consistency, planning and natural consequences. It is in providing these, our children develop a healthy backbone for their own life.

Joanne is a lovely woman, warm hearted and known to be generous to a fault. As a solo mum, Joanne wanted to be friends with her daughter, Sarah. After many years of juggling the closeness of friendship and the authoritative responsibility of being a parent, Joanne was exhausted. Sarah seemed to rule the roost as she resorted to temper tantrums and clawing cat-fights if she didn't get her way. Sarah had just turned 12 years old, when Joanne turned to counselling after her daughter violently reacted to being caught climbing out her bedroom window at 10:30 p.m.

Sarah was equally confused in the relationship and used to getting her way. It was of small consequence to Joanne, with only one child to appease, so frequently the path of least resistance delivered the desired peace.

Working with structure, we started to bring in a new way of living to enable both Joanne and Sarah to be the individuals they needed to be. We set boundaries for both, with a clear understanding of the consequences when pushed or broken.

Void of structure for her own life, Joanne had spent most of her childhood being shipped from house-to-house after the passing of her parents in a tragic car accident. For Joanne, to teach boundaries and structure to Sarah was simply not going to happen until she learned these for herself.

Structure adds containment and containment gives meaning and purpose. Let's take the example of a puddle of water. It has little boundaries and no movement, it just sits, collecting more or dries up. If we take this water and place it into a watering can, we have given it some focus and direction. By doing this, we give it purpose and it now has value. This principle applies to our parenting. By placing structure around our family, we give focus and direction with the natural outcome of this being purpose. When in possession of purpose, we feel valuable and gain a sense of meaning.

> Structure gives focus and direction, this gives purpose; with this we feel valuable and gain a sense of meaning.

Stimulation

Moving onto the third parenting element, we have *stimulation*, and I believe it is here our modern parenting has abdicated one of our largest responsibilities in being a parent. The stimulation required by our children's developing minds is immense. More than any prior generation in our history, our children have the greatest opportunity to excel with modern technology at our fingertips, opening an unprecedented world of knowledge before us. Yet, as parents, we have fallen into the trap of this power, being the convenient thief that robs our children's minds. Through the addiction to being entertained, we have almost stolen our children's ability to be stimulated.

> Natural imagination and creativity are vastly different from entertainment ... we become so numb to nature's magical scenes before us.

Natural imagination and creativity are vastly different from entertainment. I personally believe there is a direct correlation between the alarming rates of ADD and parental irresponsibility in using screen-based entertainment. The media, in all their brilliance, have subtly lowered our inner energetic life force by sucking it straight out of us. Most of our children sit in a near-hypnotised state while advertising feeds their thirst for more 'things' before they have a chance to experience life's natural gifts. As adults, we are insanely addicted to screens and we can even remember the days when it wasn't this way. Most of our children do not know of life without screens. Fewer and fewer children are able to remember holidays spent building sandcastles, damming up the streams and then racing small sticks down streams as they follow tumbling over boulders. Our children have forgotten they can lie out under the stars and see them for real, so trained have they been to watch them in close-up on some sci-fi movie instead. We have become so numb to nature's magical scenes before us that instead we revel in the brutality of violence being used as a form of entertainment; it highlights the most bizarre of all, that we now kill our own, and call it fun.

To stimulate our children's minds, we need to start young. If they are older, it is not irreparable, but we need to treat it much like an addiction towards a toxic substance such as drugs, alcohol, or cigarettes, because it has become damaging and highly addictive. We need to turn off the televisions and computer games and start interacting.

> Over the years in our home, we have turned off many screens and instead, picked up packs of cards or got out board games to play together. Children watch how to win and lose graciously; they learn how to celebrate someone's attempts to draw, guess, or act, and to give encouragement to another less than decipherable performance. They interact with high's and low's, and choose how to talk together instead of throwing a grunt or passing comment as they watch a screen as they sprawl alongside each other.
>
> We have also decided to celebrate short-term boredom because very quickly it is followed by creativity. For a long time, I used to keep the kids active, with constant activities, crafts, or games for them and then wondered why I was rung out by their bedtime. From the nothingness space that short-term boredom provides, the child's imagination ignites and fills the void, but this only happens if there is a void there in the first place.
>
> Amazing things happen. Books get read. That model plane that was given last birthday finally gets taken down from the shelf, dusted off, and an attempt is made to build it. Lego towers are rebuilt again and again to compete for their personal best height record. The musical instrument gets picked up for pleasure rather than practice. A simple block of wood is quietly chiseled into a koro, a well-chosen stick is now carefully whittled and sanded into a beautiful wand. The banging of pots and pans indicates another creation is soon to follow from the kitchen. The glue and glitter give way to the beautiful card, now being written in. Naturally age and stage dependent, the mess or supervision will vary; however, in our home we found the allowance of natural creativity, rather than normal screens, to be a very powerful influence.

Protection

For most of us, providing our children with the basics: food, shelter, clothing, and warmth is taken for granted; we provide these regardless. To protect our children from severe physical harm or emotional violence, however, is equally important. If we suspect, even for a moment, that our children's welfare is being compromised, we would be wise to gain clarity, and then act. Protection under such circumstances is likened more to a German Shepherd bitch with her pups! This is where innocent children need to be removed from harmful situations and supported while they deal with the trauma.

Beyond this foundational layer however, somehow we are subtly missing the point of protection. A young lion does not go alone to a kill. Within the protection and safety of the pride, their mother keeps them out of harm's way so that slowly these cubs learn to respect their own frailty and over time develop enough strength and skill that they can one day become the King. If they were either left alone or if they were protected beyond the opportunities to learn their physicality, they would not realise their magnificent potential.

> Many children are kept from learning the limits of their own physicalness while still young enough to gain respect for it.

Many of our children are kept from learning the limits of their own physicalness while still young enough to gain respect for it. More common than not, there are soft-mats for playgrounds, netted trampolines, fenced swimming pools and padded elbows, wrists, and bums for skates. So while I see the benefits, I can also see a distinct lack of commonsense because our children fail to learn the limits to which they should push their bodies, and the consequences of exceeding those limits.

Through cushioning the result of the issues, we appease the irritation yet we leave the cause still festering. Laws regarding swimming pools have been a major issue in our country, and in many other Western cultures. The insanity these laws have brought to our backyards is unfathomable as families are forced to spend thousands of dollars on fencing, locks, and fancy gates, while within less than a small child's stroll, there are beaches, creeks, duck ponds, and drains that all remain exposed. Why are we failing to teach our children the appropriate behaviours that are required around water rather than only targeting the restriction of backyard entry? Our focus has lost commonsense.

Our over-protective parenting style is developing children who are denied the opportunity to learn from the smaller signals of pain. In our society today, we postpone those vital learning years until they reach their late teens and early twenties, when many combine this with alcohol, sex, and depression, as they missed the opportunities to learn about the consequences to their own bodies early.

> Over-protective parenting styles are developing children who are denied the opportunity to learn from the smaller signals of pain.

> After years of being driven to school, our kids rode their bikes. During this time, we experienced riding into parked cars when checking their foot pedal, falling off while going up curbs, getting the wobbles and freaking themselves out racing downhill, along with other close calls. We also saw them gain a healthy respect for speed, skin, and the tar-seal. While I got no pleasure in their pain, or lessons, or from the phone calls for help or the mysterious damage to their bikes, as parents we saw them gain greater appreciation for their own safety and a gradual development of commonsense . . . all before they got behind the steering wheel of a car.

Physical protection is only one aspect of our job as parents. All aspects of development require staged protection to avoid overwhelming your young one's worlds with adult dysfunction. It is acceptable protection to lock doors, safety-latch windows, and set alarms to help us feel protected; however, through our own lack of awareness, we allow violence to walk straight through our front door with the latest blockbuster movie hired for a night of family entertainment. Having become obsessed with sensationalist television, we also permit cartoon characters to infiltrate our young children's minds, and believe this is acceptable because it is so common.

Our children came into this world as a blank canvas, blessed with every ounce of opportunity to live a life of rewarding fulfilment and inner abundance. Through our interaction with them, and their's with the world around them, they form their view of the planet. By infusing them with corruption, violence, greed, and all manner of low energy forms, we force their masterpiece into mediocrity and hopeless normality. The control our media has over our minds is like a worldwide cancer that subtly programs us with what is deemed acceptable behaviour; it implants the very behaviours our children mimic when reacting to pressure. We wonder why senseless violence is on the increase, yet we know the multi-billion-dollar advertising industry works — what part of this simple equation are we missing?

Protecting your child's mind is the greatest protection you can offer them. This doesn't mean raising them in a bubble, isolated in your home, but rather to prepare them for when they meet the world. It means ensuring they have developed appropriate tools to allow them to handle what they see and hear, whilst you carefully and gradually expose them to more. Bombarding them with a distorted perspective of normality at an early age robs them of the opportunity to view life as beautiful and kind. If they grow up believing the world is a friendly and abundant place, they will more likely experience it this way.

> There's a mantra I used for myself as I went through my divorce; it has remained with me ever since: *"I'll let everyone into my heart, very few near my body, no one inside my head."*

Why, as parents, do we protect our things so viciously, and yet allow our children's minds to be polluted and eventually conditioned to violence, distorted sexuality, and mind-numbing indifference?

Chapter Three
Ages and Stages

"If kids adjust, why are there so many dysfunctional adults?"

That quality line expresses a belief I personally hold, and reveals the core of my passion for increased awareness in parenting.

Many people comment on my well-adjusted children, with the intention to express a compliment for how unscathed they appear while coming from a family where divorce has featured. In their clumsiness, they automatically assume I agree with their paradigm where the level of expectation is lowered because of the disadvantaged life my children were born into. This is yet another example of the subtle grey cloud that hangs over those inside a Complex Family.

Do children *adjust*? I believe they modify behaviour, change expectations, absorb patterns, shut down, and become resigned to situations that are beyond their ability to solve. I also do not believe this is the intention behind the complimentary words. As for *adjustment*, it could be said the children get used to it, reconcile, alter, and rearrange. This is far from coming to terms with it. While outwardly they may appear to adjust, perhaps inwardly, it would be more accurate to say they *cope*: that's a strategy that underlies personal survival.

> While outwardly they may appear to adjust ... it's more accurate to say they cope ... dysfunction will wait to surface in their adult years.

If we take comfort in our children's ability to adjust, we miss the opportunity for potential development in their ability to face challenges, process and resolve issues, through life. As parents, we clearly recognise the gap between an adult's and a child's physical abilities, so why would dealing with the complexity of divorce or separation be any different? We do not expect children to carry out tasks, nor handle pressure more competently than an adult; this would be an inappropriate level of expectation. However, we do place enormous expectations upon our children who have so few tools or resources to assist them in this growth. Understandably, children do not adjust, they cope; their imminent dysfunction will wait to surface in their adult years. This temporary facade of coping does not give us license to embark upon the path of ignorance and overlook the impact our actions and attitudes have upon their lives.

Mariner and the Storm

If we struggle to give up our judgements regarding the effects the separation has on our family, we can create a damaged stage of development in our child. This is not said to inflict further guilt or condemnation upon those who are struggling; rather, it is meant to highlight the need for an inner *acceptance* of one's circumstances. It is important to note here, the word acceptance does not carry the same meaning as agree with, condone, or resign. *Acceptance is surrender*.

A wise sailor knows it is better to work with the power of a storm than to vigorously fight it. Although our sea dog may not enjoy the storm, he accepts the weather as it is, and he works within the circumstances that currently face his boat and crew. Making appropriate adjustments to his tactics, sail choices, crew positions, and even his personal wardrobe with wet-weather gear, he surrenders to the forces around him. Resistance to the circumstances the storm presents sees issues escalate with possible gear failure, breakages, and worse yet, at times, the loss of life. While surrendering to the weather, this does not mean there will be no fallout from the storm, but the negative effects are minimised.

Your inability to work with the forces surrounding your relationship's demise has repercussions; if you ignore these, the outcomes could be worse than anticipated. If you are able to accept what you see, you grant yourself and your children the opportunity to make wise choices. In this way, you will continue to learn and develop skills and wisdom as you help your children to grow into healthy adults.

Stages are Natural

Natural child development occurs in phases as focused attention enhances learning, growth, and evolvement. We accept it as normal for most children to learn to sit up by the time they are five to six months old, to crawl at about nine months before they progress to walking by the time they reach their first birthday. Of course, these are approximate averages, and we all know children who have walked earlier, and some later, depending on circumstances and surroundings.

In much the same way physical development occurs, our children develop their perspective of life through various stages that conveniently coincide with age. The filters through which we view the world as adults is formed during our first 20 years of walking the planet. If we have healthy, stimulating, and constructive growing years, we are more likely to experience the world as a healthy, stimulating, and constructive place — albeit we clearly see the contradictions. If we are raised with fear, paranoia, and anxiety, we are more likely to experience the world as being hostile toward us.

The intention of this chapter is to provide a road map of your children's development. When you understand the implications of your actions and attitudes on their lives at each stage, you gain insight into their subconscious development. This will increase your opportunities to focus attention at pivotal times and most effectively use practical tools and techniques to bring about healthy growth.

Using Age as the Gauge

In this chapter, we will focus on children's development within each stage — reasonably aligned to an age, but not defined by it. While age is an approximate indication, stages of development may well blur at the edges. Sometimes, the result is months of overlapping development; at other times, the transfer will be as significant as a light-switch that is turned on: a signal that the next stage has begun.

By being aware of developmental stages and using age as the gauge, we can recognise when a limitation within the stage is present and is often lived out during adulthood; this is the reason many counsellors, psychologists, and psychotherapists look back to childhood to establish the root causes of dysfunctional adult behaviour.

Using the Stages

As you read, you may find yourself saying "Wow, that's me" — this is okay. Not only is this perfectly normal, it's what makes the journey of parenting so meaningful. The more aware you become of gaps in your own life, the more compassion you can develop towards the gaps you notice in your children's; this gives you the heart to help develop healthiness in both. It is understanding the damage, trauma, or abuse within each stage that enables you, as parent, to effectively help your children grow through these years, and retrospectively, to heal your own affected layers. The stages outlined here may also spark pangs of guilt, questioning, or blame. If this happens, pause and mark the spot. It is by paying attention to these subtle impulses that you will expand your knowledge and increase the opportunity to help your children to grow.

This chapter follows the same format for each stage: first, an explanation of the key areas of development and identifying what is seeking to be formed, and then when this is done in a healthy way, what the external characteristics and behaviours will look like. The next section will explain how this relates to our beliefs, to what we feel we deserve, and the negative outcomes should this stage be under- or over-developed.

Once we understand the theory, I will bring this into the Complex Family environment. We look briefly at what this means for the Leavee and Leaver, and then move on to supporting your children if they are currently in this stage of development. If your children have passed this stage, or you recognise some limitations for yourself, there are also suggestions of things you can do.

Experience and Wisdom

One of the things I've seen in my years of working with parents (irrespective of family structure) is a frequent source of confusion and discontent stems from excessive parental expectations — a belief that their child ought to be more advanced than they are. That is to say, we assume we have the ability to save our children from developing wisdom through experience. We hope they will be able to avoid all the painful lessons and pitfalls we experienced, and we hope they will do this by listening to us. The irony is that *wisdom comes from experience*. Our attempt to save our children from painful experiences robs them of the opportunity to gain their own personal wisdom, and builds a destructive dependency on external structures.

Part of us learning to walk was accepting that we would fall. There was no problem in falling; it would have only become an issue if the pain we felt hindered us from getting up and continuing our development. Living in a world blessed with sensors and feelings, we learn through experience. If we block this process, life becomes a theory class where the most we can attain is *belief* — without ever *knowing*. Knowing is at the core of wisdom — therefore, the purpose of having an experience is to invite wisdom to reside within.

Stage 1 :: Womb – 12 months

Naturally, this stage is initiated while the baby is fused with the mother, so the child has not yet experienced separation. Only after entering the world do they gain their sense of self. Depending on culture, the degree of trauma this separation experience creates for the child will vary, but it is a major event regardless. Through the comparatively recent practice of separating mother and child, this developmental phase is damaged before we get much parenting underway. Fortunately, as more people are becoming sensitive to the naturalness of childbirth, we see increasing numbers of mothers and babies staying close.

The Essence and Focus of Stage 1

The first stage focuses on *survival*. It deals with the *physical* world into which the baby is born. The little one needs nurturing, love, food, warmth, clothing, time, stability, routines, and a certain amount of things that build up their world so this can be happily accomplished. If all of these are provided, the child feels *welcomed into the world*. With this feeling of welcome, they find it easy to *trust* the world they've entered. If the atmosphere of welcome is missing, mistrust is developed as the infant feels their basic survival is under threat.

Some parents can testify that their child was born with a chip on their shoulder; they came out ready to fight with everyone and everything. This common signpost points towards some trauma the baby suffered while still in the womb. It could have been an initial rejection by the mother as she tried to come to terms with being a parent. It could have been the separation of the baby's parents during the pregnancy, the death of a family member and the great loss felt, or the vibrations of hostility in war-torn countries that permeate the mother's consciousness. With so many possible factors that can influence the unborn child, and even more that can occur in the first 12 months of development, the potential for this kind of trauma effect is significant.

Healthy development within this stage builds on trust with an increasing sense of *hope*. Hope emanating from the very core of their being, it flows into natural expansion, inviting security at the foundational level of development. This person maintains a great sense of expectation; aspirations ooze from them; it is often the unexplainable difference felt when one is around them; they project a sense of grounded optimism. The trust built in this foundation for life underlies all other layers waiting to be developed; therefore, their solidness is intrinsic.

Consider for a moment the construction of a building. We wouldn't dream of taking shortcuts with the workmanship on the foundations of a building just to save time; this would be considered irresponsible. We inspect what has been built, make corrections, alter time frames, and typically increase budgets to solve any issues with the foundation before we continue with construction; in this way, we ensure the safety and soundness of the building. In much the same way, during the term of pregnancy and throughout the first 12 months of life, we need to build a solid and balanced foundation for the child's life: a healthy, stable, comfortable place where the child is free to relax and grow, and safely explore their physical surroundings. With strong foundations, the child gains an inner security, a sense of *self-preservation*, and improves their innate ability to survive. If gaps are left in this layer, they affect the integrity, authenticity, and stability as growth continues.

The Rights and Thief of Stage 1

Fear is the aspect of this stage that haunts the child who is developing with poor foundations. Even with the best of foundations, your child will at some point experience fear, but it will be their trust and hope that outweighs the fear, so that fear ceases to be the controlling force in life.

The ramifications of unresolved fear manifests in children through extremes. A deep belief in their own *right to be here* has been stolen from them, so they may well find themselves at either extreme of the *having continuum* that ranges from having absolutely nothing to holding on to everything as in hoarding. They may struggle with weight issues, and be either obese or noticeably underweight. Perhaps they will display financial greediness, or the opposite, continual financial difficulties. They may have very poor boundaries, be insipid or fragile in temperament. Or they may head for another extreme, the rigid person with no flexibility, or one whose ability to handle change is almost nonexistent. This person doubts their *right to be here*, fears personal discipline, and is frequently found struggling with focus and concentration. They can also be lazy and display a certain tired sluggishness they feel unable to shake.

As we begin to understand the importance of this stage of development, we gain an appreciation for the struggle so many young people have with life. As their foundations have not been well developed, they are left to simply grow older as the clock ticks, yet somehow we still expect greatness from them. Children are left to build their masterpiece on shaky foundations.

Inside a Complex Family

If you have an unborn child or one who is less than one year old when a separation occurs, the most important thing to remember is that your own acceptance of the separation will minimise the impact on the child. It is your ongoing *resistance* to the divorce or trauma that creates the issues, not the event itself.

The following explanation reflects the intention and attitude that this book intends to develop; they are introduced here as goalposts to indicate what we aim for. The Leaver and Leavee will each do what they will, but the examples below provide the essence of responsible parenting in each role.

Leavees: Understanding our child's needs powerfully motivates us into a place of acceptance even if, initially, it is only out of love for our child. Through our desire to provide the best for our child, we can seek more assistance to deal with the trauma in a positive manner. We know that the longer we carry the hurt, the more damaging the brokenness becomes. Knowing the main negative factor that causes the damage is *fear*, gives us our clue for healthy development.

Leavers: We do what we can to continue to provide a safe and stable living environment for our children during this period. We work to overcome the paralyzing effects of fear, along with the negativity that has been imposed upon our child's environment; we look at our fears, accept them, and make constructive choices while we take practical steps to minimise the fears. If our Leavee is in a fearful state and our child is with them (especially during pregnancy), we know we must avoid placing more pressure on our Leavee by telling them to *'stop being fearful'*; instead, we do our part to support and ensure that daily survival and practical economic challenges are met. We look at their fears and become the support that provides relief, without allowing ourselves to be sucked into a vacuum of emotional drama. We have left — this was our choice — therefore, we accept that the path ahead is shared by both parents and the children as we look to the *Highest Good of All* as our guide rather than seeking a good feeling here and now.

Growing Your Child in Stage 1

If your child is in their first year of life, you must ensure they feel safe. They need to be in an environment they trust, one that builds their sense of a *right to be here*. This means you need to be wise in your choices of living arrangements and social surroundings. Any physical or emotional harm, volatility, and instability, breeds fear. This fear robs children of trust at their core, stealing their belief that they are welcome in the world.

During this stage, do everything you can to keep yourself and your children in good health. Eat sensibly, sleep as well as possible, and remember to appreciate your physical reserves may have changed. Sometimes, this heart-wrenching time needs an antidote; the good news is, the best one available is also free — spend time in nature; your children absorb through their senses, and nature (by definition) feels more natural to them. Make daily appointments for yourself and baby at beaches, trees, parks, wide-open spaces, and anywhere you can be in touch with nature. Get away from the cafe culture and concrete jungles by losing yourself in the beauty of nature. There is a groundedness there that builds your child's innate trust. Give them time to absorb it by soaking it in; let your young ones play on the grass while learning to crawl. They may get a little mud on their hands and knees but that's okay; the benefit they gain from nature will outweigh the laundry later. Wrap up your children, take them out, and make sure they touch nature.

Put down the schedules and pick up your child. Take the time to do nothing; just sit and hold them. This is not to sit and cry with them, (this won't assist their development), it is to sit in quietness. Just Be. Allow yourself to be still with your babe in your arms — practice it. Even in the middle of screaming colic, it is possible to hold an inner peacefulness for an aching baby. Most of us know, when we have exhausted all other avenues, all we can do is hold them, provide comfort, and wait for it to pass. In the same way, you can hold this inner space and allow your baby to continue feeling some connection to you; you allow them to trust. You may not have any of the answers right now, but if you *accept* all your shortcomings, frustrations, and hopelessness, rather than resisting them, this surrender is contagious.

Revisiting to Grow Stage 1

For those whose children have passed this stage and who have felt a pang of recognition as they read, take heart, it is possible to fill in the gaps and smooth out the peaks and troughs, in your children's foundation. The hitch is the children need to be willing to do it. The older they are, the more important personal desire — coupled with willingness and commitment — become; but it can still be done.

Fundamental in building stability is the child's need to reconnect with their body — their physicality. This may sound a little strange considering they are still in their body, so I'll explain further. People are able to tolerate amazing physical pain by disconnecting their minds from acknowledging pain. When children live with traumatic situations, a disconnect can occur between what their senses feed into their brain and what is permitted to be recognised. Prolonged states of fear can break vital connections that need to be rebuilt, and it is physical activity that helps to develop the reconnections.

Invite your children to do things that connect directly with nature; build sandcastles, climb trees, dig gardens, chop firewood. Be creative and be sure that only earthy things, things of nature, are touched; avoid artificial or simulated objects. Walking, playing sports, dancing, running, or swimming, all help children to recognise their physicality. This is so simple, we overlook how good these are for us.

Touch is the most important sense involved as you revitalise these connections. Consider massage as this is an obvious touching activity, whether giving or receiving, it encourages increased physical sensing. Some people choose to take up yoga, pilates, or tai chi that focus on physical grounding through attention to movement that is also very beneficial.

As you participate in such activities with your child, the intention is for the child to develop a belief that it is safe to be alive. You want them to truly know that the ground they walk on supports them rather than have them be fearful of every step they take. Seek to inspire them to love and respect their own bodies as you teach them to listen quietly to the messages their bodies send; encourage them to acknowledge those signals rather than ignore or reject them.

Finally, as you spend an increasing amount of time in nature, encourage your children to fully attend to the beauty and abundance that nature provides, and see that it's not just the picture-pretty backdrop that we so often take for granted.

Stage 2 :: 6 – 24 months

This stage introduces emotions, sensations, differences, and movement. Here the baby becomes mobile, and we watch as their attention turns to ever-broadening horizons. The child begins to explore their world, often in raptures over something you have long come to take for granted and no longer acknowledge its simplistic beauty or worth.

The Essence and Focus of Stage 2

Young ones begin to understand duality: hot and cold, up and down, in and out, day and night, pleasure and pain, close and distant, on and off. From their perspective, they form interpretations of their surroundings and life is simplistic duality: On : Off. They are free of the limitations that labels and names provide, and their distinctions are more felt and recognised than understood. They are free to come close or move away, and this movement creates sensations that they explore. As they begin to recognise how it feels to move, whether closer or farther: Do I feel good or do I not? Does this cause pain or give me pleasure?

The focus here is on *pleasure* as the sensations interpreted through emotional feedback from their movement form these vital connections. Healthy development at this stage will allow both distance and closeness to occur with pleasure. This identity of *self* builds on the trust developed in Stage 1 and allows for secure movement.

As this stage is about pleasure, it is innately bound to sexuality, an aspect of early childhood development that is only exposed in later years when the memory of this formative period is very faded. By the time a gap in this stage of development is revealed, one's beliefs regarding pleasure are so ingrained in their subconscious thinking, the gap is often interpreted as a sexual issue; however, the issue is not about sexuality, but rather about the formed beliefs surrounding *self-gratification*.

As you meet your child's needs while they explore the new-found freedoms that movement and sensations provide, you help them to grow healthy connections between pleasure and pain; this will enable them to experience separation without linking it to pain or loss.

When this stage is healthy, you will see an explosion in emotional intelligence; your children move gracefully and naturally nurture themselves and others as they continue to grow. These are children with healthy boundaries, they receive great enjoyment from feelings of pleasure. When they give, the give has a feeling of lightness, and we feel it is genuine; it's not a trade or something that comes with the strings of attachment.

The Rights and Thief of Stage 2

Stage 2 children are all *Need, Sensation,* and *Desire*. The *Wanting Cycle* — *desires* birthed from *sensations* that come from *needs* — explains why we find it so difficult to know what we want. When the foundation is not formed in a supporting, healthy manner, we wind up out of touch with ourselves and left to answer, "I don't know" when faced with the simplest of choices.

If problems are opportunity's paper wrapping, here we introduce *emotions as the clothing of feelings*. Emotions help to expand the experiences the body offers; emotions give feelings a voice that says, *"I feel; therefore, I am."* To know what we want is intimately connected with our *right to feel*. If this right is not developed, damaged, or goes unnoticed, it will produce a slow inner numbness.

Further damage can occur at this stage when needs are treated with hostility or emotional manipulation. The need becomes disguised within the entangled emotion of *guilt* that is infused into our child's psyche. The normal parental line of *"You've made me so angry"* damages the integrity of the *right to feel*. Anger is the result of feeling helpless, hopeless, or powerless; it is not the feeling itself. It is not the children who make us angry, it is we who have become angry as a result of our own loss of control.

Then there is the adult who admits they feel guilty about everything and can't work out why? Even if they have no direct involvement in a situation, they still feel guilty. This adult-child has been unable to fully appreciate needs, sensations, and desire as being a normal process in realising pleasure. The voice of *"I feel; therefore, I am"* becomes stronger if it is infused with guilt. To handle such destructive powers, avoidance techniques are subconsciously used; we deny desires or become numb to sensations as we ignore our needs. Such an unhealthy belief in either giving or receiving pleasure turns into blame or sabotage, and causes us to avoid any opportunity for self-gratification.

If the haunting spectre of guilt sits on one's shoulder, they are likely to express the extremes of the *pleasure continuum*. We may see either addiction or denial of all forms of pleasure: alcohol, sex, gambling, shopping, sunbathing, eating, sports and fitness, entertainment, and so on. We find those who refuse to look after themselves, (even modestly) because they feel bad about doing so. Others are incapable of knowing when to stop spending on themselves; they are addicted to short-term pleasure, regardless of the pain. We may see excessively strong emotions (hysteria, drama-queens, panic attacks) or the opposite end of the spectrum; with the death of both desire and passion, this person is emotionally numb — the walking dead as we call them. There will also be those who are emotionally dependent on others, or obsessively attached and unable to create healthy boundaries for themselves.

Inside the Complex Family

If your separation has occurred at a time when your children are between six months and two years of age, your children will be at the stage of living through the emotions surrounding connection. Considering that separation anxiety is natural for children to experience at this time, it is here you can begin to understand a little more about how your children interpret their surroundings.

As stated in the previous section, the examples below are intended to provide the essence of responsible parenting for both the Leaver and Leavee.

Leavee: We acknowledge that we often transfer our hurts and judgements of bad and wrong, pain and distance, onto our children with more negative energy than we realise. As understandable as this is during a time of great turmoil, we know that our children's lives are being affected as well. We need to find a way to carefully acknowledge our feelings while we continue to stimulate positive, guilt-free movement and pleasure in our children.

Leaver: While we may believe separation does not equal 'bad', depending on circumstantial changes, we understand that our young child may well feel it is bad — or at least, not good. One of their parents is no longer going to be living in the home. Life is changing. We remember that at this stage of development, our children operate with simplistic duality; hot - cold, on - off. If it doesn't feel good, it will be bad.

As parents, we both must stop any emotional manipulation or transfer of guilt onto our children. Comments such as "You've made me so angry" or "Now look what you've done" as another thing falls apart, gets broken, or is forgotten, need to stop. We understand that at this stage, the guilt we build into our children's lives will force them to deny what they truly feel, and take on the manipulation as being real. We acknowledge that no child can make their parents angry; they can do things that we choose to become angry about — but ultimately, the choice is ours.

Growing Your Child in Stage 2

Growth through this time is made possible if we take the focus off the divorce and pay attention to the children's needs as we allow them to explore the related emotions and sensations. They need to know very little detail of the separation at such a young age; what is critical now is that they are *free to feel*. At this stage, children are not yet able to interpret what they are becoming a part of; it is through our vibes, our attitudes, and behaviours that they will begin to learn what they believe they should be feeling.

At this stage, it is particularly important for parents to assist their children to continue to explore the world around them — to implant their *right to feel*. This is not about *feeling right*, it is about their *right to feel*. We will be wise to avoid comments that deny them their feelings — especially while their physical surroundings are changing. It will be through their emotions that we will see their feelings expressed; we want them to express these and feel safe in doing so however they come out. They are the child — innocent. They will not be able to articulately verbalise what they feel, but they will feel all the same. To scold them for expressing these emotions will cause them to slowly become numb. Therefore, if we are constantly guilty, fearful, or insecure, chances are our children will absorb these feelings and develop them also.

As we want them to feel, and to fully feel, it is therefore important to have our children learn boundaries. This builds the understanding that they are connected yet separate. If they can connect with the feelings they experience when there are no boundaries, when they overdo and experience excess, they will come to recognise that over-indulgence becomes pain. To teach this principle, boundaries are vital.

Revisiting to Grow Stage 2

To retrospectively fill in developmental gaps within ourselves or in one of our older children, we need to focus on *movement*. We need to practice with the kinds of movement that involve *coming close and moving away*, in activities that give equal pleasure to both — such as dancing. This will turn our focus away from being in a state of loss and onto the recognition of flow as expressed through movement — regardless of the direction of the movement. If we only focus on the pleasure of coming close, we are more inclined to create a dependency on attachments.

As we explore all types of movement with our children, it is important to include conversation to stimulate the connection between movement and the sensations they may have become numb to. Include all sorts of things: some healthy, some easy, some outrageous, but all fun. Kick a ball, have an ice-cream, enjoy a warm drink, soak in a warm bath, linger over chocolate ...

Our children deserve pleasures in life and to withhold pleasure is to damage this vital area of development. On the other hand, to have excessive pleasure is also to undermine the very existence for which pleasure was intended. If they continue to experience life as pleasurable, they will have an *increased capacity for passion and desire that stimulates movement and action.*

Practice daily the process of absorbing information from feelings. Instead of ignoring these feelings, take the time to pause and absorb them fully. Start with simple physical tactile sensations gained through the five senses, and then extend into emotions as we become more sensitive. Enjoy the feeling of the warm water in the shower. Take the time to feel your breath as it moves in and out of your lungs rather than ignoring that it even occurs because it is automatic. Focus on the pleasures of eating, absorb the variety of flavours and textures. Savour each moment. If your children are indulging in some happy moment, allow them to thoroughly enjoy it. If it goes on too long, allow them to feel how the lack of boundary has produced pain rather than pleasure. Of course, use commonsense here and gauge the age-appropriateness.

If you see your children wallowing in emotional drama or stricken with guilt, allow them to understand the part their emotions are playing while they become aware of feeling the sensations. Do they feel pleasure or pain from the emotional drama? If they begin to connect with the short-term pleasure they believe they find inside the drama, they will be able to find the pain beneath it far more quickly. If you try to force them by saying, "Snap out of it," you are asking them to deny their feelings instead of learning from them.

Stage 3 :: 18 months – 4 years

This stage is all about the time our delightful little ones use coming and going to recognise they are separate from us. As they grow beyond the locomotive development of Stage 2, the child experiences duality at its core; they come to know separation. To confirm this separation from their parents, they play with it and attempt *autonomy*. Indeed, it is a challenging time for parents, and perhaps even more so if the importance of this developmental stage is not understood.

The Essence and Focus of Stage 3

Suddenly, your rather peaceful, fun-loving, exploring child starts to say, 'No' in a whole new way. Where previously it was cute, now it rings as a warning bell for emotional outbursts that can make you want to find a place to hide. Now is the time you swallow all judgemental words you may have previously uttered while in the supermarket scorning some other bewildered parent, as you frantically rummage through your memory banks hoping to discover some piece of brilliance to stop the morphing monster in front of you from taking hold.

The dynamics of *power* are explored and developed through experimentation with personal will; as your child experiences their first identity crisis, the way it is handled will influence the way they will deal with future ones. If Stage 2 was about your children being *On : Off*, then Stage 3, is about them creating *change*.

Whilst in this stage, children are developing their ego. The ego's job is *self-definition*. It wants to define who we are because it understands we are separate. To enable us to identify ourselves, it uses our will, actions, and behaviours. As part of this defining, children discover the power to choose actions, hence our ego says, "*I am what I do*" as this ego is birthed from within the previously formed physical and emotional stages.

When this focus and essence are in balance, that is to say there is a healthy developing power and sense of self, we see an inner authority. A warm confidence with a well-developed sense of humour is obvious. This is the child who rises to meet challenges throughout life, and one who understands appropriate self-discipline. They are the ones who will put themselves to bed because they feel tired, yet light up the room with the sparkle in their eye — even when they're pushing the boundaries — because, intuitively, they know they are acting. They are free to be, and they thoroughly enjoy being it.

The Rights and Thief of Stage 3

As the growing child comes to believe they are what they do, they enter a time of action. Children become so clever in their action and acting, they begin to believe their play. Because the essence of *ego* is about autonomous self-definition, the power we seek believes in *power over* rather than *power with*, hence the power struggles begin. The main purpose of this power struggle is for *transformation*. Toddlers are looking to form self-definition autonomously; this means they demand to be in charge of the change. If we can change the focus to explore the beauty of *power with*, we will find the freedom that comes from inner authority.

As the sense of our *right to act* develops, a healthy person who is responsible and reliable emerges. In the role of parent, if we understand this required transformation through power, we validate the child's *right to act* which is their natural form of experimentation. If this activity is restricted, their will and spontaneity is squashed, and we see decreased vitality.

Without healthy self-definition and an understanding of power, people develop with poor self-esteem and poor boundaries which, in turn, produces a sense of *shame* that undermines all the positives that can flow from healthy autonomy. Here we see someone who is unable to be an individual. This stage holds the *control continuum*, where we see manifested through weak-willed and easily manipulated personalities, the victim personality and those who constantly blame others. These people can also express the other extremes of dominating and controlling forces: the temper tantrum-throwing adult, given to violent outbursts; the arrogant and those with low self worth; the competitive and the passive; and the hyperactive and the low energy person.

Let's look at the power struggle stripped bare. The key to developing healthy respect for power is to understand the difference between *power over* and *power with*. It is a weak (very insecure) person who wants to dominate a toddler and then celebrate that they have won. It's not about winning or losing, but rather about developing a Learning environment where competition is removed and learning occurs. Attempting to hold *power over* our children will inflict shame and doubt on them. They will struggle to develop their own personal boundaries because their childhood 'no' held little weight. The same words, used by parents, had harsh consequences, and yet their own attempts were ignored; this confusion goes unanswered.

It can be challenging to understand the most appropriate ways to have our children explore the *right to act* and still keep boundaries present. It may help to understand that forming the ego is likened to creating an inner executive. It executes our intentions. The conflict comes if our ego self-promotes to CEO. We are wise to remember the ego is useful, but only as a middle manager.

Inside the Complex Family

Going through separation with children aged 18 months to four years, will have them try to flex their power as they attempt to gain their own stamp of change over the situation, which of course is hopeless. After all, while this is not about them, through their own senses they may come to the conclusion that it is their will, behaviour, or actions that have caused this to happen. This can plunge them into a deep state of shame. If you try to logically undo this inside the mind of a young child, it simply does not happen. Instead, you must do this through the demonstration of who you are and provide a model, an example of power, through your actions.

As stated in the previous sections, the examples below are intended to provide the essence of responsible parenting for both the Leaver and Leavee.

Leavee: As the children at this stage are preparing for life and learning through change, you will be anxious about the physical changes such as location that may occur during the separation period. However, what is more of an issue is the constructive way you handle the struggle with the Leaver. You know that your children will mimic your behaviour and learn power from what they witness.

Leaver: You know that change and transformation are exciting for children in this stage; this means the strength of your emotions surrounding this change is what will affect your children's development. You will be sure to keep your ego in check, especially when around your Leavee and will practice *power with* rather than *power over*, and avoid all traces of threats.

Growing Your Child in Stage 3

Our children believe they are what they do, so this means they need to do a lot. If we squash their natural passion for being busy, we will watch them lose their appetite for life. They need to be free to Act Act Act. Do Do Do. Find all manner of things that will keep them busy doing. The more they are focused on doing, the more the transformation, that they are seeking to explore, will be played out with things, rather than through their parents. They will still turn to you — do not be mistaken — but the majority of it will be channelled into their doings. Viewing television, computers, and other screens are not doing, so turn them off and make sure this is vigorous doing.

During this doing phase, transformation is the compulsion, so to channel this we find ways to celebrate the completion of doing tasks rather than being overly chaotic in the dismantling of bedrooms or homes. Keep the tasks easy to accomplish, and add risk or complexity as age-appropriate development occurs. This way we can turn random doing into constructive action, and build on the pleasure receptors of Stage 2.

When the Battle of Wills strikes, listen. Remove any language from your vocabulary that might shame or threaten your child. Hold respect for how they feel; reassure them that they are safe and loved while we, as parents, learn to honour the power within each other. We do this through constantly looking for ways to remove typical *either/or* thinking, and replace it with *and*. As we expand our child's black and white world of duality formed in Stage 2, we begin to add in shades of grey. It is by adding warm and chilly to hot/cold; dawn and dusk to day/night; and spring and autumn rather than only summer/winter, that we find ways to expand their worlds where we transcend competitive winning or losing, and move beyond right and wrong, that begs yet another power wrestling act to follow.

Remember, autonomy and transformation are the craving so be sure your conversations always leave your child's dignity in tact. Remove all thought that you are trying to cause harm or are wrestling to win, as egos have memories like elephants.

Since we currently live in an ego-driven society, you will do well to remember this power comes about from action and doing. It is not so much that the ego is bad, but rather that it can become destructive when it is out of place. It takes control when we so fully believe in the act of becoming what we do that we forget it is but only the third stage of seven.

Using *power with* instead of *power over* is an art. It is a state where our stated boundaries are vital; where our "no" means no, "maybe" is maybe, and "yes" is yes. When you grant freedom for your children to act, while having established consequences, they will experience the autonomy of power through choice. With no boundaries and no consequences, we restrict the power of choosing. If you find yourselves resorting to techniques like raising voices, dominating stances, or bullying, you only teach your children *power over* rather than provide a living example of *power with*.

Revisiting to Grow Stage 3

In those who experience excessive control or aggressive or dominating behaviour, we see a tendency to need to be right or to have the last word. Typically, this person is arrogant, competitive, and in possession of driving ambition. While many of these characteristics have been thought to be the keys to success in our ego-based society, (driven largely by false perceptions of success), it is the realisation of this power excess that holds the key to our true power.

We also meet those who are within the opposite spectrum of our *power continuum*, the weak-willed, lacking in energy, with poor self discipline. These people are often passive, unreliable, and suffer from low self-esteem.

Gaps in the power stage can cause either excessive or deficient behaviour; in the case of excess, we need to build our child's sense of inner power, and let their self-esteem have less requirement to continue to prove itself externally. In the weak-willed child, where the opposite is displayed through trying to avoid being noticed, we can help by providing opportunities for our children to be responsible and reliable, to act with confidence, without giving our personal power to them. It's a matter of balance.

To begin to shift towards a powerful centre, if we are towards the excessive power end of the scale we need to use relaxation techniques; should we be at the weaker end of the spectrum, it is best to start on vigorous exercise. Spend the time in emotional contact with others, establish your own sense of autonomy, and at the same time be open to listen and learn. Learn to honour the development of power through practicing *power with* rather than *power over*. This developing power keeps the ego where it should be, the middle manager.

Stage 4 :: 4 – 7 years

The butterfly years. Emerging from the chrysalis, stretching their tender wings, our children develop their awareness of social living. As you build on Stage 3's well-practiced principle, *actions have consequences*, they start choosing to adapt their behaviour to either gain or express *love*.

The Essence and Focus of Stage 4

The purpose of Stage 4 is the development of *love* and balance. Our children's new focus is gaining depth through experimentation with how things relate to each other. Concepts evolve from objects and things; by adding in the complexity of people, we can see our child's interpersonal relationship patterns and the basis of social identity begin to take shape.

This maturity causes a shift in our perception of our self. Instead of being based on the more egocentric forces of doing and power, we see a shift into roles of serving others. *Serving* is the intention and attitudes we hold while carrying out the doing, not the doing itself. When this is truly lived, it becomes evident through the emergence of a strong sense of *self-acceptance*. This builds compassion and the acceptance of both oneself and others; it allows healthy intimate relationships to form, where strong levels of devotion occur without neediness. In this position of balanced acceptance, we witness the natural flow of reaching out and taking in, both of which are needed for the continuing flow of relationship energy.

When you collect your child from school, you will hear the next installment of their tumultuous friendships unfolding, and it is easy to begin questioning if something is wrong with your child. While there is probably nothing wrong with them, how you handle what they are experiencing is important. This normal push-pull young relationship tension is assisting your children to develop their persona. Our persona is the part of us that our ego (Stage 3) allows to become visible; it is the way we want the world to see us. We experience this through our relationships with others; therefore, it is a relative comparison that we are making, moment by moment, that builds this persona within. This explains the importance of group dynamics, our choice of friends; it is this which develops our levels of self acceptance. A wise question to ask is, "Against what or with whom are we comparing?"

The Rights and Thief of Stage 4

This stage develops compassion fueled by initiative; in the ever-increasing expansion that love and self-acceptance brings, there is a peaceful balance within the cycle of giving and receiving. When this balance is being lived through a thriving heart, it naturally creates the promising platform for ongoing, long lasting relationships, and our child develops direction and purpose.

Wrapped up in the nucleus of this delicate stage is our child's *right to love*. The other side of the same coin is our child's belief in their *right to be loved*. If our children struggle to accept themselves, they will struggle to believe they have the right to love or be loved by another. When this belief takes hold, they become stricken with *grief* at the very core of their being, and feel unworthy. We will see these children begin to close down, and have difficulty in reaching out to us and their friends. This obvious inability to reach another is a signal to us, as parents, that our children are struggling to reach themselves.

Poor development in this stage, will see our children become either antisocial and withdrawn from others, or cling to those relationships they believe they must keep. As parents, we often feel for them, and we genuinely do as we feel our own sadness and loss inside. We want to defend. These are the parents who blame schools and other children, and who put down others who they believe are causing the harm. Sometimes when we see our darlings close their hearts, it becomes a painful reminder of our own survival. Sometimes these children are so lonely and isolated, that they fall into depression in later years because it has not been understood and helped. Many become so fearful of intimacy, they reject relationships entirely.

Then we find the other extremes; children who become codependent and demanding. They find it difficult to differentiate themselves from another, and jealousy is considered completely normal behaviour. Our child may have this over-sacrificing willingness, substituting themselves in the hope of being liked, because they simply do not understand the value within themselves. Their little hearts are grieving for a loss they feel inside, yet they are attempting to control it physically, rather than face it emotionally.

If the ego of Stage 3 has become too strong (climbing its self-appointed ladder towards CEO), it covers up for the hurts our heart finds too painful to acknowledge using new initiatives of busyness through our mind's clever distraction techniques. We witness inventiveness based in egocentric pastimes. This is easily identified through the loss of compassion and attitude of service, and it is here we self-serve instead, as we attempt to gain self-acceptance; the result of this is that our creativity is hindered by the lack of genuine service towards others.

When there is a healthy balance between loving and being worthy of love, we feel a lightness of heart and a sense of compassion. This natural expansion continues to develop as we mature, and brings with it the freedom to love and to be loved.

Inside Complex Family

Patterns of relationship intricacies and stability form what is acceptable, normal, unacceptable, and out of the question within the Complex Family. If your children are between the ages of four and seven when separation occurs, they will automatically assume they are not worthy of being loved. This, in effect, can rob them of healthy relationships in years to come. To counter this assumption, we need to focus on building their sense of self-worth and self-acceptance. No amount of verbal persuasion will do the trick; this will need to come from within themselves. Although we, as parents, desperately make our promises to them, explaining that it's all different, our words hold little merit as they have seen the flaws in one set of promises already.

As stated in the previous sections, the examples below are intended to provide the essence of responsible parenting for both the Leaver and Leavee.

Leavee: Although your heart may be sore, you must refrain from lowering yourself to say, "I didn't leave, it was ...". If you do this, you can cause even further damage to your child's understanding (or rather misunderstanding) of love. You understand that the Leaver has made a choice that is an individual's right to do. In speaking about this with your children you avoid laying blame and use the situation as an opportunity to teach a lesson of choice, acceptance, and love.

Leaver: As this stage is about love, it makes it even more challenging to deal with what will appear to be the exact opposite of this. However, in some instances, the act of separation is actually an act of love for both yourself and your children, one that they will only come to understand later in life. You understand your children will experience a level of grief and that you are in the more constructive position to assist them through this. All your communications with them will be reassuring and supportive of the Leavee and consistently reaffirm to the children that they are loved by both parents.

Growing Your Child in Stage 4

Irrespective of the ages of the children, this stage takes a blow as divorce occurs. As adults, teens, younger or older, there is an innate desire for connection with another; in this case, it has proven to be impermanent. The fairy-tale did not work in this family. The ideology of unconditional love being strong enough to win over everything else is rocked. This creative, expansive, and purpose-driven stage of development is so tender and delicate that it feels an inner contradiction: between what happens and what we want to happen. It is when the concept of unconditional love is questioned by the enquiring mind that they realise a lifelong promise can be broken. It is then only a small leap in their minds to conclude: "Is it possible I might do something to make my parents change their mind about me too? Is it possible that I can make them so mad they may want me to move out?" The unspoken, unable to be articulated, feelings of grief can bring to your child the saddening of their eyes and the restriction of genuine compassion from their heart.

Many children who go through divorce believe their love has to be split; their understanding of love as a single portion means they, metaphorically, split that portion of love into two pieces, one for each parent. They are ignorant of love's true nature, and we need to remind them of its very essence. Love expands. Love does not divide. It is infinite. If children (of all ages) understand that love expands, it allows them to begin to experience divorce as a time where their family dynamics change, but this does not have to equal less. It is very important for children to know they are free to love both parents equally, although uniquely.

If your children are going through the normal ins and outs of friendships at school, you can use this to demonstrate the parallel experience of your divorce; but this must be done carefully. When Sally no longer wants to play with your Jane, take the time to get inside Jane's world and talk warmly of friendships moving on. It's not about the details of who said what to whom, and when; these are circumstantial. It is about getting the child to feel secure as they develop their own acceptance of what is happening. There are friendships that last only a season. It is wise not to draw comparisons or fixate on your divorce example, but rather to insert the principle while you allow them to make the connection in alternative circumstances.

If they have been wronged (which does happen), take the time to teach them to forgive; this is an unpopular word in a world reluctant to release. Forgiveness is the most valuable lesson to learn as we release grief. Spend the time with your children to show them their playground incidents are important, that these are the practice runs for their adult world experiences.

Through practicing the releasing of friendships, the choosing of goodness in our lives, we enrich their relationship expectations. Releasing as a principle is the opposite of the way we live in our modern society. We are very quick to hold onto things, gather, hoard, and store. There is a hesitation to release, to give away, and let go. Questions such as, "What if there is no other? There might not be enough? This might be as good as it gets." are normal; such limitations are believed and cause us to hinder the natural flow of expansion.

Revisiting to Grow Stage 4

This stage of development is about expansion or contraction; with the use of focused attention on a simple action, we help to become more aware of this natural rhythm. Breathing is a powerful exercise for exploring the genuine feelings of drawing in and releasing out. The use of arm movements help to reinforce this giving and receiving. With children, this can be a game; try catching and throwing a ball, or giving and receiving hugs. Think of simple things that will naturally move their arms, focusing on the movement of reaching out and taking in.

For those who are a little older, try taking up journal writing. Girls and women usually experiment with journal writing — far more so than boys. Take this naturally creative time and give it a little direction for your child, being careful only to suggest, not to control, as this is their creative time. (Tip: It is important that we do not read their journals as breaking confidence is extremely damaging.) Giving direction is as simple as suggesting they may like to write about feeling angry, hurt, misunderstood, or struggling in any way at all. If this option is taken, let them know it is important to continue to write until peacefulness comes. It is in the peaceful space that while there may not be answers, there is an acceptance of the event or circumstance. This acceptance space does not condone what has been wronged; it does not forgive the person with whom we are angry; it is a space that says, "What is, is." It is as simple as that. The resistance has gone, and for a moment, we can leave it be. If we can help our children, of all ages, to reach this place on paper, they will start to unlock doorways towards healing.

Gratitude is the single most powerful tool I know of to touch the very core of this stage. While *forgiveness heals grief, gratitude fuels expansion*.

Gratitude is a way of directing our minds to change perspective, to become aligned with our heart's singing. When we are fully grieving, we make music; this is the beauty of tears; gratitude allows this. Contrary to what we want to think, our mind has us feel sorry for ourselves — but this is far from grieving, as grief is of our heart, not our mind. To turn your mind towards health, write lines of gratitude until you feel the subtle shift towards your inner music, that you will feel coming from the heart, instead of your mind.

There is a real grieving and relationship disappointment when divorce enters a family's world. Whether for the Leaver or Leavee, or for the child, the end of the relationship has an impact on our hearts. Some people believe they will never love so deeply again, that they will be too scared to try. Others dare to become vulnerable, and believe that only then can true intimacy develop. Some children make childhood promises never to repeat this in their adulthood, and they lock their hearts away in an attempt to avoid possible future pain.

Discovering the healthy aspects to this stage will radiate to all other areas of your life. When we know we hold the *right to love* and *to be loved*, it defines our actions. When we know love is infinite and indivisible it defines our thinking. When we know it is our choice to reach out and draw in, it defines our healthy balance of living.

Stage 5 :: 7 – 12 years

The years of the outward development of your children are wrapped in the confusion of physical development and some early hormone changes. Having built upon the layers: physical, pleasure, power, and love, you will now start to see a significant change in the expressions that come from your child.

The Essence and Focus of Stage 5

Stage 5 is where *communication* and *creativity* bloom because expression is typically demonstrated by what we say and what we produce; it is here that verbal expression is highlighted. Your children can talk but communication develops at new levels during this stage. Many of you notice the awkward phase that occurs when your children are developing their sense of humour as you watch them move beyond retelling a joke from a book, and start creating their own methods of making people laugh — and even if sometimes it's simply not funny, they are still learning.

It is during this time that children come to understand the dynamics of themselves and others as their social patterns emerge; this stage is all about *self-expression*, and if it is built upon healthy layers beneath, a strong sense of self who is vital in energy and emotional well-being will emerge. The child will speak fluently and clearly, and equally, will be a great listener with a smooth sense of timing and rhythm to their communication and creativity.

Self-expression is developed through energy, diligence, dedication, vigor, hard work, and productivity, and through it all we see the engine of creativity churning. If one lacks these attributes, they struggle with inferiority; but even then, by continuing to apply the attributes of creativity, they can gain competence, and thereby increase their feeling of satisfactory self-expression.

The Rights and Thief of Stage 5

Communication forms a strong portion of our identity; therefore, with maturity you will begin to see your children take responsibility for both words and actions. The combination of communication and creativity introduces our core *right to speak*. On the other side of this coin is our *right to hear truth*. When we are free to speak, we gain authenticity in our expression. As this healthy communication continues, it becomes a stunning extension of our immediate self, and radiates into the world. With healthy self-esteem, coupled with social confidence, and a great sense of compassion for others, this is the time for this to be fully explored.

Developing into this maturity invites our *right to hear truth*. After all, if we refine authenticity through speaking, the balance is in the hearing. The hindering of this freedom occurs when we are faced with *lies*. They are the antithesis of truthful communication. Lies will damage this vital stage by twisting your relationship to the outside world through distorted information.

Frequently children's lives are negatively affected by parents, cultures, teachers, relatives, and others who will not allow a child to speak truthfully. While it may appear to be harmless, it can severely damage a child's right to speak and hear. Most of us can think of times we have told our children 'white lies' in an attempt to protect or cover up; we have twisted something to avoid conflict when we know they suspect differently; we try to cover up instead of fully exposing.

Our culture has fed us an even greater level of duplicity. The right to hear truth is eroded through television newscasts, magazines, papers, billboards, and media everywhere. We are fed parts of stories by reporters who create their story from part truths, deliver it emotionlessly, and abuse our sensor for truth. We are lied to through advertising that seductively leads us by creating a sense of need for something we didn't really want. Most of us who live within cities know that even on the quietest of nights, we still hear car horns, street noise, people, dogs, alarms, and the hum of the city. That constant noise belittles our belief in being heard, or equally, being listened too. Silence speaks, yet we are unable to hear because of the incessant noise.

On the *expression continuum*, we again find extremes. Those who have a faint, small voice and fear speaking, find it a challenge to articulate their feelings and become shy as a way to externalise their introverted preferences. On the other extreme, are those people who cannot stop talking, who are completely unable to listen, and often have very poor comprehension. Typically, people like this have gossip as a favourite pastime; they avoid meaningful conversations as they dominate by interrupting the flow of communication.

Through violation of our right to hear or speak, we turn away from the natural flow of self-expression. Instead of following a natural desire to become contributors to the larger system, we focus on a microscopic world and become insular; we lose the vital connection with others and our environment.

By developing a healthy stage of self-expression, both in communication and creativity, we begin to see glimmers of our path ahead, the realisation of our personal contributions towards a larger group, perhaps even society-wide, and the natural flow of listening and speaking while we gain our authentic, creative identity.

Inside Complex Family

Within this age group, as you move through the process of divorce, you will need to pay attention to your children's *right to speak*, their *right to hear the truth*, and the interpretation, in practice, of what this means. Parenting is about age-appropriateness. The wisdom of walking with children through the divorce lies in dealing with the changes to their external world while allowing them to both speak and hear truthfully. Tip: remember, Less is More. The details of circumstances should be kept to a minimum. As the confidentiality and dignity of all concerned is maintained, it offers security and assurance to the children's future ability to confide. If we expose only what they need to understand, we will give them the freedom to continue loving both parents, irrespectively.

As stated in the previous sections, the examples below are intended to provide the essence of responsible parenting for both the Leaver and Leavee.

Leavee: If we as Leavees feel we have been wronged, this is not a load for our children to carry. It is our time to learn to express appropriately, and with integrity.

Leaver: If we Leavers believe we need to be free, this is not a burden to be shared. It is up to us to fully respect the individual choices we make and lift the focus beyond communicating rights and wrongs, and to express the most appropriate choice we can make given our objectives.

Growing Your Child and Revisiting to Grow Stage 5

This stage is about creative expression, and involves communication with your Ex privately, in front of the children, and with others. To measure appropriateness of communication, let's look at children's playground conversations. This can be a guide to what is important to them in their world. They neither want, nor do they need to know, all the details. A point commonly raised here is the confusion between lies and withholding truth. While it damages children's *right to speak* and *hear truth* if we lie, if we avoid involving them in adult-world perceptions, this is protection. As they mature in years to come, more may be unveiled. The growing into understanding goes hand-in-hand with the signals we see in their personal lives. For many Leavers, their story may only be told and better understood when their children have married and encountered similar challenges.

> In my personal circumstances, slowly over the years, a little more comes out at appropriate moments as my children make a connection. One such moment occurred while watching a movie as a family one night. A child asked, "Is that what happened to you, Mum?" I could answer, "Similar, but it was how we chose to handle it that was quite different, and of course, the most important part." This then led into an age-appropriate conversation about our divorce. It wasn't a news report, or facts without emotions, nor was it dramatic or embellished. I told them

> what happened, acknowledged the pain without blame, and reinforced positives by highlighting the advantages of being a Complex Family.

If you're in doubt, or find it difficult to work out what to say, it's best to err on the side of compassion for all, including the Ex. Words cannot be taken back; it's better to speak only kind, gentle, and compassionate words in such conversations.

> In over a decade of parenting with an Ex, my children have not heard negative comments about their father or stepmother come from me. They will say things to me against their father in moments of frustration, and while I may smile inside, I only say that I understand, and leave it there. Any comment that would reinforce their momentary irritation or dissatisfaction with their father would not assist them through the challenge, and could later build a wedge inside our family unit.

If you find this too difficult to do, perhaps consider how you would wish to be treated if your children were bleating to your Ex about you. Would you like your Ex to support you and give you the benefit-of-the-doubt? Good communication is equally listening and talking. It is sharing in fullness, both facts and feelings, and it leaves both parties with a sense of creative contentedness when it concludes.

Your ways of communicating are mimicked. During the 7–12 years, young people are going to mimic and absorb your communication styles and creative outlets. If you have a habit of raising your voice to gain attention, expect this to come from them when they're frustrated by your inability to focus on them. This often becomes a wake-up call to highlight your own parenting style.

Take the time to evaluate what you hear yourself saying to your children. Are you speaking the truth? Do you say negative things to them, and reinforce lies? Common lies slip out easily from busy, over-scheduled parents. An accident as simple as milk being spilt or keys temporarily misplaced results in, "You're stupid." Your children are not stupid, what they do may be stupid, but they never are. Do you have a habit of yelling, nagging, or talking over the top of them? Do you continually correct them for using the wrong words in forming correct sentence structure? If you do, you need to consider the lies, lack of truth, and blocks to creativity that are being fed to them on a daily basis.

Creative Expansion: While this period can produce evidence of beauty all around, it can also produce the reverse. At this time, children focus on productivity; if you constantly correct or pull apart their expression (verbally or otherwise) they will stop expressing themselves in words or actions or worse yet, in both. This stage is different from the busyness of Stage 3, as it is now focused expression, not just a busy doing, regardless of productivity. Learning music, taking up painting, arranging flowers, curling paper, baking cakes, carving wood, and all manner of things, bring evidence of creativity. This is more often caught rather than taught, so lead the way. It is the atmosphere inside your home, with the willingness to explore ideas and flow with a hunch, that sees you let the normal boundaries go as you watch yourself begin to colour outside the lines of prior restrictions.

Allowing your children to focus on creative expression will take their minds off the changes that are external to their control and allow them to reach within themselves and bring the flow outwards as they effect change externally. Start simple if it is foreign. Gain confidence in expressing yourself verbally first, and then branch out from there. Encourage storytelling to young children. Try singing; keep it simple by singing along with great fun music while you're in the car or around the home. Perhaps take up some kind of music lessons. These are often run through schools, and if finances are tight, group lessons are fun and offer an economical way to let your child explore. Story writing can also be a great way to express imaginative creativity. If they can write well but struggle with illustrations, grab some magazines and get them to cut out the pictures instead. The key here is to have your children explore various means of communication creatively and without deadlines; remove all possible measurements of failure.

Stage 6 :: Teen years

These are the years in which most parents spend their nights in sleepless worry and their days in raging battles of will. We watch our children's physical size overtake current emotional and mental abilities as we see them begin to grow into adulthood. Many parents mistakenly believe the teen years demonstrate their success or failure at parenthood, and leave them wondering why they have produced this result.

The Essence and Focus of Stage 6

The purpose of this stage is for teens to begin to *recognise the patterns* they've already formed in their lives, and to start to *apply* them to their life decisions. This is the point where *conscious choosing* occurs, rather than choices coming through habitual programming.

If this is to happen, it means teens need to start to question; and question they do. They want to; they need to; because the way they experience choice is by reexamining everything through their social identity. Stage 4 was the formative stage of this, the years to potentially attain levels of self-acceptance. If those years produced trauma and self-loathing instead, the teen years can be very challenging. Within the Complex Family, Stage 4 conditioning has taken effect in all of us so we need to be particularly mindful of working with the How To's suggested in Stage 4.

As recognition and application of patterns is the purpose, the work at this stage focuses on developing your teens' abilities for *self-reflection*. It is vital they begin to question within a supportive environment, and with activities based on learning rather than on performance. This way they can begin to take ownership for what they see; they begin to discern themes, repetitious behaviours, structured outcomes, and connections that can be made between various inputs and perceived outputs.

The life of a teen comes with inherent inner conflict; this arises from a lack of understanding of the difference between their *Identity* and *Function*. Teens are on a mission to identify themselves by looking at where they are right now when compared to their family, friends, community, society, and the world at large. The problem is not whether they will naturally draw these comparative conclusions; it is how they undertake the process.

To most of them, the difference between *who they are* and the *function they are carrying out* is almost indistinguishable. They are a student by function, but is this who they are? Many will answer yes, believing themselves to be what their ID tag labels them as. In this way, they are missing the crucial difference of understanding who they truly are.

We are not our function, albeit many parents fall into this common trap. To be authentic to ourselves, we need to learn to establish a healthy difference between the *function* we perform, (being a someone who studies) and the *identity* of our self, (being genuinely joyful, spontaneous, intelligent person). If your teen can understand they are engaged in study for a time to learn more, it will not define them, but rather let them explore the great depth this phase of their life has to offer.

You can assist them by separating these two conflicts and enhancing their recognition of ongoing life patterns; this way, they can begin to apply these patterns with greater clarity. They can see the similarities of what they do as they perform many different functions, the different skills required, the attitudes applied, and the characteristics that matter in their roles as student, employee, sober-driver, friend, confidant, daughter, son, brother, sister, and so on. They see that while they perform various functions, this does not define them; they begin to understand themselves in a variety of settings, and learn to recognise particular patterns that have predictable results. As such, they begin to realise they are the leading lady (or man) of their own life show; they grow to understand how to work with the surrounding stage and props as they create the plot and write the script.

The Rights and Thief of Stage 6

This stage builds our core *right to see*; this is our ability to interpret what we see as being real or not real. This ability is challenged or damaged by two common occurrences in any home, but more so within a Complex

Family: 1) things are deliberately hidden from us, or 2) we are told what we see is not real. When either of these occurs, we can damage our seeing ability, and fall into the trap of *illusion*. This causes an inner confusion where we find ourselves seeing or perceiving something as being obviously real, yet our desire strongly wants to believe something contradictory to this reality. The intensity of the conflict is irreconcilable logically, so we plunge this contradiction into denial, and force a type of blindness. In this moment, we are unable to see what is actually there; and one fragment at a time, this slowly robs our clarity. Left unchecked, it will reach a point where we believe ourselves to be part of the illusion itself.

Along the *intuition continuum* is where we will see our teens oscillate. What does a damaged Stage 6 look like? You may say, that's easy, just look at the delinquent teenagers everywhere; but let's pinpoint the signs that refer to Stage 6, rather than those that include previous damaged stages. Typically, we see those insensitive characters whose world still revolves around them. They struggle with poor memory and poor dream recall, and a severe lack of ability to visualise the future that produces very short-term focused actions. They may suffer intensely with nightmares and even have great difficulty concentrating throughout the day; they are unable to study or enjoy school at all.

Often their physical vision becomes affected when strong areas of denial are apparent; this validates their inability to truly see what is happening around them. Something that is apparently obvious to us, they are blind to; this leads many to become obsessed and quite delusional about their own power, abilities, and thought processes. Often this damaged stage of development will leave people stuck in believing there is only one true right way forward, as they hold this very rigid and inflexible outlook on all of life.

In contrast: successful development in a healthy teen grows valuable *intuition*. They become insightful, perceptive, and have a great imagination. Their ability to visualise is high with a strong understanding of symbols and signs; as this form of pattern recognition is applied to life circumstances it becomes a strong asset. As they establish their personal identity, they become very comfortable with the world around them; they see it for what it is, with all of its faults and failings, opportunities and adventures. They see themselves living as part of society and yet they are free from the effects of peer pressure because they are comfortable in their own skin; they understand the balance between who they believe themselves to be and the function they are currently performing.

As this stage gathers maturity, it leads to the formation of our classic, quintessential identity. This becomes our model of who we believe ourselves to be. As part of this, we find our own life themes expressed within society at large. It is the time when we may watch a news report and hear ourselves say, "Wow, that's me.", or we watch a movie and almost believe they knew about our own life to make a film that so accurately reflects our feelings. The fairy tales, mythology, and media all start to make us feel that there is a larger part of us that is understood by the masses.

If this stage is constructively developed, as they realise the movement from individual insular thinking is being expanded, they may be encouraged to explore religion, mythology, or philosophy. It is through an inner impulse to reexamine patterns that the teen starts to follow their intuition of scrutiny. As they grow closer to adulthood, there may also be a time of dabbling in spiritual interest as they seek to gain greater understanding of themselves within larger structures and expansive concepts.

However, if the teenage stage becomes a battlefield of lies, quick fixes, and scare tactics, when they reach the point of feeling they are part of the larger worldwide story, your teen may well feel overwhelmed — as if they are stepping into a void without lifelines or compass. Their sense of personal insignificance and hopelessness is increased as the limitations and gaps within the previous five stages of development over the past decade and more are highlighted. This is one of the reasons teens turn to delinquent behaviour; they do so in an attempt to mask this hopeless inner conflict, and then experience a sense of personal insignificance as they reexamine their inner codes. They are genuinely, although negatively, in search of meaning and significance for themselves so they can begin to see what is real.

Inside the Complex Family

Marital separation during the teen years is no more, or less, challenging than during the earlier stages; however, it presents different issues. Your children are in their own space of *self-reflection*, as they examine their beliefs in the context of their life inside a larger whole. When your marital relationship changes and your teens are changing, there is a double movement. Instead of life remaining relatively consistent externally while they choose their relationship to it, you now have both elements moving. It's like being in a boat and pulling up alongside a free-floating platform rather than a pier. The solid pier gives you stability in focus and direction, something to aim for and bounce off. A floating platform is at the mercy of the currents and winds, forever a moving target.

Helping your children to gain anchorage and creating stability are your primary focus points as parents. Your teens need to be given the opportunity to venture out and explore beyond, and it is parents who are the best ones to provide a safe-haven for them to refuel and dock when needed.

Leavee: If you're upset, your children will see this, and that's okay. What is not okay is when you tip the scales and start wallowing or blaming. You then create the illusion.

Leaver: As your teens may be angry at you for the change, take the time to build up the communication, and let them see your authentic self rather than your attempt to keep up appearances. Be respectful towards the journey; however, remain free of blame or control.

Growing Your Child and Revisiting to Grow Stage 6

To have our *right to see* validated is to have our attention focus on things as they are; this allows us to see accurately, much like a lens. It just is. The paradigms you have raised your children to think and believe within will either make sense or not. If you hold rigidly to your beliefs, but they don't make sense to your teen, conflict is inevitable. You have all witnessed the dismantling of outdated paradigms, those within your home, those that have inflicted terrible suffering onto countless millions, and those of insanity that are quickly destroying the planet — the very source of all life. It is the crumbling of such significant prejudices that would have parents, pay attention to the questioning of teens. There is much to be learned from listening and watching the hypocrisies and insane patterns that are being exposed.

The greatest strength your teens can develop during this phase is their ability to see accurately. If they are able to avoid fixating upon the illusion and learn to develop their intuitive and perceptive abilities, they will grow healthily. All gaps in earlier development — within other stages — are going to surface throughout these teen years. It has taken 12 years to develop through five stages, yet this Stage 6 lasts between six and eight years. During this time of exposing the gaps, your teen will either choose more appropriate actions or beliefs, or plunge further into the apathetic hopelessness that such inner contradiction provides.

Many times, it is your single-minded views as parent that cause the conflict with your teens. The teen years are meant to be fun, and they are the years during which you can watch your newly-formed bud come into bloom and greet the world with full beauty. These are also the years you are meant to have your teen push boundaries; how else can they begin to recognise the patterns and hence make choices. They need to have you act as their mirror to let them see their own self-reflection.

Your teens have their own emotional rides triggered by hormones and relationships during this stage, so if you, as parent, behave as if you've returned to the sandpits, scrapping in playgrounds and throwing sanitised punches, you cannot provide the required safe haven or anchorage. It is from your position of responsibility and leadership that you can lead by example, and live the best way you can. If not, they will dismiss or reject connection with you, and turn to their peers as their source of wisdom, counsel, and confidence.

As this stage naturally fosters the inquisitive watching of movies and the media that allow us to see ourselves as part of society-wide, we need to be mindful of what choices are made in selection. (Mindful is quite different from controlling.) A worldwide phenomenon within the explosive entertainment industry sees teens at the centre of advertising and media frenzies as it vies for their next buck. The mindfulness allows your teens to see things for what they are rather than the illusion that is presented through all forms of media. Discussion about what they are watching and learning is the key here. If you can expose the hypocrisy, deceit, and illusions that are contained in their entertainment, while they may continue to watch, you are able to add a balancing perspective that will help to encourage the healthy development of their *right to see*. As you provide the balancing perspective, and alternative views, it increases their opportunity to expand their awareness of cause and effect, and to consciously choose the way they form their quintessential selves.

If there have been some gaps in the earlier years of development, focus on visual stimulation and the effects of light. You can use photography, painting, interior decorating, and presentation of food; really anything can be used to create a visual feast. Experiment with light, candles, mirrors, glass, and observe the difference colour makes to what we see. As you begin to experiment with your perspective, you learn how altering ones perspective changes what is seen — in both the micro and macro. It is the visual demonstration of the non-physical part of ourselves, highlighting the fact that delusion is usually only a choice away, only an altering of perspective. You can begin to make the connection between *what you see* and *how you feel about what you see*.

You can try a little meditation or quiet prayer. Meditation is a powerful way to bring your focus and attention towards self-reflection. It will help you to understand the difference between your own *identity* and the *function* you carry out daily in your life. There are plenty of techniques to assist you to learn either prayer or meditation; however, it is more about accessing the space of stillness and silence, than perfecting any technique you try to practice.

You can also start playing with the power of visualisation. Visualisation works because the feelings that come as you see or do something before it is physically present trigger the same brain responses as if you were doing it. Great sports people visualise their winning, but this is done through specific visualising of each individual step towards winning, not the trophy collection moment itself. The feelings that arise as each moment is carried out with precision is where the power comes from. If you only focus on the *result*, you've missed the point of the process.

Stage 7 :: Young Adulthood

This is the final stage of development. This era of young adult growth concludes our subconscious development. Beyond these years the subconscious mind is left to drive one's life, as it forever radiates its subtle and limiting messages of beliefs, fears, and expectations.

The Essence and Focus of Stage 7

The purpose of this last stage is to allow us to gain *understanding*. It is the pursuit of knowledge and the application of all we have learned — the evolution of *Wisdom*. Wisdom comes from the experiences we have had and the application of the lessons gained. It is only foolishness to repeat an action and hope for a better outcome when we have already tested and produced predictable consequences. Looking at our world, it is easy to say that for most people this stage seems to have suffered significant issues in reaching development.

Reflecting on our construction analogy back in Stage I, it is the foundation upon which all seven stages are built that comes into play here. It makes sense that as our building becomes more of a challenge to stabilise with the damage done to each succeeding layer, we spend much of our adult life living through repeated cycles until we develop sufficient wisdom to make the changes. Our lives have a concentrated learning time during our first two decades; the highs and lows, deficiencies and excesses, all provide the structure and framework with which we will live our adult life.

Before the seventh stage of development can be whole, the preceding layers must be whole. However, without losing heart, certain key characteristics are more likely to occur if we begin to assimilate knowledge. As the purpose of this stage is *understanding*, the focus will be on *self-knowledge*. This is achieved by moving *information* from an unstructured space into meaningful *knowledge*, and with maturity, this knowledge transforms into *wisdom*.

As we expand with our assimilation of wisdom, our identity expands. In much the same way as we see our world oscillate between feeling vast and universal, while small at the same time; we begin to expand beyond our micro-sector left over from the teen years as we take in global and universal recognition. Often this is linked with a spiritual awakening where the focus is largely on the search for meaning.

The Rights and Thief of Stage 7

This stage concerns our *right to know*. It has been said by many that knowledge is power, and it is this power that has been hidden, through elitist control, from the vast majority of human existence. When our *right to know* is hindered, we become afflicted with unruly *attachment* — a plight upon our planet, currently demonstrated by our materialistic and consumer driven society.

While attachment is more often referred to in a physical sense, (our unwillingness to depart from what we have acquired), a more powerful and yet subtle form of attachment is our beliefs. Attachment robs us of being willing to learn more while remaining open to broader perspectives, because we believe we know the one way, the right way. Instead of taking this resourcefulness, that comes naturally to Stage 7, as knowledge expansion, we throw ourselves into enhanced learning to defend or justify our current knowing.

Our *right to know* includes receiving accurate information; this is part of our *right to truth*. It is the *right to know* what is really going on as we build forward from Stage 6, our *right to see*. If we can gain this knowledge and build upon the previous stages of development, the opportunity for freedom awaits. It was with a willingness to question the belief that our world was flat that we discovered the freedom of endless travel as we were freed from a perceived fear of falling off the edge; and when man dared to question that the sun did not revolve around the earth, modern science had the opportunity to expand our world perspective.

It is the same willingness that moves us beyond religious dogma and invites us to question and follow natural impulses. This is the change from diversity being viewed as right and wrong to looking within the depths of unity to find wholeness. To deny this opportunity to explore is to damage and restrict the importance of our final stage of development.

If you have been raised in a strong religious environment or within a culture of racial prejudices, extremes within the *connection continuum* may occur; these can range from cynicism towards spirituality to religious addiction. There are those who hold very rigid belief systems and are uncompromising in conversation, and those who tend to over-intellectualise life. There can be a disconnect from the messages your body subtly sends; and more often than not, there may be a tendency to dominate others. Usually, there is a strong compulsion towards materialism that can lead to greed and reaffirm an attachment to physical gains. There is also the other extreme that can be seen as an apathetic character who lives in constant confusion, feels disconnected from all life has on offer, and often suffers with learning difficulties.

However, in contrast, a well-developed seventh stage is evidenced by the ability to perceive, analyze, and assimilate information. This is the person who is aware, thoughtful, and possesses innate intelligence. They are secure and therefore have an open-mind to acquire knowledge; they develop a natural questioning that constantly challenges the accepted norms, a sense of connectedness, and an inherent belief system that is often a well-developed sense of spirituality.

Inside Complex Family

More often than not, we expect our adult-children to deal well with the divorce of their parents; some do, but the vast majority find this a particularly challenging time. It becomes difficult because the layers of instability that have built up over the years, are suddenly and dramatically exposed. The adult-child who is unable to comprehend, feel, or even articulate their emotions is left with the sense of a deep dislodgment within. The dissolution of your marriage, the life-long commitment to be together forever, rocks your adult child's belief in solidness. It is often the contradiction between what they have believed, and what they perceived non-intellectually, that comes to a head;

however, it will travel deeply into their beliefs that surround such choices.

Leavee and Leaver: If this is handled well, you will see an acceptance quickly followed by relief for the adult-child as pieces of the jigsaw puzzle, that previously seemed blurred, fall into place and they gain a sense of clarity. If not, this will reinforce the confusion they have felt as a result of these contradictions, and our adult-child will become more attached to what they believe. As this is a time when they are searching for their own self-knowledge, if wisdom is gained, they will bloom; if not, they will become one of the extremes of the *connection continuum*.

Growing Your Child and Revisiting to Grow Stage 7

Our physical world uses marriage as an external metaphor for the offer of an internal connection to divinity — a life-long connection, unconditional, all-encompassing, and unifying. It is the beauty of a shared vision and the witness to our life, a feeling of significance in a space of such vastness: this is our spiritual connection. Equally so, the ideal of marriage, this gentle essence, that awaits invitation, is consistent in both love and its forever presence; it is unwavering and unconditional, the dream image of two people inside one relationship. However, the very core of what we call marriage has sadly become the attachment to one person forever.

Marriage has been a poor substitute for our yearning for full spiritual connection. Is it any surprise then that the breakup of our marriage is often regarded as the most devastating time in our lives? One of us attempts to compensate for another's inner spiritual connection, that can only ever be a substitute. The beauty marriage offers, when fully accepted at this level, is that these two lives assist each other as they journey towards individual realisation, and build towards a freedom that is beyond attachment. It is through assimilating knowledge, that is shared as a couple in intimacy and vulnerability, that we see the development of such wisdom. This is the awesome beauty of lifelong relationships.

Encouraging our children during this final and longest stage of development comes from a place of leadership. It is by walking the talk and living consciously that we begin to develop wisdom that is contagious.

Attempting to convince your adult children of some religious belief, or entering into intellectual arguments where it is difficult for them to explore knowledge, will only hinder the process. Open, inquisitive communication while you support their own exploration is where you will assist them most in their journey of development. The practical application and reconfirming of your own inner divinity will quietly invite them to develop in their own unique style.

If you have a hankering towards learning and study, take it up and explore. If there is a new enquiry towards times of silence or meditation, have a go and allow yourself to be open.

Be open to learning and consider the natural cycle of information transforming into knowledge, and graduating as wisdom.

Beyond ...

With the seven stages accomplished in two decades, the *masterpiece* is now free to grow in both definition and intensity of colour as the years unfold; the framework and design have been defined. Adult life is the creation where with open invitation we can use the chisel of choice as our refining tool to live the life we believe we were been born to live. Is it destiny? This is for each of us to choose.

I believe every parent does the best they can do whilst drawing on all they know and using the resources they have to give their children the greatest possible start for their lives. We can only teach what we know, and you pass on what you live. It is up to us all to take responsibility, as adults within this world, to create a better place for our children and the generations yet to come. We do this by refining, growing, and continuing to develop ourselves as we come to learn and understand more.

> *"You must be the change you wish to see in the world."*
> ...... *Mahatma Gandhi.*

Parenting is the most important place to start; the effects of this grand adventure are expressed in the lives of our sons and daughters forever.

Chapter Four
Concerning the Children

How to practically manage the emotional and physical changes.

Given the absence of an Instruction Manual delivered at birth, carefully tailored for our child's specific requirements, we as parents have to make it up as we go along. Obviously, there are some parts of parenting that are easier than others, and leading our children through divorce is not one of the cruising moments. It is instead a time we could quite frankly do without — but be encouraged, I'm about to take the cover off many of the biggies asked by others over the years, and give you a head start.

Realistically, sometimes I bumbled along crossing both fingers and toes, and hoped it would work; at other times I screwed it up so completely I had to retrace my steps, but I learned along the way. What I am passing on is both what does work and what definitely doesn't, tested over and over by others who have walked this path, albeit each in their own way.

Let's take a look at the nuts 'n bolts of how to manage the emotional and physical changes with our children. Each topic is addressed with key points of focus and suggestions, followed by answering some of the most Frequently Asked Questions compiled from my years of coaching and counselling.

If you will, take these points and work with them; apply the suggestions offered, and modify them for your own situation. By personalising the suggestions to your own life scenarios, you will breathe life into them, and in doing so, move beyond common ritualistic following into a practical day-to-day integration that enables the knowledge gained to be experienced, and that grows your wisdom.

Breaking the News

For most of us we dread this part. The reality of telling the children highlights our own frailty and vulnerabilities, as we force open the doorway to the children's youthful innocence, the fairy-tale is prematurely ended. This natural desire to protect and provide seems incongruent with our announcement of separation — a cutting blow we know they will remember.

Leavee, Leaver, and the Children

With some Leavees, any positive tone or word diminishes their very real sense of pain, that for their own reasons they take comfort in as it justifies the betrayal they feel.

The Leaver, attempts both to reassure him/herself, and to offer relief with assurances that life will be greater and better.

The children want to know their world is not going to get worse. They can handle change, but naturally resent worse.

Underneath all the confusion of our disparate emotions, the truth is simply that neither parent wants to disappoint the children, and currently, this feels like the ultimate disappointment.

Until this point, if the children have known of divorce, it is through the experiences of others. They may have little or no idea what is ahead, or they may have watched some terribly traumatic times shared by friends or relatives that we fear will haunt them. Regardless of their current knowledge, it is crucial you understand it is your job to provide the perspective through which your children will view your divorce.

Gaining Bearings

This is your first chance to excel as a Parenting Team beyond marriage. For a few children, this will come as welcomed relief; however, this is rare and usually only in cases of abuse. The vast majority of children who have been through their parents separating remember being told, and most agree that this point was negative — unless they were particularly young.

If your children already have a preconceived idea that separation is devastating, you need to be conscientious in adding a constructive balance to this picture. This doesn't mean you pretend you aren't suffering, but rather acknowledge the appropriateness of having your children share the experience and be able to see this as a learning experience for their own lives. If they are naïve to the entire ordeal, keep it positive. Above all, keep in mind that your responses and attitudes will set the tone and guide their feelings — not only about the divorce, but about handling any traumatic change — as they move forward in life. This is fundamental. Even if you are devastated, if you can at least attempt to show some acceptance, your children will accept more easily, and therefore learn. If you show resistance to everyone and everything that is occurring, your children are more likely to do the same.

Important Ingredient

Before speaking to the children, take some time to become comfortable with an integral part of parenting: as parents, we will forever affect our children's life masterpiece. In the face of this, you will very soon announce the addition of real complexity; but let's not burn, cut, or destroy anyone in the process. If you do not respect this important ingredient, you will project judgement and blame in your conversations. While I fully appreciate that coming to acceptance is the intention of the journey ahead, it is wise to at least be at the starting blocks when you break the news to your children.

Intentions

Begin by understanding your true intentions behind any conversation you will have. Do you require yourself to be made to look right or good? Do you want your soon-to-be-Ex to be wrong? Do you want the children's sympathy? Do you want the children to accept you and your choices?

As you answer these questions, take the time to consider the long-term perspective, regardless of circumstances. While it is normal to find it a challenge to maintain an attitude of acceptance in the face of a current adversity — and to want your children to understand and accept your decisions — remind yourself that this will all develop over time as you continue to use constant and consistent communication and contact.

Conversations

When you tell your children, your job is to help reframe the window they will look through as they view your divorce. This first conversation should not be about defining the separation, the reasons, or about the details of the changes that are going to occur. While some of this may come up during the talk, the primary purpose should be to explain how the family structure will be changed as the parenting of your children continues. It is meant to reinforce the importance of them in your lives, and their innocence (that they are in no way responsible for what is happening), as you acknowledge that they are naturally affected.

> Your job is to help frame the window your children will look through as they view your divorce.

Be sure to make it very clear to the children that they can always talk and ask more questions as they think of them, or share their opinions and feelings about it when they arise. A little bit more often, works better than a large download and expecting your children to process such critical information all at once. Limit the focus of any conversation to one point at a time, and constantly bring the topic back to your children's world, not yours.

> TIP: If you can monitor your own conversation content, as a rough guide, keep at least 80 percent focused on their world and 20 percent on yours. This way the conversation consists of 20 percent that outlines the facts that the children's parents are separating, and 80 percent is about the solutions and results of that decision — not dirty laundry.

Emotions on Display

While it is perfectly natural to have open displays of feelings from time to time, you must be very careful with how (and how often) you do this while in front of your children. To see either parent emotionally upset because one parent has made a choice affecting the other puts children instantly into a situation of feeling divided loyalties. If you have a natural flood of tears, draw strength and take courage, saying, *"This is natural and may happen from time to time, but I know this is going to be okay for us all."* The reassurance of it being okay, is not promising anything more than a realistic future. You will be okay, you probably will not be fantastic right now, but by making such a statement, you reassure them and yourself that you will not be lost within this. This also helps your children avoid blaming their other parent for the current pain.

FAQs:

Do we both tell the children, or just one of us?

This needs to be answered with another question; Are you able to agree on how you will both tell the children? Can you both refrain from any personal digs or cutting remarks while telling them? If the answer is yes to both, then doing this together is a very constructive beginning. It adds the demonstration of family togetherness albeit the opposite is being said. This is a powerful display of the new Parenting Team in action from the earliest of stages in an atmosphere of communication and cohesiveness; it enhances the children's feeling of stability and sense of security; they know it is okay.

> Together is a very constructive beginning ... demonstrating family togetherness.

If the answer is *no* to either one, perhaps it is best both parents take some time to decide if, for the moment, they are able to place their children's welfare ahead of their own private battles, and then reconsider if they are able to reach *yes*. If *no* remains, it is best if the parent feeling the most constructive speaks to the children alone.

While the parent feeling particularly destructive is well within parenting rights to speak to their children, it is best to avoid early stages of 'dumping on children' just because we are hurting. There will be plenty of time for conversations to be had in the weeks, months, and years ahead; this is only the first of many conversations, so keep it in context. At the moment, this is all about focusing on communicating the change in the children's lives, and not airing dirty laundry.

What do we say?

What you say is important; how you say it is critical. Be straight up, don't beat around the bush and expect your children to get the general gist of what you are saying. Say it as it is. *"We are no longer going to be living in the same house..."* This statement passes no blame, makes no excuses, promises nothing more. It is as it is. Depending on the type of communication you have with your children, you are able to add stability and comfort to the new story of your lives. The entire focus of this conversation is the effects this decision has upon your children's lives — nothing more. This is all about them!

> What you say is important ... how you say it is critical.

The first question asked in return is going to be Why? Your children have been asking this question since toddlerhood, and they expect a good answer. To ignore or invalidate this question is foolish; so how do you answer it without getting yourselves into blame, excuses, or finger pointing? Depending on the children's ages, your answer might be a version of this:

> Although we genuinely believed we would be able to live together forever on our wedding day, it hasn't happened this way. However, we are both grateful and fortunate to have had children together, and although we will be living in two homes, we both agree to keep parenting together because we want to, and we love you very much. One upside to going through all this change is something I have learned ... relationships need a big investment of time and energy, and we will now begin to spend more time together. This may sound like cold comfort right now, but I have been told that after separating, many parents have

discovered their relationships with their children gets better, and I'm looking forward to that happening with us.

Focus back on the effects on their life and remove the attention from the marriage or lack thereof. Continue to always build on the positives, while you give many reassurances of love for your children.

The key points to convey are:

- This is not about them — although we acknowledge how much it affects them.

- They are not at fault regardless of how grumpy we have been with them lately.

- We will keep talking as questions come over the weeks, months, or years ahead.

- Although we no longer live together, we are still parents, and our children always have access to both parents through coming and staying, phones, text, etc.

I want the children to know the reason; my Ex doesn't. Now what?

Why do you want to tell them? Normally one wants to be vindicated or free of finger-pointing. You want to be understood or made right. If the reason you want to explain the cause of the divorce diminishes the other parent in any way, wisdom would say, it is not to come from your lips — regardless.

Here is the reason I speak with caution on this point; telling your children the reason assumes you accurately know it. The tricky part is usually you will not want your Ex to tell their reason because it's wrong. If the full truth be told, it forces us to look at our part in the demise of the marriage, but usually, we convince ourselves the other party is the delusional one.

If you give your reason, it is likely to be from a narrow perspective that immediately invites divided loyalties and judgement from your children. As tempting as it may be, refrain from giving reasons, as these usually come out as excuses. As the years pass, many of your children's own life experiences will give the opportunity for more reasons to be explored free from the immediate emotional time of change. It can take years for pieces of the jigsaw to fall into place; meanwhile, the Parenting Team is able to begin its new journey on a solid foundation.

May I add, the only exception to this rule is in the area of abuse. In the case of separation under abuse, we must explain that one never deserves to be treated this way and therefore you must move to keep yourself safe. However, take the time to add that the only reason someone acts so badly is because they loath themselves intensely — even if they themselves cannot recognise this yet. This additional comment opens the doorway for your children to later accept their other parent without needing to condone the witnessed behaviour.

> Telling your children the reason assumes you accurately know it ... immediately inviting divided loyalties and judgement from your children.

> In my own example of the marriage ending, our children would have been sorely misguided had I attempted to tell them the reason at the time. Although my reason was justifiable by me and onlookers, it would have only passed on blame. I wanted to blame because I was hurting. Had I chosen that path, I would have avoided disclosing the deepest undercurrents that were within our marriage, not because I wanted to deceive, but because it was only in hindsight that these were revealed to me in years beyond the divorce.
>
> Although circumstantially, it seemed both obvious and fair to tell the children why our marriage had ended, that would have robbed me of the potential learning, them of a respectful relationship with both their father and stepmother, and all of us, of the rich Parenting Team.

I have no plans, and don't know what we are all going to do; what do I say?

Be honest about the limited answers you currently have while being very clear about the security, stability, and priorities you hold for your children.

Many things are going to change over the years ahead, and it is okay not to know all the circumstantial facts straight away. It is also perfectly reasonable to ask for more time, and say that you'll let them know more by the end of the week, or something similar, as you give yourself time to find your answers.

Whether you tell them as a Parenting Team or on your own, begin to teach your children that sometimes we all need to walk one step at a time; and although this is not always easy to do, especially in times of such uncertainty, it is an invaluable skill to learn. Your children will learn as they watch you in action; so lead the way.

While there will naturally be much you do not know, take the time to explain what you do know; *"We are going to find a house with three bedrooms and a place safe for the dog. Once we have done this, I will look for a new job close by while you all stay in the same schools with the same friends. You will go and spend nights with Dad too; and remember, you can always phone him ..."*

> Let them feel secure in a plan, and you have their well-being as top priority ... if they feel safe, children are content.

These are the things you know. While the routines may change, the job scenario might be a bit of a blur, the house search may be hard going at the moment, you can spare the children the emotional details, and limit the conversation to the facts. You don't need to give them your full list of 27 things to do; all they need is the top few to let them feel secure that there is a structured plan, and show that you have their welfare and well-being as your top priority. Generally, if they feel safe, children are quite content to leave the details to you.

Even if your children are older, continue to protect them from shouldering adult responsibility. Although they may appear to be mature, if you understand the developmental stages as discussed in Chapter 3, it will give you insight into how easy it is to damage a developmental stage with parental issues. Confide in adults, not your children.

What if the children get really angry and don't want to see me again?

Some do, most don't — if it is handled well by both parents. (Unless in the case of abuse.) The overwhelming evidence shows that when children get really angry and choose to reject a parent, it is when the parent is resistant and struggling, and as a result poisons the relationship between the child and the parent who has caused the pain — usually the Leaver.

There is a part of each one of us that seeks acceptance and love from our parents; however, when we, as parents, fail to live up to the child's expectations in such a devastating manner as to no longer want to live together, it is understandable that their core sense of acceptance and love is challenged. This confusion is masked through the blatant anger that is expressed in isolation. While no child really wants to continue to be estranged from either parent, this will continue to be a source of resentment in their lives until they are able to make peace with what occurred. Sometimes, the only thing we can do as parents is genuinely love and support them while they take the time they need to grow to understand this for themselves.

> Genuinely love and support them while they take the time they need to grow.

If you can talk openly with your children about their anger, you will leave the door open for further engagement. Even if you are unable to talk, your willingness to constantly be available to them, in their time and in their way, is important. In the case of a toxic parent, strong attitudes of judgement against one parent will generally come from children who are 12 years or older. This is not to say those who are younger will not struggle, but usually it is the older ones who make the choices of defiance and rejection. To counter this, around this age there is also a reasonable level of personal independence that will allow for communication between you and your child without inconveniencing the other parent. In this way, the responsibility to build understanding and develop the parent/child bond rests heavily on you as the parent, so take the time and learn new skills to invest in constructively building their lives.

I have fallen in love with someone else; should I tell the children?

If you have plans to build a life with this someone, then yes; if not, keep it to yourself. Many relationships that have been the catalyst for the breakup of a marriage fizzle within months of the heartbreaking demise. Of course many may answer with, "Well, I think it will, but I don't really know, we're just taking it easy right now." If this is the case, this is clearly not a committed relationship; therefore your children are better served to be sheltered from the intricacies of such adult behaviour.

> If you have plans to build a life with this someone, then yes; if not, keep it to yourself.

However, if you believe there are great possibilities of a sustainable relationship, it is best you tell your children; if you don't, someone else will. The most important factor in telling your children about someone else being involved is to be sure that the new person does not carry the blame for the end of the marriage. To have your children believe the new stepparent should shoulder the responsibility of the marriage demise is both devastating and inaccurate. The marriage breakup may have had a catalyst (being the new partner); however, as with all catalysts, it needed to have elements to work with, which means there must have been significant unresolved issues in the marriage relationship.

The question then is surely not an *if*, but rather more *how*? Be honest and open with your children about introducing your new partner — but I have a hesitation with this statement: how deluded have you become in your belief in honesty? In fairness, this is one of the biggest traps you can fall into while going through such delicate stages of change. Hence, before being honest with your children, be sure you are truly honest with yourself.

> TIP: If you cannot see your part in the marital demise, the hurt you have inflicted on your Ex, and the acknowledgment of your emotional turmoil between jubilation and guilt, you are no longer being honest. If this is the case, it is best to postpone making too many statements to your children about someone else until you have dealt with yourself first.

The answer to *how*, is as simple as giving your children the freedom to genuinely like and accept the new soon-to-be-stepparent into their family. The older your children are, the more they will decide what judgement is to be cast, with the main measurement based upon their perceived quality of relationship their parents had before the separation. With this in mind, there is little more powerful than both mother and father knowing and accepting the new adult into the family unit. In doing so, you offer your children the gift of true freedom of personal choice. To follow this path takes true courage and strength for everyone involved, but especially from the parent who is without a new partner.

> In my particular situation, following my personal choice of embracing our new stepmother into our family, we introduced her as a friend of Dad's for the first few months. Our children were spared the emotional manipulation of divided loyalties and isolating tactics trying to appease one parent's hurting heart. While I grant this may be too challenging for some, it has been my greatest act of love for our children, and while I didn't know it at the time, also for myself.

Day-to-Day Care

This section is focused on the daily happenings inside your home and focuses on the patterns of care rather than the routine that houses these patterns; it is those aspects of caring for your children that involve daily interactions and frequent choices. It is more about alleviating the minor frustrations than solving larger issues with the Ex. Remember, day-to-day care is quite separate from legal guardianship. While there can be shared guardianship of the children, often one parent has the majority of the day-to-day care for the benefit of the family as a whole.

Leavee, Leaver, and the Children

Leavee: The Leavee typically views all agreements with the Ex relating to day-to-day care as issues that have been forced upon them due to the change in circumstances. This base resentment means that if the Leavee is the one with the major responsibility for the day-to-day care, they will want no contradiction to the way they go about fulfiling this; they are also the one who is either gaining, or reclaiming, control over their world. However, if they are the one without the day-to-day care, they will often feel they've been robbed of involvement in their child's world, even if previously they were quite distant.

Leaver: The Leaver, on the other hand, is the one who believes all things can be worked out with just a little adjustment. If the Leaver is the one who has the major responsibility for the day-to-day care, they will tend to continue to express their freedom of choice with definite boundaries being placed upon both children and Ex. If they are not the one with the day-to-day care, Leavers tend to want freedom within the agreed routine, allowing them to remain in contact with the children irrespective of the Leavee's desires for it to be otherwise.

Children: Your children simply want things to flow smoothly so that the discomfort of their parents living in separate homes doesn't interfere too greatly with their daily lives. If there is constant tension or confusion, your children will feel powerless to influence their own day-to-day choices, and as a result they will experience anger.

Important Ingredient

It is most important to realise that the day-to-day care of your children is what imprints their expectations of life, and predictability add robustness, growing an awareness of stability for them. If you have regular schedules and predictable patterns, your children are then free to make choices for themselves, and gain a real sense of control over their lives. Without this, your children are likely to relinquish their decision-making powers to others, and thereby they often create lives of mediocrity and blame.

> Day-to-day care imprints your child's expectations of life, and predictability gives stability ... they are free to make choices for themselves.

Culture

Day-to-day care is vital in the creation of the culture in which children begin to learn what is appropriate, acceptable, normal, and tolerated within the family. The little decisions you make daily are the specks in life's tapestry that infuse your children with larger cultural preferences and expectations; this is then enhanced by the milestones and major celebrations that openly display your family culture. For this reason, your day-to-day care is so important; it is also the area where the focus turns to developing strong parenting styles.

Flexibility

While predictability is important for your children's day-to-day care, it is also essential to maintain flexibility within this structure to allow for spontaneity, fun, surprises, and the welcoming of new opportunities. If expectations are established within your family culture, deviations from this hold greater significance, and therefore are often more highly treasured. When this occurs, you have created the platform from which both predictability and exceptions can be meaningful.

FAQs:

My Ex calls the children every day and it's invasive.

This is one of the most common irritations for both the Leaver and the Leavee — and sometimes also the children. Many parents have ended up fighting with their children in an effort to make them talk on the phone to their other parent. Completely disinterested, the child reluctantly comes to the phone and leaves the phoning parent feeling a tad disappointed and disconnected. The desire to stay in contact with your children on a daily basis is often important during the early stages of separation, especially when the children are young. However, it is natural for your children to be focused on who they are currently with, and they, more often than not, adopt an *out of sight, out of mind* mentality. It is therefore questionable exactly who it is that needs the calls; is it the parents who want the contact, or the other way around?

To avoid this constant irritation, the parent who has the day-to-day care of the child needs to accept that both the Ex and the children may have a strong desire to stay in contact. This being so, it is reasonable to put some predictable timeframes on when it will be least disruptive to the family's flow.

> If children are secure in knowing they can contact you when they need you, they are less likely to need to and more likely to want too.

For the parent who makes the calls, ask yourself, am I building independence for my children, or a neediness? As a member of a Complex Family, non-daily contact with your children is a byproduct of this environment and one you are best to quickly accept. If your children are secure in knowing they are free to reach you when they need you, they are less likely to *need* to and more likely to *want* too. If you can grant this freedom to them, and become comfortable with contact during your established routines, you will help to remove complications such as guilt, emotional manipulation, or interpreted pestering. The other benefit gained from such ease is that it will diminish your children's constant hankering to be somewhere else other than where they currently are. Practice in resolving these issues now will greatly assist them throughout their lives.

Trying to solve the constant contact problem by mobile phones does not so much provide a solution, but rather opts to avoid the irritations and neediness experienced by either parent. While it is convenient for both parents and children to keep in touch by way of mobiles, it is a poor substitute for dealing with any insecurity we may feel because we are not in daily contact with our children.

> I spent much of my early separated years demanding that my children come and talk to their father on the phone as he called on his way home from work. His phone call would normally come at a time that never seemed convenient for the children, or for me, and always left me feeling frustrated. I had to deal with my frustration, but did my Ex discover the calls were more for him than the children, and realise he was often left with the feeling they were disinterested? I don't know, but eventually the calls were replaced with a natural security; they all came to know they could make contact when they wanted to, rather than following a preset schedule.

The Ex wants the children to do activities but does not help out.

Extra-curricular activities are a time-consuming part of day-to-day care. This is a common frustration families struggle with and one where the parent who has the day-to-day care of the children needs to establish where the source of their reluctance towards the activity comes from. If your child is going to benefit greatly, and you can manage such undertakings, then regardless of who was the instigator of the idea, it is worthwhile doing what you can to be accommodating. However, if you genuinely cannot manage any more commitments (financially, emotionally, or within your schedule), it is not unreasonable to express this clearly to your Ex and leave them with the issue to solve. If it is truly important to them, they will find the time and resources for the children to partake in the activity, if

> *If your child is going to benefit ... it's worthwhile doing all you can.*

not, it obviously was not as significant as you were first led to believe.

A healthy sign inside a great Parenting Team is where the parents are comfortable with recognising their strengths and weaknesses. Since you are in a Complex Family, you no longer need to live with the weaknesses of your Ex, so you may as well make the most of their strengths. If you dread doing particular activities, ask if your Ex would mind doing it instead. Often they will be delighted to help out their children in a field they excel at. If they are particularly good at being a 'weekend parent,' goofing off and having a blast with the children, and you are far better at keeping your children disciplined in homework, schedules, and sporting practice, it may be smart to construct your routines around these natural tendencies.

> In our family, my Ex was determined our children were to learn sailing. I was convinced I had neither the finances, nor the time, and while I was in favour of them learning an additional sport, I wanted to see their passion equaling that of the Ex's before I added to my juggling game. Leaving it with him to rally the troops and arrange all the details, it soon faded, as it was clearly not important given the sacrifices required.

> Likewise, I do all craft, hobbies, and practical hands-on building type activities. He takes them to the latest blockbuster movies and provides the consoles and screens. Our children know who to ask for what and we can all enjoy our strengths for what they are. Being different is celebrated, and accepting this diversity builds strength inside our Parenting Team.

I want to look after the children at home until school age.

Many agreements that existed during your marriage are now up for review, and this is another one. While you may hold very strong opinions about this parenting option, your Ex is not obligated to continue to agree; that is their choice entirely.

Whether they agree or not, you can opt to continue to be an at-home-parent and hold true to your beliefs; however, with that comes a level of reality. How you are financially supported during this time? While some country's welfare systems provide assistance, you need to act responsibly and with integrity, and carefully assess the tradeoff in the messages that are sent to your children. A mother with a newborn needs support, and should the father be unwilling to provide financial assistance for a reasonable period, our legislation ensures there is a safety net so that mother and baby can be at home together. While you may consider this path, you can also look at options for at-home work, especially in modern society where you can use the Internet to enable your home to be the workplace. You may be able to provide a sustainable livelihood and still uphold the original desired commitment to your children's formative years.

The main point here is that as you understand all agreements are up for review, and you acknowledge the powerful reality of the effects divorce has upon your life. This can remind you of why it is so devastating, and that it is also an opportunity to review your choices. As discussed previously, who you are being while you are an at-home parent is the most important part, rather than fulfilling any right you believe you are owed.

> Who you are while you are an at-home parent is most important.

My Ex expects me to look after the children, and won't help out.

Or the reverse, *my Ex expects to look after the children, and won't let me help out.*

Either way, one parent has firmly misunderstood the importance of two parents in children's lives. Day-to-day care is not about the routines of who goes where when; it is about the consistent provision of all that is required to keep the wheels turning within the routine. The day-to-day care is making sure children get up in time for school, have breakfast before they leave, and take lunch with them every day. It's about making sure the washing is done and the homework gets completed, the taxiing around for after-school activities, and the required purchases of clothing or extras. This is the level of care we are talking about here.

If you are either isolated or isolating from both parents' involvement in this part of your child's life, you create distorted perspectives. If you are shouldering the entire responsibility of raising your children on a day-to-day basis, you are best served to seek comfort through your best efforts and release any expectations of what your Ex ought to provide or do. This is parenting; it is a function you perform, irrespective of the inconvenience of little or no help from your Ex. To help, instead turn your attention to the upside of the isolation; there are fewer controlling influences; more opportunity for structured timeframes moulded to your schedules and commitments; less friction caused by differing opinions; and it does become easier to establish a predictable culture of expectations. These are all very real upsides. While you can become rather tired from the busyness, you can also learn to manage your workload as the counter-balance, and be very real about what you can and cannot achieve.

> This is parenting; it is a function you perform, irrespective of the inconvenience of little or no help from your Ex.

If you are the one struggling to partake in the day-to-day raising of your children, unable to overcome the isolating tactics enforced, you need to do your best to take the initiative to stay connected. You can be proactive in other areas where physically it is nearly impossible for the courageous Super Parent not to drop the ball. It will happen, and you need to be there, ready to catch it for the good of your children (and avoid the temptation to show up the foolishness of their isolation). Get along to meet the teacher; take the time off work to do some class field trips or school camp parent help. How about becoming the coach of their sports team? Through removing the focus on what you are not permitted to be part of, start adding to the value for your child in realms your Ex will otherwise over look or simply be too busy to attend to. There is a definite limit to every parent's resources; so find a solution.

Do we use a nanny, daycare, or after-school-care programs?

There are benefits to all options, likewise there are drawbacks. Weigh these up for your unique family circumstances and remember it will change as the ages and demands of your children change. Be flexible, while being willing to hear your children's preferences but remember they may well manipulate situations to suit themselves rather than for the good of the family as a whole.

Nannies can provide some stunning advantages, especially when the nanny becomes an extension of the family; however, this does not substitute for time with parents.

Advantages:
- Children are in their natural home environment.
- There is reduced exposure to early childhood sicknesses.
- It is cost-effective with three or more children cared for full-time.
- Light housework duties are usually included in the nanny's time.
- Children may receive individual attention and customised care.
- The nanny handles the hand-overs with the Ex.
- Belongings are easily gathered for time away from home.
- There is consistent care, and bonds of friendship form.

Disadvantages:
- As parents, we leave their world because the nanny is in our home.
- The nanny has a great independence, with significant responsibility for our child's welfare. e.g.: driving in cars, friends dropping in.
- DVDs or TV can become the baby-sitter without our knowledge.
- Can be upsetting when the nanny leaves.
- Children can manipulate the situation to have the nanny leave.

Daycare or an early childhood centre for preschool children is very popular and many caregivers do a great job. Consider the resources available and the number of hours per week your child would be in attendance, because we can all get rather scratchy when tired and away from home too long.

Advantages:
- You know where you left them and have designated times for picking up again.
- The child leaves your world, not you leaving theirs.
- The separation from the home environment and total dependence

on the at-home parent encourages the child's sense of self and their independence.
- There is a stimulating environment with variety of activities and resources.
- It can be cost-effective.
- The house is intact at the end of the day.
- Handovers can be covered through the daycare although, belongings sometimes are trickier to keep track of.
- Good friendships are developed and socialising skills enhanced.
- It is a good place for supporting parental friendships to develop.
- Local areas encourage friendships to continue.

Disadvantages:
- Your children may be exposed to influences that are not consistent with your values.
- May be difficult for strong observation of your child's needs.
- Many childhood sicknesses are passed around.

After-school-care programs are becoming more popular with the increased demands of working parents. With the increased awareness that it is illegal for children to be home alone, and the desire and responsibility to keep our children safe and cared for, many parents seek this alternative.

Advantages:
- Handovers can be covered through this program.
- Homework is usually supervised; this extends your child's perceived school day, but homework gets completed.
- It can be cost-effective.
- The house stays intact as you left it in the morning.
- Some programs provide great stimulation where children experience extension learning or opportunities for activities they otherwise would not be exposed to.
- Avoids too much TV time.
- With supervised time, you know your children are safe.

Disadvantages:
- It makes for a very long day for the children.
- Children know they are there in a 'waiting pen' until home time.

While these lists indicate some pros and cons, it is to your advantage to thoroughly check out what is on offer in your community — and the costs involved. Local neighborhoods sometimes organise their own shared-care groups where points are earned and spent amongst the group for childcare; this assists those who are on limited budgets. The idea is to be proactive, and to keep your children's well-being as the top priority.

Day-to-day care is just that — care. It is the ability to balance the need for predictable patterns with valid expectations while maintaining harmony and forward momentum. It is being able to keep the somewhat mundane routines of daily living happening around us in a caring and constructive manner, while we encourage the flexibility that will be required as other people become part of the family unit.

When considering the most appropriate alternative for your children's care, be aware this is impermanent, and will change as the demands of each stage become evident. It is a juggle, and as parents, it is simply about doing the best you can while being the best of who you are.

TIP: If possible, have the children leave your world, rather that you leave theirs. I wish I had figured this out earlier, as the power of perception means they believe they are leaving us; we watch them leave our world in anticipation of what is next; their focus stays in their positive forward space instead of feeling deserted because we left them. Usually the children become free of feelings of rejection, inadequacy, failure, and all manner of negative emotions that stem from being out of control. When they are very young and unable to fully comprehend why their parent is leaving, children's beliefs about their own sense of self-worth are developing. The feelings associated with someone walking away from their world can reinforce these limitations.

> Have your children leave your world, rather than you leave theirs.

Have you any ideas or tips for solving the petty things?

Often, it is the little things that tip the scales and suddenly you are off, having a rant at your children — again. Here is a small sample of suggestions I've used to help smooth the waters at home:

Whose turn: *"It's my turn, not theirs — that's not fair — you said last time it would be my turn."* Often, we simply do not remember, and it seems insignificant in the scheme of our life, but it's enough to get us all going. Solution: We made a single die (one of two dice); it is oversized, 4 cm square, with two sides for each child, as we have three children. If you have two children, three sides each; if there are four children, one side each plus add the dog, or a free roll for fun; but you get the picture. We rolled it for things like who got the first pancake on Sunday morning or who gets to carry in and give the birthday present, who gets to choose the movie, pick the type of takeaways and so on. It has been used for anything a little irregular that needed to stay light and fun.

Who sits in the front seat of the car: Put it into a routine and take yourself out of the equation of being judge and jury. Our routine has stuck for a decade just because it works. Three children into seven days; one has Wednesday and Weekend, one has Monday and Friday, and one has Tuesday and Thursday. If two adults, they are all in the back. Although Wednesday and Weekends is three days, because we are together every second weekend, it balances out. The key to the success is to keep it simple, easy to remember, and fair all round.

What are we doing today? Stop being the Entertainment Guide and have your children create the family weekend agenda. Solution: Make a Family Day box. Use any box or container and colour-coded cards, perhaps yellow for outside activities, and blue for indoor activities. Make up a card for as many outings and projects as you can think up. We put a $ sign on those that were above an agreed threshold, which meant we needed to save for these or reserve them for special occasions. Establish a monthly budget for the Family Days and get your children to work organising it. They will amaze you at their resourcefulness and the fun these outings provide because they have been part of the planning and decision-making process.

Help out around the home: These are the routine things like setting the table, doing dishes, taking out rubbish, but not cleaning the house, just the daily tasks that keep it rolling. Your children should be helping out; it's an important part of healthy parenting, so make it a routine. Work out together what is believed to be fair and equal. In my house, we have one who sets the table and clears it, and two who do the dishes. This kind of simple routine lets everyone know who is expected to do what and when, so reminders work rather than nagging or debates.

Housework: Again, find a way to remove yourself from the nagging and demanding. A couple of options here: put it into a routine, or you can make another box depending on their ages. If you decide to use a box, make it a Dip & Do box; write on pieces of paper all the jobs that need to be done; take turns to pull out a task and do this for as many as seem to be reasonable. Our Dip & Do's happen for everyone at the same time; everyone pitches in before we take our Family Fun Day outing. We put the music on and make it fun; this hive of activity for an hour or two precedes our celebration of achievements.

If you choose to post your routine on the wall (or similar), make sure it's written down, with clear expectations and timeframes set out. Before you begin, agree on the consequences of non-compliance, and stick to carrying them out — your teens will often purposefully push it just to see if you're serious.

Untidy Bedrooms: All rooms need to be healthy and hygienic, but this does not include tidy — as most children can show us. On top of the normal childhood chaos that most parents experience, a certain level of leeway is given for children who are moving between homes frequently. The Dump 'n Dash patterns that encourage less tidy behaviour and more rushed reactions, genuinely don't help them; however, this having been said, many children are just untidy and that's how it is. Most parents feel frustrated by the lack of orderliness inside their children's bedrooms so we need to work out a way of solving it. Solution: Don't! Agree on some standards, and have your children take the responsibility to complete it, and then leave it at that. We agree to curtains opened daily, and during summer, open windows too. They must put their washing into the basket, in the laundry. They are expected to clear and vacuum their bedroom floor on the weekends they are with us; it may all return, but at least it's been vacuumed. Beds are changed on their designated day and remade. For young children, no food is allowed in their rooms; as teens, food must be out of their rooms each day, and rubbish goes in the bins (although near enough is often good enough while practicing their hoops). Other than this, their bedrooms are their domain, and I often choose to close the door. The proviso for staying out of their bedrooms is their respect for the balance of the house; they do not leave their things lying around. Some things can be left on their computer desk and surrounding work area but all other belongings are taken with them to their bedrooms nightly. Every six months or so, I am known to arrive with rubbish sacks and begin a clean-out; this is usually hurriedly supported by the child hoping to save some favourite article I may deem as trash. This gives them a fresh start and we all feel better for a day or two ... then back to normal.

Routines

Agreements on the day-to-day care of the children is only one aspect; the routine in which this care is carried out is another. The variety of routines, and the beliefs held as to what routine is best, is immense. When considering routines, it would be fabulous if we had a simple answer, but the truth is, there isn't one. There are some key principles, however, that make routines work.

Leavee, Leaver, and the Children

When considering the routine, does it really matter if you are dealing with a Leavee or Leaver? It is easy to dismiss it, but there are motives that drive some predictable behaviour; these are often a result of which side of the separation coin you find yourself on.

The routine may irritate the issues concerning where temporary control resides; it can be a means of giving privilege or pardon for the parenting responsibilities that effect both you and your children.

If you are a Leavee blaming your Ex for the demise of the marriage, and struggling to accept the consequences of such a decision, establishing a routine that will cause more emotional pain for your Ex to contend with is sadly normal.

If you are the Leaver who has strong opinions about parenting and believes in a better way for the children, irrespective of your Ex's wishes, it is very common for you to want to restrict the number of nights your children will be away from home.

Children simply want a routine that makes their lives easy, predictable, and provides opportunities for them to enjoy the differences between both homes. They will love and loathe the best of routines simply because it causes them to move, creates inconveniences, and the routine sets boundaries. Keep in mind that, above all, your children want to have the opportunity to gain control over their own lives while living within the restrictions of the Complex Family routine.

Natural vs. Normal

It is natural for your children to make suggestions about their routine and let you know what they prefer; it is normal that you ask your children to help make the decisions. It is natural for your children to resent the coming and going; it is normal for you to invalidate or magnify their resentment. Your job in parenting is to work with what is natural, and to overcome what has now become normal.

Power of Choice

A major factor to consider regarding your child's living routine is where the power resides. This is to say that if your children have the authority to chose when they will be where, it removes the benefits of structure and discipline, and makes it very difficult for you, as parents, to manage natural consequences when the need to correct behaviour is immediate; it also becomes difficult to set and uphold levels of expectations.

While it is important to have flexibility within the structure, it is equally important to ensure this does not become the means of emotional manipulation with any members of your Complex Family. Both children and parents need to be free to challenge the status quo, without threatening and intimidating tactics that destroy the benefits of any routine you can put in place.

FAQs:

What is the best routine?

This is a million-dollar question for which there is no one answer, but I have seen the best routine is the one that works for the entire family, not just the children — and not just the parents. Some professionals lead us to believe we need to choose if our parenting is child-centric or parent-centric while arriving at the conclusion. I would rather say that to form a great routine it needs to be family-centric, otherwise someone is losing, and it will be the quieter person or the first to buckle under pressure.

The reason no one routine is the best becomes apparent when we consider the number of aspects involved in formulating a great routine: geographical challenges, schooling requirements, after-school activities, and naturally, parents' commitments. When deciding on a routine, be aware that the requirements will change as the children grow. While the children are preschool age, frequent contact with both Mum and Dad is preferable because three days is a long time in their world. Once they reach teen years, three days becomes comparatively short. If you live close by to your Ex, the routine can often be a bit more flexible; if you live far away, changes to the routine can add hours of travel time and increased expenses.

> A great routine needs to be familiy centric, otherwise someone is losing, and it will be the one who holds the weakest power.

> For many years, the Ex and I lived in the same street; this allowed for convenient drop-offs and pick-ups. I kept a very open-home policy, and we maintained a routine of them with me for ten nights per fortnight. This geographical closeness provided ease of access if Dad and Stepmum liked to pop in, or if the children had asked to see them on their way to and from work.

In alternate week routines, sometimes younger children find the gap too long between visits, but there is a nice simplicity with them being settled for a week in one place. One of the main considerations with this routine is the times things are forgotten. This can particularly affect the child regarding their classroom activities; while many 'forgotten' items can be done without for a week, it becomes quite a disruption to teachers if they constantly have to compensate for the child's forgetfulness, while trying to be supportive of their home life. One way to resolve this is to work out a way to remind your children of all they need before leaving for the week. If you need to have a checklist, make one. It is a balance between growing awareness of their own responsibility and your understanding and acceptance of the complexity in their home scenario.

Forming the agreement can be a little tricky at times. Over the years, we tried most types of routines, including the parents moving while the children stayed in the same house since they were the innocent ones. To be fair, it didn't work; but at least we knew we had given it a go. We have had great challenges in agreeing on routines. Whenever it called for a review, we would go back and forwards for several weeks until we had viewed it in the context of the family as a whole, instead insisting on the principle or timetable we initially wanted to fulfil. Upon reflection, one of the routines that stuck for years, I shouldn't think any court in the land would have assessed as satisfactory, yet it was the best for us all and one that we could agree upon as a Parenting Team. Our children were mostly happy, and we, as parents, were satisfied — although I had strong feelings for an alternative. The reason that routine stuck for many years was because it reasonably fulfilled the core principles of a good routine even though it saw a fair amount of coming and going.

The routine was I had the children every day after school to do after-school activities and homework, and it gave them a place of consistency. For the nights, the first week they would stay with me, next week with Dad, changing over on Friday. Stepmother collected them from me at 6:00 p.m. for the week they were to be with them.

So far, so good. Here is the twist — and the part that caused issues for us to form agreement.

Dad played sports on Tuesday nights so seemed pointless to him to have the children. As a result, instead of a full week at each place, we had Monday nights at Dad's and Tuesday nights at Mum's with the balance of the nights in the week-about pattern. This caused more confusion than you care to imagine, but we all managed to work with it to accommodate Dad's preference.

Establishing a great routine is not about holding to an ideal, but rather doing the best we can while allowing for flexibility. A good routine has some key characteristics:

- **Reasonable time in each place:** not sleeping in a different bed every night.

- **Not too long between change-overs:** able to survive when something is forgotten so it ceases to become a calamity.

- **Consistency:** easy to remember and able to book time for future dates, working out who has who when.

- **Flexibility:** when the unforeseen happens, we can call upon our Ex's support.

All this being said and done, the greatest routine will provide both benefits and perhaps an element of inconvenience for all involved. It is about focusing on what works and continuing to refine the parts that do not flow as well.

Are we meant to have one home or two for our children?

Some families definitely have one home and the children visit the other parent. Other families have two homes and the children go between, living almost parallel lives.

There is no right or wrong answer here; it comes down to parents' differing styles, resources, and choices. If your children have one home, this typically means they spend significantly more time with one parent than the other. Sometimes, one parent has a family-sized home while the other parent's home is a studio-sized place that struggles to lend itself to child-friendly living. One may have pets; another chooses to have no pets. One may work long hours; one may not work at all. There are all sorts of influencing factors, but in the end, a home is not about the house, it is about the heart.

> The word home is not a title to demand; rather a word of recognition for what your children feel about where they place their heads at night.

There are parents who become very particular with their children's terminology making sure they always talk about having two homes rather than visiting another parent. Sadly, it is frequently contradicted by the other parent who wants to clarify their sense of importance in parenting too, so we overhear parents saying, "No sweetie, this is home; you visit ..." To say such a comment to your children is damaging and quite unnecessary. If you genuinely want to raise fantastic children, create a great home or homes, and allow them to feel at home whenever they are with you.

The word home is not a title to demand, but rather a word of recognition for what your children feel about where they place their heads at night. If they are allowed the freedom to express their understanding of belonging as home, it flows naturally as a response to the environment rather than to your command. If it is on offer in both places, all the better.

Do we keep the children together or have one each?

Keep them together — All or None. It sounds very direct but I have seen more negative fallout from splitting them up than from keeping them together; so I suppose it's a gamble I don't want to throw the dice for. While some families choose to have their children divided, it is normally met with a certain level of regret during the years of adulthood. While it may well create more peace for the short-term, as parents are free of sibling rivalry, it does not contribute to the creation of valuable family bonds.

Although some research has attempted to provide statistical analysis of the effects of such a decision upon the children, this has usually been conducted in developing children rather than retrospectively with adult siblings. These reports suggest siblings get on better when they are in each other's company; it is hardly surprising since they see each other so infrequently. Adding to the complications in decisions such as these, are situations that include living with step-siblings and half-siblings; this lends further weight to the benefits gained from keeping natural siblings together, and learning to deal with the issues such as divided loyalties.

If there is more than one child, the bond of constancy they develop between them as they live a life of comings and goings, helps to cushion them. They take comfort from each other's company, although this is infrequently seen in action as their usual bickering tends to negate any suggestion of camaraderie; however, it is there and is usually reflected upon with warmth once they have left home and gained full independence.

While one child may have strong preferences towards a particular parent, the avoidance of the other parent does little to build or strengthen a much-needed relationship. The frequent split where fathers have sons and mothers have daughters, negates the importance both parents have in their lives. This being said, it is invaluable for fathers to have strong contribution to their son's lives during teen years; however, this does not mean it should be done at the cost of daughters gaining fatherly time.

> The bond of constancy they develop between them as they live a life of comings and goings, helps to cushion them.

While the opportunity to spend one-on-one time with your children is valuable, it is not necessarily the best way to live. It is better to arrange for activities where you create some one-on-one time. If you have flexibility in your time-sharing arrangements with your Ex, they may be very happy for you to pick up only one child once a week for an outing or some quality time together. If this is not the case, it may present more of a challenge to get this time out of the house; however, you can get creative and arrange to have the time at home.

> We enjoy one-on-one — one child, once a week, for their special time. It has occasionally caused issues of competition and irritation, but it also gave us some great conversational times and kept us focused on being together in their unique style. As they get older, the one-on-one time became is easier to have because we were free to go out without needing another adult to be present for their siblings. But just because it became easier, we didn't assume it would happen without some conscious effort and planning. Every month we book our one-on-one time together and continue to do so.

My teen wants to move in with the Ex.

Many Complex Families go through this time where a teen stipulates they want to move in permanently with one parent, stepping out of the alternating routine between homes. Again, this answer is not black and white; although at first glance, it may sound contradictory to the previous question and answer. The difference here is the teen has made the request and therefore it needs to be dealt with appropriately.

> The motive for the request is where the answer is found ... if motivated by discord ... it only postpones the inevitable.

The motive behind the request is where the answer is found. Sometimes your teen will act out of rebellion towards you; maybe they think they will benefit with financial gain or perceived freedom; maybe the youngster wants to avoid their siblings; or perhaps they are simply sick of moving between homes. The intention of the request will give you the clue for the most appropriate action.

In short, if this decision is motivated by discord between parent, sibling, and/or teen, it only postpones the inevitable. That is to say, if the key reason for this move is to avoid resolving interpersonal relationships, the issues will still need to be addressed. Teens generally believe they know what is best for their lives, and given their perspective of the world, they do. However, as parents, our job is to guide and to add balance to their view of the world through the addition of our longer-term perspective. So, should they be in a place of avoidance, it is better to deal with the issue than to ignore it by allowing them to move in with the Ex.

On the other hand, if you can see that your teen will benefit from being with your Ex, be willing to let them experience it. Any form of control over such a change may be more a reflection of your unwillingness to let them go rather than any feared damage to their development. After all, you know who they will be living with, and they may well be back before long.

When it could be useful for the family as a whole, is in the case of containing toxic attitudes. However, this is not a strategy I would easily promote considering the control and power struggles that are frequently at work. If your teen is in a toxic space, isolation is not usually of greatest benefit; instead, practicing good communication and firm boundaries often helps. If there are unique circumstances where siblings need to be protected and kept safe, separation may be the obvious choice.

I dread the hand-overs, what can we do?

It is quite possible your Ex dreads them too, so here are a couple of pointers to help. Stay focused on what the hand-over is — it's a time when all attention and focus should be on the leaving and greeting of the children. The natural excitement, the hurried organisation, attempts to collect belongings, and the beautiful heartfelt embrace as they say hello or good-bye.

> Stay focused on the hand-over ... all attention and focus should be on the leaving and greeting of the children.

Regardless of location, as parents, we need to get past the emotional negativity; this detrimental mindset is absorbed by the children when either parent (or both) displays such unfavourable emotions in the presence of their Ex. This is the child's other parent, and it is unhealthy for them to be around toxic interactions like these. To make these times workable, return the focus to the purpose of the hand-over and establish some boundaries for yourself; these will eventually flow across the relationship, although it may take some time.

1. **Appropriate timing of conversations.**
   While tension is felt, even if it appears to be the most opportune moment, it is unfair to your Ex, yourself, but most of all to your children, to begin discussing differences, opinions, schedules, or next steps at hand-over times. If something is important, arrange a time before or after the hand-over to deal with the topic, (this may include the topic of not arranging meeting times during hand-overs).

2. **Be courteous and friendly.**
   Always be respectful. It is not unreasonable, regardless of how

difficult your Ex is. The children already know that you do not like each other — but there is a level of respect that is deserved just because you made babies together, and your children need to see this respect in action. If your Ex becomes rude, threatening, or intimidating, stay calm and remove yourself promptly. If the children are with the Ex, falling apart in floods of tears in the car is okay, but keep it out of sight of the children. If they are with you, do your best to keep yourself together by focusing on them until you are alone. Practice, practice, practice.

3. **Constructive comments only.**
At pick-ups, if you are expecting shoes to arrive with your children and it's a no-show, sure it's disappointing, but catch yourself before a comment is passed. It is frustrating, but it is inappropriate to criticise or judge whilst in the presence of your children when trying to parent constructively with an Ex. This also relates to age-appropriateness as older children are quite capable of getting their own things together; however, if they are young, protection from negative comments is all the more important.

As your children get older, the hand-over's fade, so try to keep it in perspective. While some parents choose to do hand-overs at a neutral place such as McDonalds, if tension is present, even there it will be felt by the children.

Saying good-bye is always emotional, what do I do?

The quality of the relationship between the parents and the ages of the children involved, will determine the best solution. If your children are young and still struggling with natural separation anxiety, generally this will fade as further security is developed. If your children are a little older, you may need to consider looking at why it is happening.

Sometimes your children do not want to leave you because it is uncomfortable moving from home to home and they simply don't want to be bothered. However, if you buy in to their emotions about saying good-bye by personalising these feelings, (that is to say you believe it is because of hardship that has been caused in their lives) you disempower your children's opportunity to gain independence, and rob your Ex.

If, however, they are regularly distressed in the moment you say goodbye, it can help if you turn their attention forwards by mentioning something to look forward to with their other parent. Encourage them to look ahead rather than backwards. Do your best to genuinely bless them as they start a new mini-adventure; release them from any emotional neediness you may feel, and allow them to move into another area of natural growth for themselves. If this becomes a frequent occurrence and your Ex sees the children being emotional, it may be just the encouragement they need to step up and form a better relationship with their child and thus avoid such scenes in the future. What is important, however, is that you neither amplify this situation, nor hinder what is naturally there. If you try to disguise or hinder, you will only further invalidate their anxiety about separation. The balance is to ensure you release them to freely enjoy their time away from you as much as you want them to enjoy the time they are with you.

> Release them to freely enjoy their time away from you as much as you want them to enjoy the time they are with you.
> … Let them know you are content.

Particularly in the case of solo parents, your eldest child can find it more difficult to leave because they sometimes have feelings of responsibility for your welfare. It is important for your children to be secure in the knowledge that you are content and comfortable during their time away, while still being careful not to go too far and make it sound like you have more fun without them. You can point out that during their absence you like to use the time to catch up with your adult friends and do some of the things they find rather boring. Even if, truth be told, it turns into bliss when you have a chance to read a book in your PJs until noon, they don't need to know the details. The point is, you want them to be happy, free of a sense of responsibility for your happiness that hinders their enjoyment of being with their other parent.

Drop-offs / pick-ups never go as planned; it's frustrating!

The three most common frustrations are being late with times, forgetting or missing items, and no-shows. While many believe they are the only ones with this hassle, we know that's hardly the case. If your Ex was consistently erratic with timeframes before the separation, don't expect it to get any better now that you're apart. If they're the type who would lose their head if it wasn't screwed on, why would you expect it to get better? If you have experienced being stood up, it shouldn't be a surprise when it happens again; you know how hard it is to deal with.

There are two things you can do to help with the timing issue:

- The first is to *accept your Ex* as they are. Perhaps, even use your feelings of frustration to remind yourself of an advantage to no longer being married — either way, learn to accept that this is them, and stop believing they are doing it to annoy you personally.

- The second strategy is to *place a gap* between yourself and the drop-off / pick-up occurrence. Use an intermediary such as school, daycare, or the nanny; use one who has their own way of penalising the tardiness without involving you. Many after-school-care programs sting the late adult $1 for each minute they are over collection time. It doesn't take long for the message to register, and saves you from any involvement.

If you cannot seem to avoid being affected by their lateness, steer clear of any attempt to teach them a lesson through reciprocal behaviour. Learn to focus on the positive time you had free of child-raising responsibilities, and learn to become wise when specifying the handover time. Perhaps, add a little buffer of extra time to ensure you remain free of unwanted pressures considering it is almost predictable they will be late. Most of all however, avoid scolding your children because of your Ex's casual approach towards timeframes.

The second major frustration is forgetting items or losing them along the way. Children can innocently leave things behind as they don't always remember two days in advance what is required; they can find themselves with the wrong thing at the wrong house at the wrong time.

> In our family, we have packed suitcases, lived with two wardrobes, and had one wardrobe spread around what feels like the greater part of our neighbourhood — and still, there has been no completely satisfactory way to do things. It is a hassle for both sides of the family. Most of us become convinced that school socks are gobbled up by some mysterious creature, and we eventually become comfortable knowing that one week there will be a dozen pairs of underwear at Dad's, and the next week there will be none! The great new jacket we purchased last week, thinking it would last a few seasons is now lost, and brand new shoes barely last six weeks. Eventually our children figured out what clothes they want in which house and take the responsibility for it themselves, with the occasional catch-up trips still being made for appropriate exchanges.

To all of you, everywhere, be encouraged, it's very normal — your children and your Ex are not out to get you — it just happens.

A few things that may help:

- *It is never about the children;* however, don't let this become an excuse either. It is not their choice to live between two houses; so regardless of how irritable you may feel, resolve the issue in a kind and respectful manner.

- As parents, use *reminders* and keep reminding (not nagging). There are no games, just reminders. Avoid the temptation to withhold reminders just to teach them a lesson; there are enough mishaps that occur naturally to teach the lessons.

- Get into *routines* that assist in what is needed where and when; this makes it easier for everyone.

With all this being said and done, the emergency runs, drop-offs, and pickups continue to occur outside the bounds of the greatest intentions. In moments like these, your children want to know they are loved and supported even though they have forgotten, lost things, or screwed up repeatedly.

Finally, there's the heart-wrenching disappointment of being stood-up. It's hard enough to deal with as an adult, so protecting your children from being wounded by their other parent's insensitivities can be one of the more tiresome events to deal with. Sometimes, the desire to keep your children inside the innocent childhood bubble of love can even cause you to cover up for what you judge to be wrong, and you can feel that your personal integrity is in question as you defend the very one who is failing them.

> Two children's bags packed, house tidied, and all ready in anticipation for Dad to be arriving full of warm hugs and welcome. They wait, you wait, the dog waits, and slowly you get the dreaded gut feeling of "gulp, he's not coming." You call him, no answer. You wait and watch as your children are about to transform your now-tidied house into the play-ground it was only an hour ago. Still no response, and still directionless, children are left hanging in the gap between two houses.

The worst part — if you knew he wasn't coming, you could deal with that and carry on living, but you don't. You have no idea if he's five minutes away or five hours or not at all. We all know how long ten minutes seems when you are waiting for someone and they are late, imagine how long it feels for a child.

Here are a few suggestions that may help:

- Like the lateness issue, *place a gap* between yourself and the drop-off / pick-up occurrence. The reason their parent has not turned up at an agreed day or time is not about the children (although they are the innocent ones we are here to protect), it is more they hold little respect for you and your life, but they know you will not do poorly by the children.

- While it is a supportive team player who covers for their Ex with the children, there is a balance to be had between supporting them and them mistreating you. No child should ever be confronted with their other parent's lack of priorities but reality is many have to face this too early in life. The way this is done is important rather than a debate over whether it should be done or not. Keep it as a fact rather than an indication of where they rank in the other parent's list of priorities. Reaffirm the safe, secure, and loved environment they have with you, and encourage them to love their other parent for everything they are — and accept what they are not.

- Have a *back-up plan*. If the Ex's lateness is predictable, and you cannot make connection with them on the mobile phone, be sure to give a sincere warning. Not a threat — a warning of what will happen next time. Next time continue as if it was a weekend that you had the children.

The hard part of this back-up plan comes when they do arrive. To protect the children, go somewhere for the weekend (camping or similar) so you can avoid the conflict in front of the children. Whatever you think of, take the lead and be inconvenienced, but let it be known to the Ex that they are missing out on that time with the children. While it does not help with all the disruption this will bring to your life, if you can accept that the Ex is going to disappoint, hurt, and cause emotional pain, you will be better equipped to handle these events when they happen.

Children deserve protection and you are wise to do this when they are young. When they are developing teens, providing a cover-up only produces further confusion; in these instances it is about appropriate boundaries and having the courage to enforce them. Do not ask your teen to confront their other parent in the hope of greater effect. As always, arrange a meeting time to talk with your Ex about the situation and ask for their solutions. Make sure it is away from the children.

When home from the Ex's, the children take ages to settle.

This is very normal and it's not necessarily because things are wildly wrong at your Ex's place either. It is because two homes are different, and it can take some time for your children to transition between them.

A few tips to help:

- **Debrief:** Spend some time to genuinely show interest by talking about the fun and positive things they did.

- **Transition:** Arrange your schedules to do something that will assist with the transition; e.g., you get them on Friday afternoon, so perhaps you could go for a long beach walk after school and have ice cream on the way home.

- **Reminders:** Remind them that in your home, some things are a little different and repeat the core expectations again — avoid lectures.

- **Accept it:** As much as you may find it frustrating, your frustration will only fuel the issue further. Accept that there is nothing wrong; it is normal when living between two homes. Hold a reasonable expectation that your children will need some time to settle back into your routine and environment.

> A little practice in transitioning your children from the Ex's place, and a focus on the positives you share will assist.

A little practice in transitioning your children from the Ex's place, and a focus on the positives you share will assist enormously. As you grow in your acceptance of your uniqueness, and embrace the differences you know exist between your two homes, a strong family culture can develop where your children thrive. The inconvenience of the differences dissolves; replaced with a celebration of diversity they fully enjoy.

Friends & Family

Friends and family dynamics change as a result of a marriage or relationship ending, and sometimes it is more difficult to deal with the dynamics of the family and friends than it is with the Ex themselves.

In this society it is recognised that the bond of marriage carries with it a bond to the extended family. Your family in-law becomes part of the agreement, and although you do not marry the family, you certainly marry into it. Sometimes family acceptance can take a while, at other times a flood of joy comes in welcoming a new in-law into the fold. Whichever way it happens, as we enter into a long-term relationship with our chosen one, it invites unspoken commitment to their family as a whole. It is the depth of these unspoken relationships that often is only revealed once the married relationship concludes.

In much the same way, relationships with your friends may be affected. The friendships that developed over the years you were together will go through a time of significant change, and many simply will not make the transition. Some will fall away because they find it difficult to understand what true friendship is; some may have been the catalyst for the change itself; others are repelled by the drama; some are concerned it's contagious; some want to protect themselves; others are good time friends, and separation is usually not one of those great times, and so on. Likewise, we find those friends with whom, through this time, we build greater and more meaningful relationship as we begin our journey to build a Parenting Team.

Leavee, Leaver and the Children

It matters little which position (Leavee or Leaver) we're in when inside our own family, and sometimes even with our friends. Although it can have an impact, it does not normally define who we will be continuing to see post-divorce, since most friends choose ongoing friendships based on the relationship connection rather than on the reasons for separation.

Inside the family, we come to understand the saying of 'blood is thicker than water' in a whole new light. Although your husband or wife may have been part of the in-law family for years, usually post divorce, blood wins and the bonds with the in-law family fades.

Being a Leaver, we are more likely to be kicked out of the in-law family than treated to a natural fading over time; whereas the Leavee is often the one who gains further support and ongoing welcome as they have become the victim of the villain's choices.

However, when it comes to the children, both families tend to rally around the children; to this end, we applaud our aunts, uncles, grandparents, and wider family who take the time to continue to build the sense of belonging into our children's lives. This is especially important when their immediate family structure is changing.

Predictably Unexpected

> Once the separation occurs, your Parenting Team needs great support and understanding — sometimes more so than before.

The relationship you had before separation, and the reason for the separation, along with the bond your Ex has with your family and friends will dictate the level of complexity ahead. Articulated in a variety of ways, one of the most common phrases uttered by your friends and family will imply the long-harboured doubt about the suitability of your choice of partner. Such remarks are usually made to encourage you, but they can have quite an opposite effect. It's the comments like 'He was never good enough for you' or, 'I always thought she ...' or 'Finally! Wondered how long it would take.' Comments like these, that are made from ignorance, often make you struggle to gain your balance quickly enough to have some decent reply. They can also mould your perspective and cause a greater divide between all parties: family, friends, and your Ex.

Once the separation occurs, your Parenting Team needs great support and understanding — and sometimes even more so than before divorce; it is a true friend and a wise family who get this point early and avoid speaking with such belittlement about your choice of partner.

FAQs:

How do I stop the gossip, because I always end up defending?

Part of what we go through when a relationship ends is acknowledging that it is not only about us and our children; it affects our family and friends as well. The demise of your relationship provides an opportunity for others to express their judgements about what could have, should have, or ought to have been. It is normal for your mixed emotions to be highlighted by the conversations or actions of others, especially when it comes from within your trusted and respected friendships.

The important part of this situation is not so much the defending, but rather asking yourself what you are saying or doing that would encourage others to speak negatively about your Ex? Although it may feel comforting to complain about your Ex, it doesn't take very long for this to become normal behaviour with the result that all conversations centre on the doings of the Ex. As tiresome and draining as this becomes for you and those who are doing the listening, it invites participation into a mudslinging match; people cannot be expected to listen without offering comment.

The strongest way to avoid the cycle of defending and loathing is to stop complaining. If you are genuinely seeking advice, be sure to be careful who you seek advice from, and ask directly. A direct and sincere approach can quickly focus your attention on the solution rather than the dramatic retelling of an annoying incident or two.

> **The strongest way to avoid the cycle of defending and loathing is to stop complaining.**

> Believing it was my duty to protect the children and allow them the beauty of loving without influences of judgement, it took me nearly a decade to finally silence the critics.
>
> I had chosen to build a healthy Parenting Team, and this required that every shred of remaining respect and trust my Ex and I could muster be cultivated, not destroyed. If, as a result of talking with someone, I felt

more unified and stronger in my commitment to building my Parenting Team, I would continue the conversation; however, if it left me feeling disenfranchised, frustrated, and emotionally drained, I would choose silence as the better future option.

There were many months when I did not have the personal strength to defend my situation, so I opted for silence. This gave me the time to neutralise and observe my thoughts and feelings while I heard the blatant half-truths being espoused as absolute facts upon which judgements ought to be based. This silent phase allowed me to transition towards a constructive way of ignoring the ignorance of others, rather than attempting to defeat the ignorant. I could uphold rather than defend — and this changed the tone of conversations about my Ex and his family.

My in-laws are my friends; what happens here?

This is just one reason why divorce is so incredibly life-changing for most of us. There are some who remain close to the Ex's family post-divorce; however, for the vast majority, the family dynamics change so significantly that connections with the Ex's family become centred only on the children.

> Although you may not want to lose the bond, maintaining it can result in prolonged anguish.

Consideration of the reasons for separation and levels of acceptance towards the decisions ahead will all contribute to the quality of the relationship with the Ex's family. Although you may not want to lose the bond, maintaining it usually results in prolonged anguish for everyone. Whilst you can enjoy the opportunities to catch up when you join in the time they share with your children, you are wise to also allow the Ex's family time to adjust to the changes.

If you graciously lead by example in such situations, it will give the Ex's family the permission to be free from judgement as you gift them with a great act of authentic love. Although you may feel the vacuum for a while, it will not remain long if you have the courage to fully release.

> My in-laws were a strong and wonderful clan for me during my 10 years in their family. I enjoyed the family dynamics, the contrasts with my own upbringing, and the way they warmly welcomed me and my children into their lives. I found it difficult to accept the distance that would inevitably occur when the marriage ended; however, I chose to treasure the memories and time we shared.
>
> Today, I see the pleasure my teens have in retelling a story they have been told, stories of the bonds shared between myself and their grandparents, aunts, and uncles years earlier; these highlight the beauty of a former marriage through which they entered this world. The stories increase their belief in their expanded family unity.
>
> To this day there is genuine warmth in our exchange and the strong respect for our positions in the children's lives is obvious; it is expressed in an ever-present friendship. This is partially because I chose to release and freely give my In-laws the opportunity to become my 'Out-laws' (in the most nontraditional sense of the word), without resistance from me; the family was then freed to welcome a new member into their clan — my Ex's new bride.

Friends take sides and it's ugly; what do we do?

Stop talking to others and start building a Parenting Team together. The relationship is obviously in disarray, and issues that have caused its demise do not need to be resolved; however, the ongoing commitment to raise your children does. All the finger-pointing currently going on will do little to assist anyone in the future, and the future is where your attention needs to be.

Take control of the situation and allow your friends to make their own choices. Friends will have opinions about the choices you make — in or out of relationships, and depending on their own life story, it will affect the type of advice you will receive. If your friends have been through a difficult divorce, they will warn you of all the doom ahead. If they know of others, you will become the receptacle of all the woeful stories into which doubt and insecurity can be poured.

> Stop talking ... and start building ... ask your friends to help you find a constructive way to build a great Parenting Team.

If you can, guide your friends away from the game of slaughter and slander by giving them a job to do. They often feel helpless and unsure of what they can usefully do, so ask them to help you find a constructive way to build a great Parenting Team. If they can't do this, you are wise to refrain from conversations that involve the change in your relationship; instead, opt to confide in others. If they are able to be helpful, you may well find this to be the start of a more meaningful friendship.

Protect what remnants you have of the relationship with your Ex, and turn these into positives for your Parenting Team. Your friends may change, or they may grow to accept the change, but if you give them permission to negatively affect you or your children's acceptance of the new family structure, it diminishes you all.

Grandparents want to tell the children what happened; it feels like a time bomb.

This is not at all unusual, nor is it surprising considering your parents' natural urge to protect applies whether you are the Leaver or Leavee. The desire your parents feel for fairness and truth combines with their belief that age provides perspective and a bird's-eye view of the married relationship even before the separation; it suggests their version needs to be known by their grandchildren.

The way your parents communicate with your children would be wise to follow the same basic principle you abide by: avoid any remarks that would diminish your Ex in the eyes of the children; to do otherwise would only diminish themselves. Naturally, as ages and stages progress in your children's lives, questions will be asked, and further discussions will be had — and it is very healthy to have these — provided they are carried out in a manner that respects your Ex and the choices you made in both entering and leaving the marriage.

To have your parents (the children's grandparents) transfer their emotional turmoil onto your children does not assist them to build a picture of their other parent in a supportive environment. While you may temporarily enjoy the feeling of support and back-up you gain from your parents, you only need to think how you would (or currently do) feel when the Ex's parents have a word with your children.

Sometimes, you may need to discuss this with your parents to help them understand how objectionable it can be to have the children caught in the verbal confusion between two sides of a family. Guiding your parents concerning your beliefs and choices for your children in this matter doesn't mean you defend or ignore the current situation; rather, it gives you the opportunity to state your preferences in a kind, respectful, and direct manner, and then leave the option with the grandparents.

> *Grandparents are wise to avoid any remarks that diminishes your Ex in the eyes of the children; to do otherwise would only diminish themselves.*

In spite of your stated wishes, your parents may go ahead with their own conversations, and maybe you will hear a sincere rendition from your child. Instead of reacting or scolding your parents for their choices, take a deep breath and when speaking with your child, add the appropriate balance to the picture they have been given. Take the time to explain the dynamics that drive grandparents; help your children accept that they see things a little differently at times, and that's okay. Highlight the special position grandparents hold in your family, and how much you can learn from listening to them.

If your parents watch you in action as you create unity rather than division — even in the smaller family unit comprised of you and your children — you will do far more with this powerful example than by any conflict that demands they do it your way.

Being with the Ex's family is awkward; what now?

Your path from awkwardness and anger to support and respectful interaction starts with you — not them. They may choose to hold grudges and negativity towards you for the rest of their lives — and there is little you can do to change this; however, if you begin to remove the anger and awkwardness from your own life, you will dissolve the toxic levels that affect you when you are around them.

It takes time for your Ex's family to transition into a new relationship with you, and the quality will depend on the level of closeness that existed before the separation and the choices made since. A new level of relaxed conversation may take time to evolve. Time is a valuable tool in this case; however, it is not enough on its own; it also takes commitment to yourself, and being careful to speak constructively and treat everyone with respect. Take the time to understand the situation from their perspective, and remove any requirement to defend your position.

> Your path from awkwardness and anger to support and respect ... starts with you not them.

If you hold on to negative emotions when you are in the presence of the Ex or the Ex's family, your children will feel your energy change. If you feel inferior, intimidated, superior, or arrogant — they will know. If you are angry or tense, your children will feel it, and even more so because they are around the Ex's family without you so have a comparison. Perhaps they may come to recognise it feels better in your absence.

For best outcomes for all, take the time to encourage the memories you hold of even the smallest fragment of great times shared with the Ex and their family. Focus on what your children gain from being part of this extended family. For some, even if it is only as an example of what they may chose not to be in their own futures; if nothing more, you can be grateful for such a powerful example within their lives.

Work

The need to effectively balance work with daily life is a topic more often spoken about than practiced. The expectations and requirements of employers who want more from their staff to increase their revenue or decrease expenditures in the effort to grow profitability has seen long hours at the office become normal. Our standard working week of 40 hours seems to have crept up in both intensity and length, with more demanded from all of us.

If you add to that the harsh reality of being in a Complex Family and, in some cases, the added responsibility to "earn a living" or "nurture the family", it can leave you feeling very stretched. The reality is, most children are now faced with both parents working. Current consumer lifestyles and increasing costs of living have forced the vast majority of families to have both parents earning; this is a stark contrast to 40 years ago. While there has been a great increase in the freedom this has provided, it has almost come full circle to bite us, with less time for our families as a result.

Leavee, Leaver, and the Children

The differences between the Leavee and Leaver are significant, and given their current emotional position, it is the ramifications of their choices upon their lives from this point forward that fuel the fire. It is not at all unusual for great emotions to surround this topic; yet underneath the circumstantial layer of work, we often find a more compelling argument linked to the issue of money — after all, most of us are working purely for the money. If you have been touched by good fortune and are doing work you love, this topic will be relatively simple; although it may still surprise you to see things from the perspective of your Ex.

For the vast majority of the children, your work in their mind is a relatively distant function you do; and provided it continues in its predictable cycle, produces expected incomes, and observes restricted timeframes, they accept it as being normal. Although I think it is great to have children know where you go and what you do for work, I want to focus on how this affects them in their world, and look at the example you set through your work ethic and your happiness as you come and go daily.

Natural vs. Normal

It is both natural and normal to work. What has become unnatural, however, is the domination of work in our lives and the suffering the vast majority of us put ourselves through on a daily basis, as we count down to a two-day respite at the end of each week. This very normal behaviour tragically robs us of our opportunity to enjoy life to its fullest.

To start living with work as it is naturally intended requires a further deepening of our perspective for life overall. It means we take the time to balance our choices to enhance the choice of work, parenting position, leisure activities and so on. It is in finding this natural balance between all areas of our lives that the advantages can be incorporated into both Complex Family parenting and work. If we continue to uphold the principle of the *Highest Good of All*, we will find this natural balance easier to maintain. The Complex Family environment offers some stunning advantages when parenting responsibilities are shared leaving us focused work or leisure time.

FAQs:

I have to take the days off when the children are sick, not my Ex.

This is not alien to traditional family parenting either, although it's probably more frustrating inside a Complex Family since it is without mutual reward. The issue cannot easily go away; however, having a conversation before the event happens is better than attempting to assert a boundary when chaos has made its call. It is fairly reasonable for either parent to be expected to take time off when their children are unwell, yet we find that more mothers than fathers do this.

When one parent resists taking the time off, it puts the other in a position where their work environment must accommodate what they would not ask their own to do. This shows both poor leadership and disrespect. While there are times when it cannot be done, if you do your part when you can, you will build a strong supportive Parenting Team that is willing to step in when you have genuine reasons for not doing so.

If you are the one who is frequently frustrated by this and all the conversations have not helped, it is time to accept that this is how it is and stop trying to change the situation. Yes, it maybe unreasonable, and it may even place certain restrictions on possible job or career opportunities, but this is parenting.

Do I get a job or not?

There is no simple answer to this question; only the one who is asking will know the true answer, but there are some strong points to consider. The age of your children is the first one. If your children are particularly young, going out to work may not seem to be your best option; but then again sometimes the stimulation of a new environment, making new friends, and giving yourself a broader focus and daily routine, can be particularly helpful — to say nothing of providing the most basic necessity, money.

It is not so much whether you should work, it is more about how you prioritise your lifestyle and schedule to ensure your children are cared for and live with an example of a positive work ethic. Your attitude towards work is contagious, so if your children see you enjoy going to work and come home feeling satisfied even if you are tired, it will help them to develop a positive outlook towards work and earning money. They may be strongly motivated towards bettering themselves, or if you're lazy in example they may slump into hopelessness and growing apathy.

> It is not so much whether you should work, it is about how you live an example of a positive work ethic. Your attitude is contagious.

Even if your children don't understand what you do for work, take the time to include them. Do your best to explain what you do on a daily basis, and if possible, take them into work so they see that environment and know where you go when you say you're off to work.

My children cry daily, begging me to stay home; what do I do?

This is enough to have any parent feeling wretched about the choices they've made. It's not easy to cope with children tugging at legs, pulling skirts and begging you not to go out to work, especially if you are already dispassionate about your job. While you can perhaps explain things away, a more powerful approach is needed; otherwise, your children are back to coping.

> Children grow up quickly; examine what matters most to you ... there are no replays ...

Consider your routine, day-to-day care patterns and those people who are caring for your children if this is causing high levels of anxiety. At times it may require further consideration of your priorities in light of the messages being sent to the children. Your children grow up quickly; examine what matters most to you as there are no replays when it comes to parenting. Keep in mind; this phase of juggling will pass. Although it feels overwhelming at the moment, often a short-term change circumstantially can help to merge security and independence more comfortably than toughing it out; it enables development that helps significantly in the years to come.

> For me, this one was particularly taxing, and a position I lived with for some years before I finally changed my work routine. I had been an at-home-mum for five years when my marriage ended and I went into full-time employment. While I made the best choice I knew how to at the time, it didn't feel that way for the children. Being left with the nanny who lived with us, they still yearned for their mother to be with them every day; the daily routine of my leaving for work was dreaded by us all. The solution came when I found a way to work at home and had the children leave my world, rather than me leave them in theirs; a compromise in position, financial reward and companionship — but worth it.

Parenting reduces my work options; my Ex doesn't compensate.

Many people can feel bitter about the ongoing restrictions placed upon their career once they become a Complex Family and no longer benefit from joint incomes or one large income that is for the family's advantage.

Again, this is part of the reason divorce can be so devastating. It is one of the ongoing effects of decisions that were made under a different agreement that has since been discarded.

Although you may feel you've been ripped off, it will not serve you well to continue the comparisons. You need to look from your new perspective and begin to accept your new parenting position. Many sacrifices are made by parents, and some of these you may not see when you look at your Ex; so while it would be easy to become bitter about the disadvantages to your career, you need to consider the advantages you give to, and receive from, your family. If your Ex is able to gift wonderful experiences to your children through the increased resources from their career advantages, be pleased your children gain. If you can spend more time with your children and have less money to spend on them, be thankful for the time you do have to develop your relationship.

> I gave up my career when I chose to become an at-home-mum dedicated to raising three children under the age of three for the good of our future together as a family. When I needed to make choices about work post the marriage, I worked my jobs ensuring I had the required flexibility and yet the structured routine to arrange child-care and timetables accordingly. I have worked for myself, others, corporates, and small businesses — all while hoping to blend family and work commitments admirably.
>
> The feelings of it being unfair and inequitable were tangibly real; I also struggled with feelings of limited choice as I pawed through job advertisements. Fortunately, I have been able to recognise that I had also gained something — the advantage of having my work/life balance enforced by what felt like a lack of choice. This ensured that I focused on work when at work, and home when at home, so I became happy being great at both. The choices my Ex makes, are his choices, and the children observe our differences in both time and financial resources.

School

For most families, the children spend a large portion of their waking week at school, where they are affected by their teachers, and to a greater extent, influenced by their friends or lack thereof. Inside the Complex Family, however, the child's week may see school as being their place of greatest consistency; it frequently acts as the link between their comings and goings.

Reinforcement

Schools tend to reinforce the levels of expectation and aspiration your children have absorbed from home; they do not create it. Do your children believe they can achieve, or do they think that is only for the lucky ones? This is a question your family culture will answer; however, the school will either reinforce this and enrich the process, or add confusion and allow the alternative to develop.

> Schools reinforce the levels of expectation your children have absorbed from home.

Although school is powerful, it is most effective when it operates in conjunction with home. This means that as a parent you need to take an interest in your children's lives at school: their friends, teachers, sports, arts, and of course their academic progress. While you may have opinions regarding the shortcomings of the educational system, if your children are going to school, it sets a poor example if your words and actions knock the very place you send them daily.

Teachers thrive on parental support and backup — not interference. It is as easy for you to find things to improve in the classroom, as it would be for teachers to spot areas that could stand improvement inside your home. If you are a parent who frequently tells the teacher how things ought to be, you might want to consider how it would feel were the reverse happening to you. Communication with your children's teacher is valuable; the trick is to keep it as communication rather than one-way dialogue of ought to, should do's and supposed to be's.

FAQs:

Do I let the teacher know we are divorced?

For the good of the children, it is best their teachers know the family situation. It is not for compensation to be granted, but rather to ease communication. Your children are not unique because they come from a Complex Family; many schools are well-equipped to handle the complexities that arise — but they need to know first.

The teachers do not need to know the details of any separation or divorce, but it can be helpful for them to know the general day-to-day care routine along with the levels of cooperation or hostility between the parents. Your teachers are usually aware from observing your child's behaviour if they are in a happy home situation or not. However, they are also trying to teach another 30 children in a classroom, with equally valuable life stories; so instead of expecting teachers to be detectives, guessing what might be happening, a simple conversation at the beginning of the year will help.

> Teachers are not detectives ... a simple conversation at the beginning of the year will help.

> In our case, while the children were preteens and younger, I ensured that each teacher our children had was aware of the Complex Family environment within the first week or two of the new school year, and explained the cooperation between our homes. The teachers were always grateful to have the insight early, although it did not prove to be particularly necessary, given our belief that no special treatment was required. This being said, there were times teachers wanted to classify our underachieving or poor-attitude child, (because we've had them too) as another statistic of the broken or split regime, rather than addressing the real issues. In these cases, it became necessary for the teachers to understand that by buying into a rather poor paradigm, it would only enhance the levels of blame and excuses. Instead, we all needed to pull together and have parents and teachers hold consistent levels of expectations, appropriateness, and acceptability.

I'm busy working and being a parent, but would like to give the children more support at school.

The feelings of being stretched much like a snapping rubber band are common inside most homes, but the full-time working solo parent, takes the top spot. It is a juggling act that operates much like a well-oiled machine with every five minutes accounted for, where for the majority of the time things flow rather well, but when a spanner falls into the works, the results are usually quite spectacular.

> Being involved is about your attitude and support, backed up by giving your time and resources, while feeling good about how much you can give.

Being involved in your child's education is not necessarily about time and money, but neither is it about the absence of these. Being involved is about your attitude and support, backed up by giving your time and resources, while you feel good about how much you can give. Teachers understand the enormous pressure upon parents today; they also know how much a little from many can make such a large difference to their class environments. The majority of teachers go to a great deal of extra effort to avoid asking too much of parents; many give more of themselves instead. It makes a difference to give them what little you can, even when you are juggling.

Keeping in touch with your children's teachers is as simple as sending an e-mail once or twice a term just to touch base and make sure there will be no surprises come report time. It means taking the teacher's advice and working with it. There is no point to be told your child needs to learn their times tables and then ignore it — or forget to do something about it. Don't make the contact if you are not prepared to follow through as that is a waste of the teacher's precious time. However, if they see through improved results in the classroom that you acted upon it, you have assisted both your child and the teacher; for many teachers, that is considerable encouragement.

During the years of full-time employment and solo parenting, I would prioritise to spend time with my children inside their school environment. One particular company made it a little easier than most through the use of Personal Days. This was one day per quarter where we were paid to take the day off and do all the personal activities people either did during work time, or threw sick-days to manage, with very few ever taking them as genuine leave. It covered visits to banks, hair stylists, lawyers, dentists, and all the other little things that can accumulate, and gave us more time to focus on our work during work hours.

For me, those Personal Days became a ticket to go and sit inside my child's classroom and do Parent Help. I glued, cut and marked, drew pictures, took sports, and did anything the teacher wanted done. My children loved having me at school, and it helped to create a sense of importance for what school means to us. I had a long list of other things I needed to get done, but my first commitment was to establish the importance of school in our family's priorities. As the years continued, employment changed, and at times I found it challenging to be available, but I would always be at least be 'back-up' should the teachers need extra assistance for an outing, and would turn up any time I could.

My Ex doesn't let me know what goes on at school.

It is sometimes challenging to keep track of the comings and goings of our children's lives, especially when things are lost between two homes.

This being said, there is seldom an excuse to be out of touch these days as most schools use technology to improve the communication link between homes and school. If you take the initiative, teachers will usually appreciate the effort and work with you to provide a solution, irrespective of how messy the relationship with the Ex may be.

> If you take the initiative, teachers usually appreciate the effort and work with you to provide a solution.

School newsletters, notices, and permission slips are often lost or forgotten even in traditional families, so be careful not to throw fiery darts at the well-intended. If you are the parent outside of the day-to-day care, it is very easy to forget what an effort it is to get through the after-school activities, with the last thing on your mind being to remember to pass on messages. It is not personal; it is the reality of juggling.

This being said, if you are the parent who is responsible for the day-to-day care, and receive messages, invites, and other notices, it is helpful if you can remember to pass these things on and keep your Ex in the information loop. Even if they do nothing with it, it helps to build the team and removes further opportunities for excuses or blame to enter into the relationship.

Attending school events is difficult because the Ex is there.

For many parents who have an Ex, these events are attended with a certain level of tension in the air, most of which is something our children have sadly become accustomed to. This is one of the reasons such a large portion of this book focuses on the encouragement and assistance for parents to move beyond the resentment and dysfunction of divorce and start to function as a Parenting Team. The majority of school events can be attended without having to spend time with your Ex if you really don't want to, but there will be those times where parents need to be mature and stop behaving as little children inside adult bodies.

> There are times where parents need to be mature and stop behaving as children inside adult bodies.

Parent Teacher interviews are an instance where teachers go out of their way to accommodate the tension of a divorced couple by scheduling two sessions so they can talk to the parents individually rather than as a pair. I think it is sad that teachers have to double their work because of such immature reactions.

In much the same way as you avoid dealing with issues at hand-overs, you deal with school events. If there is tension with an issue, choose to discuss it in a more appropriate forum than school prize-givings or sport field's sidelines. To have your Ex feel threatened or intimidated at school events will only cause more damage to your child than it will solve. If these places become repetitively uncomfortable, you will run the risk of your Ex either no longer participating in your child's life, or your children may decide to quit the activities to avoid the tension felt from the sidelines.

> For over a decade of parenting with an Ex, we have attended all school events together including the Parent Teacher nights. We have included step parents throughout, and on occasions when one biological parent was unable to attend, our children still had a cohesive example of the importance of their education both to us and to them. Since the teachers usually had three or four parents turn up to hear about our child's progress, it would be far easier to count the number of non-surprised teachers, rather than the surprised ones. The unity displayed at such events also encouraged our teachers to move from their former Broken/Split paradigm towards the Complex Family model we lived.

We cannot agree where our child should go to school.

School can be one of the greatest consistencies in your children's life as you become a Complex Family. As your children live through the divorce experience, it is preferable to maintain all that is currently established in their world, and deal only with those things that are absolutely necessary to change. As you move further into this new Complex Family environment, if you find there is still no agreement on the most suitable school, you will need to look for strong solutions.

Children learn better when they have a sense of belonging. Surveys have been conducted to examine the differences between teachers, schools, and academic achievements, and produced surprising results. The most influential aspect of your child's achievement in the classroom is neither the brilliance of the teacher, nor the resources of the school; it is the connection your child feels with their teacher. While the other factors greatly enhance their learning opportunities, this reinforces a belief I hold dearly — It's caught, not taught.

> It's caught;
> not taught.

For your children to capitalise on this much-needed sense of belonging, the neighbourhood of friends and supporting infrastructure is also part of this environment you need to consider as you make your schooling choices. The issue of parents who choose to live in a geographically isolated location is covered in another section of this book; however, to briefly recap, avoid making this your children's problem. If they are travelling long distances many times per week because of disparate living arrangements, you need to consider alternatives to the routine. If they are isolated from their friends because of your reluctance to travel, you need to find solutions. Your children need a social life and a normal part of this is usually having their friends around home. It is healthy, natural, and fun for children to spend time with friends away from school, and it is also great for parents to get to know their friends and understand those who influence their lives. Part of this sense of belonging your children need is gained through your choice of their school.

As with many conflicts discussed in other sections, you need to keep talking with your Ex until you find a solution. If you need to move your children from one school to another, be sure you have thoroughly thought through the reasons, discussed the options, and then explained them to your children.

It's good to have your children's opinion about school; however, be mindful of their ages. Most will be heavily influenced by the strength of their friendships; and while this is important, it is possibly not wise to allow this to be the deciding factor. In the end when your children are young, you need to make the final call. If, after you've done the research and made a decision with the best of intentions, your child it is really unhappy, at least you made a choice and will have learned what doesn't work. To leave your child in limbo as they wait for a decision to be made, affects their ability to learn.

To find the best solution, do the necessary homework and learn about the advantages of the school, neighbourhood, and supporting infrastructure. Investigate the opportunities for advancement or remedial assistance. Take the time to understand the school's expectations of its students, teachers, and parental contribution.

> TIP: If you are going to do the research on the school of your choice, it is wise to show respect for your Ex's preference and do the same for that school too. If you take the time to visit both, it usually goes a long way towards finding a solution.
>
> We had the situation where my Ex became agitated about our middle child's school 10 days into the new academic year. We had previously met a few incidents within the school that were less than ideal, so when our daughter passed an innocent comment over dinner one evening, it was enough for him to leap into action. The flurry of e-mails containing links to websites appeared daily, the justifications preceded the invitation to a weekend meeting. I accepted the minor comment as being part of the bustle when a new class is settling in, and strongly opposed his desire to move her to a new school after she'd started the year; I felt he should have thought about this sooner. After a few more meetings between all four parents, my opinion had not softened and my Ex's was growing in intensity — the gap was widening rapidly.
>
> Through fear of losing established friendships, our daughter ended up in tears whenever we spoke about it, and it began to cause me distress as I watched the relentless turmoil with no conclusion in sight. Realising this needed to stop, Stepdad and I visited and met with teachers and principals of the two schools in question to establish the path forward.
>
> The next day, in new school uniform, our daughter introduced herself to a welcoming class at her new school. That year was a success in every way, and I am happy to say, she had the opportunity to be taught by one of the greatest teachers I have had the pleasure of meeting. She thrived socially, academically, creatively, in sports, and in her personal development.

It is not always the first, or the most comfortable decision that is ultimately the best. Sometimes you need to dig a little deeper and perhaps — just perhaps — your Ex is holding the answer, if you allow yourself to hear it.

My children fall short of the Ex's high expectations; now what?

Holding expectations regarding your children is natural, yet they are often a source of great debate between those who have opinions about the raising of children. Expectations are not really the issue though; it is the attachment we hold to these expectations that is the issue.

If we have been raised with little or no expectation of greatness, we find ourselves living within this restriction, and believe we don't have what it takes to succeed; therefore success can elude us. If we have grown up in a family that holds high expectations of greatness, the opportunity to achieve is increased.

> The attachment we hold is the issue.

It is important to have high expectations of children and believe they are capable to achieve their desired outcomes. It is often our belief that carries them through their troughs of personal doubt in the same way we may have had others who helped us through.

If your Ex has expectations of greatness for your children, do not reject or belittle them, but rather encourage the vision while you help to create further support. Remove the pressure as you maintain the possibility. If you invalidate the expectations your child's other parent holds for them it may do more to rob them of a dream than to free them from a prison. To remind your child of the character and qualities needed to build greatness is to add the steps of balance and practical commonsense.

Most children seek to find acceptance from their parents; it is in the maturing of ourselves as adults that we gain our own freedom from this inner search. Therefore, parental expectations are part of what promotes and defines our beliefs of what life holds in store for us; hence, it is preferable to have great expectations, but to be careful about the level of attachment we have to our children fulfiling these expectations. Your children's journey includes acceptance of their other parents' views, as they learn to validate the worthwhile expectations and release those that cause more harm than good.

Pets

Pets can become an integral part of the family. Depending on the type of pet we choose, they can add humour, love, and friendship, and always a touch of responsibility and increased commitment. Children can gain a practical understanding of what is involved in the care of a life that depends on them for its survival. They have the opportunity to learn how to handle their feelings surrounding sickness and death, and many children find a friend they believe they can tell all their deepest secrets to and know they are safe.

Since pets are not born from us, it becomes less complicated for children to start thinking of their family without such rigid boundaries. It is easy for children to say they have four cats, two dogs, and a bird — even if they have two cats at Mum's, two cats at Dad's, one dog at each and a bird with Dad. Parents will also find it far easier to hear their children referring to the pets as one big family without necessarily embracing half brothers or sisters and step-siblings just yet. The welcoming of pets can provide a great testing ground for incrementally accepting an expanding family.

It is advisable to think through the commitment involved in owning pets before they enter into your home. It is miserable to have your children become emotionally attached to a dog before you realise you are unable to adequately care for it. Choose the type of pet carefully to be sure it is both age and routine appropriate. Dogs can be great pets; they can also be as much trouble as having another child in the house. Do some reading about what is important to the animal before jumping in. As an example, it is in a dog's nature to have one master, and if you buy a puppy for your children and your routine has them with you only half the time, the dog will most certainly become your dog and not the children's as originally intended. There's nothing wrong with this, as the children will love the dog just the same, but you need to be mindful of what you are doing before you bring home the goodies.

> Choose the type of pet carefully to be sure it is both age and routine appropriate.

Think through the care of the pets with the family routines; as the parent, ask yourself first, are you willing to step in when your children are with the Ex?

Practically speaking, this is not very different from what happens in a traditional family where it is usually the parents who are the ones who step in and look after the pets; however, inside the Complex Family there is no backstop, so be prepared for the extra responsibility.

Some families have chosen to have the pets move about in the same routine as the children. The dog goes where the children are to ensure the boy is kept as the master. The mice are picked up each time the children are collected along with the goldfish in their bowl and the canary in its cage. If these solutions are to be entertained, it requires consideration of the type of pet. Obviously, large fish tanks, most cats, and many other types of pets are not so easily transported. However, if you love your pets and believe it will add to your children's lives, you can find a way to make it work; but it may take highly creative solutions and a cooperative Ex.

> For many years in our home, the head-count of pets greatly outnumbered the people living there, so it was easy to think we lived in a mini-zoo. Some of our pets came and went rather quickly; others are still with us; and another has left his footprints upon each of our hearts that still bring a smile whenever we hear his name. Our pets help to create our home, sharing love and laughter while creating what can sometimes be a bridging bond of unity.
>
> While the cohesiveness of our Parenting Team did not extend to sharing pets and children, it has meant our children have had to learn to manage their duties of feeding and cleaning to fit around their comings and goings, with parent and stepparent helping to fill the gaps.

Mobile Phones, iPods, Laptops

The advances of modern communications today allows for children to be in constant contact regardless of where they live. Although this provides enormous benefit for those inside a Complex Family, it can quickly lead to a false sense of security.

Although much of this section applies to parenting regardless of the family structure, it is fair to say the Complex Family environment is both helped and hindered by technology. It provides a constant connection to the other parent, but as many have come to appreciate, this can be used against both parents. The distress of parents who have come through counselling or coaching cursing the very item they believed to be a blessing has become too familiar.

Many Leaver parents have purchased technology so they could have greater access to their children while absent, only to later realise it has been used as a tool to assist in their children's demise. In the Complex Family where there are already complications through the constant change and lifestyle contradictions, it tends to quickly remove definitive values of right and wrong from the children's reality and open those feelings discussed in Chapter 1 to be present. Parents need to be wise in allowing the benefits of technology to bloom, while the disadvantages it brings into the home are minimised.

The Infiltration

Never before in history have parents had to deal with such constant infiltration into their children's minds. The level of competition for their attention and focus is staggering, and with this comes mass distraction in the place of time for them to be in quietness. When this constant distraction becomes normal, it slowly robs children of being able to experience their feelings; instead, they become numb to gentle sensations and begin to require more dramatic events to capture their attention. This vicious cycle traps them without warning.

To have children avoid the technology available is much like standing on a beach while the tide comes in as we hope it will stop rising because of our staunch feelings against it. It simply is not going to happen. This does not however mean we remove boundaries of commonsense and allow the children to rule the roost while they hide behind technological superiority.

Pressure while Unprepared

The pressure on your young ones today to have their own game consoles, mobile phones, iPods, laptops, and all manner of other electronic devices, is huge. Mobile phone companies are marketing to this age group, and the results have been remarkable — if not scary! Mobile phones have replaced many accessories we deemed important during our teen years, with today's latest and greatest phone being a statement to impress friends and increase the youngsters' sense of self-importance.

> Children have no context in which to assimilate the information, so asking them to make sensible decisions is foolish.

Access to the Internet on pocket-size devices allows an adult world to appear at the touch of a button. Today's children are exposed to pictures, movies, and sounds that invade them before they have the maturity to know what they authentically feel about such intrusions and influences. As it is too early in their development, they have no context in which to assimilate the information, so asking them to make sensible decisions is foolish; yet we continue to do so, oblivious to the consequences.

Advancing the Advantages

The technology itself is a neutral, inanimate object that cannot, and does not, inflict damage upon our family. It is how we use this tool that causes the problems, and reflecting this below are some of the complications and how we can work with these to our advantage, as we make the most of the great technology available in today's world.

FAQs:

My Ex bought our children phones even though I said no.

This highlights the challenge when parenting with an Ex. The children will be delighted with their new toys, and for you to pour cold water on their enthusiasm is rather pitiful. You can share in their excitement and allow them to eagerly amuse themselves (as you might like to indulge yourself with such luxuries). Once you've passed through the initial glowing phase of newness, you can start to establish the boundaries (not blanket rules) for conduct in your home, and while out and about with you.

Rather than deal out rules, it is better to have conversations with your children about the impact these devices have on personal relationships; then you can agree about how it will be inside your home.

More often than not, this is a wake-up call for parents, as they begin to realise how they have been conducting themselves with their children. It's best to adjust parental behaviour before enforcing new standards upon the children — although doing it together will most likely allow for some humourous and gentle reminders to go both ways.

> Have conversations about the impact on relationships; then agree how it will be inside your home.

Remember you have no control, nor should you, over what the rules are inside the Ex's home. Over time, you may influence this through your children's preferences, but it is beyond your jurisdiction to attempt to change happenings with the Ex. Instead, this is an opportunity for your children to embrace being in two contradictory environments and to begin to learn discernment — and it may take a long time.

Discernment is where wisdom is gained through experience. It is being able to clearly see the array of options available, while you, as an individual, feel empowered to make a choice for the Highest Good of All, rather than yourself alone. This is growth in maturity, and will evolve quite naturally when fostered.

The way your children will develop this is through understanding the differences in how they feel when living in the two environments. It is not to say that the Ex's way is wrong, or that yours is better; it is to have your children begin to distinguish between the feelings their choices create. Begin to have them identify the choices that encourage creativity, spontaneity, harmony, peace, laughter, freedom, and joy — and those choices that don't. When they are able to feel the effects of their own choices — made while in contrasting environments — you give them a true Learning environment where mature independence can grow.

So let go of your resistance to the objectionable intrusion of a mobile phone (or other technology) into your home, and embrace the opportunity to establish a new form of learning for yourself and your children. After all, when handled well, the mobile phone may just become an asset that can make your life easier.

My children are the only one in their class without a phone.

Most children say they are the "only one" in their class, so while they may be in a minority, they are probably not the only ones. This aside, the real question here is what age is appropriate for children to have phones, ipods, computers, etc.?

In the same way, your children's discipline is dictated by their choices within Responsibility and Trust (Chapter 5), the mobile phone, ipod, and computer question is answered with growing levels of freedom. If you decide to set an age and wait for your children to reach this target, you have done little to grow discernment and wisdom for their choices once they receive such powerful little devices.

Many parents are disturbed by the direct access to pornographic material available through mobile phones, and yet these parents irresponsibly allow their children to buy mobile phones that support receiving such imagery. It is one part of the equation to agree to have a mobile phone; it is quite another to specify what type of phone. I remember being rather bemused as I was shown a mobile phone for the very young. It is shaped as a teddy bear with four icon buttons, one on each paw: answer, home, Mum, and Dad. No other options and no further keys. It was simply for communication between required parties. (This is if a preschool child really needs a phone?) However, the point is, the simplicity of the phone avoids further complications; it protects the child from any invasion arriving prematurely. There are phones that suitably allow your children to communicate effectively, but not have photos, movies, or web connection. Until you have observed your children developing the required responsibility and trust that builds towards greater freedom, you are wise not to give them technology to cause discomfort or harm to themselves or others. Likewise, computers and ipods are also becoming commonplace personal items.

> It is one part to agree to have a mobile phone; it is quite another to specify what type of phone.

As disturbing as it is, we are seeing families with inadequate levels of healthy food or warm clothing for winter, but who still have money for mobile phones, ipods, and computers. This is not always a matter of family resources, but rather, it is a matter of family priorities. Sadly, the addiction to entertainment is being enhanced by simple accessibility with cost-effective plans that allow children to believe the new levels of normal are now accepted as natural.

Although age appropriateness can be agreed with your children, it is also a great reality check to get them to save for their own computer, ipod, or mobile phone. Give up feeling obligated to support the epidemic, but instead of standing in the tide, take this as an opportunity to teach them how to develop their responsibility and trust while they earn the money to purchase their much-needed new computer.

> For us, mobile phones appeared when we, as parents, wanted to have contact with the children. At one stage, we had three children in three different schools, and pick-ups after school were sometimes a tad chaotic. The mobile phones assisted in smoothing out the hiccups; however, it didn't really mean we had to get them phones as we could have solved

the issues another way, but with reasonable age, good levels of maturity being displayed by our children, and a firm desire from them, it seemed appropriate. Their first phones were very simple, but greatly appreciated. As they have grown, these have been upgraded at their own expense, following the same formula for achieving enhanced freedom, for laptops, ipods, and other devices.

Can you please help out with ground-rules?

Coming up with the rules is the easy bit, making them stick is where the fun starts. The only way these rules work, is when you, as parents, lead by example. Are you prepared to follow the same structure? The key for rules that stick is to make them sensible and practical. Take your time to explore the options and educate the rationale.

Below are the house-rules for technology for our family; sort through what works for you and what doesn't; you can then tailor them for your own situation.

- Mobile phones do not to come with us to the dinner table and there is no answering of calls, texting, etc., during meal times or other designated family times (such as simply watching a movie together). If we have set aside time to engage in family time, we practice focusing on the family we are with, rather than those who are not present. Sure, there are times such as during an afternoon's bush walk when it may be appropriate for our daughter to text her best friend to exclaim her enthusiasm once we have reached the top of a waterfall, but it's the incessant distraction we avoid. Our children have all experienced being with friends and not being granted attention due to the friend being busy texting someone else rather than engaging in the current moment.

- While in the car and in the company of others, no texting, calls, or ipods with headphones being used. iPods through the stereo is an asset for most of us these days replacing CDs; but in isolation, they break down opportunities for simple daily chats. The time when iPods are useful however is for long car trips where a couple of hours may pass in blissful silence while watching a movie with headphones. So for us, it's not about making blanket rules that cause more grief, it is about protecting the benefits of being together daily and the golden opportunities to engage with our children that these devices might otherwise silently rob us of.

- Especially when driving the car, there is no texting. Not just because it's illegal, but because it's highly disrespectful to our passengers who feel their personal safety is momentarily jeopardised through such driver distraction.

- Mobile phones stay on the kitchen table until homework is completed.

- For younger children, mobile phones stay out of their bedrooms at night.

- All computers stay in common rooms such as family rooms, dining areas, kitchens, and lounge rooms.

The point with these ground-rules has always been working them out together and having agreement ahead of moments of correction. A well-functioning home is not just about what the rules are, but how the family will follow them; getting agreement from everyone, even if they do not necessarily like them, goes a long way to having them work.

I was horrified by what I found on a social networking website.

The influx of social networking sites has seen these become a normal part of our daily interactions. Addictive, popular, and immensely time-consuming, some resist them whilst others live virtually connected. It has left many wondering what they are all about, while some are questioning the levels of personal information available for security and safety issues. However, they are with us and here to stay for a while yet, with the power of the Internet being undeniable. It is best we educate ourselves, and our children, in sensible usage.

Being far from an expert in this area, I delved into the mechanics of the social networking psyche to attempt to understand what it is that drives people to publicly reveal so much of their personal life. It seems that as we sit at a computer, one step removed from reality we tend to believe we are somehow protected (even if there may be evidence suggesting otherwise) we want to flaunt our life and express our uniqueness yet sameness. We want to attach some significance to our otherwise mundane existence, and feed our need for simple interaction. We mask the craving of the very real human need for connection with another by a momentary call for the spotlight. Much like a lighthouse sending out it's light, our beam may well go unnoticed by most yet we post to the void in case we get a reply. This being said, many connections and friendships are established and maintained thanks to the clever marriage of programming brilliance and our inner desire to be recognised.

> Explain the consequences ... playing along with peer pressure ... can lead to blackmail and bribary ahead.

The message to convey to your children about social networking is the power of the Internet. There have been some horrific examples of this power being misused to destroy and hurt others. There are malicious and cruel examples of 'friends' posting inappropriate photos of someone on a website and having it viewed by millions to destroy a reputation beyond repair. This has been so toxic that we have seen young people take their own lives through sheer desperation, humiliation, and regret.

It is important to explain to your children what the consequences of some acts are, whether they are the perpetrator (ignorant of the devastation), or if they are the victim, through doing something naïvely dumb one day while playing along with peer pressure. This is not to freak them out so they become consumed by fearful suspicion; it is to fully expose the seriousness of personal responsibility.

One such powerful example was when a young teen's boyfriend was begging her to send a photo of her breasts during sexting. Naïvely, she followed through and sent the photo, only to have it be used for emotional blackmail when the time came for the relationship to end. Trapped by a stupid act some eight months earlier, this poor teen was manipulated into a ploy, one step at a time, leaving her feeling powerless. The story ended horrifically, with two parents carrying the devastation with them for the rest of their lives.

By taking the time to talk with your children and exposing the reality of what can happen, you will give them the opportunity to think a little before they indulge in some spur-of-the-moment pleasure that could lead to serious blackmail or bribery in times ahead.

Inside social networking websites, we want to emphasise the importance of appropriateness with your children. In much the same way as they take care and pride in their personal appearances, teach them to be mindful of the audience and the reputation they are establishing. As it is today's way to keep up-to-date with the happenings in other people's lives, use it, but accept the limitations and equally its power.

It is noteworthy to add, during one of President Obama's conversations with students, he mentioned the power of a naïve post on a website today and the ramifications in the years to come. He called for the students to be aware of the consequences — and if someone would know, it would be an American president, given the scrutiny he has to live under.

Computer protection: net nannies, random checks or snooping?

In short, you are giving your children access to an adult world so some form of protection is sensible. The more questionable parts of this issue are to what extent do your children know you are using this protection, and what level of personal invasion do you deem appropriate.

There are many forms of computer protection; most claim to block inappropriate Internet sites from loading, while another system sends an e-mail to parents if obscenities or disturbing content is found inside e-mails, documents, chats, websites, etc. Blocking, along with many other adjustable security measures, is put in place to raise an alarm if your children are exposed to the array of poor material available.

The fact is, you have given your children adult tools. Without adequate protection, it would seem you are setting them up for failure, and this is not part of creating a healthy Learning environment. While they are still developing their responsibility and trust, it is not a matter of 'catching them', but rather about protecting them until they are ready to learn further steps. Providing net nannies and software for spying, is one way of doing it, but providing the same software with the intention of protection has a different tone to it, one that creates levels of expectations that can be openly discussed.

> If you want to have your children develop healthy relationships in adulthood ... spend time to develop a trusting relationship.

If you want to have your children develop healthy relationships in adulthood, don't snoop to find out if they have visited porn sites, or sites about how to make bombs, commit suicide, and so on. Stop the porn sites from being accessed until you can have them learn the significance of their choices. Spend time to develop a trusting relationship where your children can discuss sexuality, depression, confusion, and other emotions with you.

If you are using net protection, once the alarm has sounded, as a parent, what do you do now? If you have snooped to get it, do you admit your snooping? Coming down hard on them will only drive them into further tactics of secrecy; however, avoiding dealing with it only perpetuates what we know is damaging.

Snooping is not a technique I recommend for parents to use. While some parents find catching the child's crime worthy of invasion. The damage you can cause through breaking trust is still hypocritical; therefore, just don't snoop. Although a few parents have disagreed with this over the years, I have come to see the damage this fallout brings and it far outweighs any benefit of snooping. Your children need trust; it is a gift you give and they learn to respect this; snooping is counterproductive to building such trust. It focuses your child's energy on becoming better at hiding, and you need to do more snooping, creating a vicious circle of distrust.

I beg to offer an alternative — this answer becomes clear when you look at what is most appropriate to work with your children. You need to explain the issues and provide the protection to ensure you maintain a constructive Learning environment for all. Keeping the technology both appropriate in functionality and in its positioning within the home, while you place boundaries that are followed by consequences already agreed upon, keeps technology as an asset and not a liability to your family's health.

> The children all know that along with technology in our home, there are expectations and conditions for its appropriate use. We discuss this during dinnertime conversations, afternoon catch-ups, and family meetings. These issues are treated in the same manner as my standard of 'violence as a form of entertainment' being inappropriate in this home. As one of the conditions for the children's use of technology here, they understand that while spontaneous searches of computers, mobile phones and ipods may be made, it is always with their full knowledge.

Chapter Five
Changing Tack in Parenting

How to practically manage the changes in parenting.

New Techniques

The need to change tack in the way we parent slowly creeps up on us in the Complex Family. Methods that have been touted as correct parenting, or the best way to discipline, simply no longer work in this new model. One of the most significant changes is that children now have the opportunity to use emotional blackmail; this puts fear into the most steely of parents. A penetrating comment of, *"I'm going to live with Dad since you won't let me do it."* is a threat that cuts most mothers to the core, and sends them reeling in hurt, disbelief, and utter powerlessness. This is but one of the unique challenges that parents in the Complex Family face.

As you begin to sort out the emotional and physical well-being of your separated lives, you need some new tactics to help you adjust your parenting styles to suit the new family dynamics. These new techniques need to be free from rigid dogma; instead, they must have sufficient strength, elasticity, and durability to stand all the tests that will come your way.

Parenting Positions

Sometimes it's tricky to work out just where you belong inside parenting. Do you lead your children all the way to adulthood, or walk beside them as their friend? Are you meant to get behind and push, or position yourself in case catching is required? What if you happen to be nowhere at all for a while; then what?

Each parent has a comfortable position, a place they feel normality resides when they are with their children. They revert to this position to resolve tension, celebrate successes, and unconsciously it becomes their status quo. It's the friendly Mummy who struggles to set boundaries that allow independence for fear her child may not continue to need her . . . or the father who believes that growing 'tough' boys requires them to be dragged, or pushed, or bullied through life.

> A master of parenting knows the most appropriate position and when to use it.

Today's parent is so busy parenting they have failed to recognise that such positions exist, let alone determine where they feel comfortable. While most parents will swap and move between these positions unconsciously, by highlighting them you can gain some understanding that will allow you to choose what is most appropriate for different circumstances. Stepping away from situations and changing perspective usually highlights an alternative; with this change sometimes the solution becomes obvious. Perhaps it's better to pull instead of push. Occasionally, you will need to become the crutch to lean on, instead of leaving your child to stand alone, wobbling in fear.

A *master of parenting* knows which is the most appropriate position — and when to use it. They have learned which one is most suitable to provide the greatest benefit. This takes practice with all four positions so that you can be equally at ease when any circumstance dictates the best one to use.

Parenting positions do not depend on family structure; however, inside the Complex Family, especially in times of tension, these subtle differences can become amplified. Since there are no longer two parents in the same house; their different default styles can no longer act as a balance for the other; your children feel the comparison.

Ahead

Ahead is our position by default — an attitude held by most parents. After all, we are older, wiser, and have lived longer — and as such, we brought our children into the world and accepted this as our responsibility. Some parents want to prove they can do parenting; often this is to demonstrate they are better than those they have critiqued during years of ignorance. Remember that supermarket tantrum where you swore *your* child would never do that — ever! As we have all discovered while walking this parenting journey, it begins in naïvety as we think we know best, and it isn't long before we begin the humbling discovery of our own inadequacies.

> Ahead is to lead by example. It's to walk the talk.

Ahead is to lead by example. It is to *walk the talk*, to ensure you minimise the contradictions your children see or experience. A parent's job is to smooth the path, point out obstacles, and encourage their children to develop awareness within their surroundings. To be successfully *ahead*, it is wise to have a plan, direction, and expectations for handling threats and opportunities as they arise.

When tramping through native bushlands, our confidence grows when we know the direction we're heading and the desired destination. Likewise, it's challenging to attempt to lead if we are constantly look backward in the hope of finding direction, or if we warn of every tree root or mud patch encountered. This would become dull and repetitive and undermine the confidence of those who follow. If instead, we naturally teach and guide, and allow our children to stumble, if we pause, encourage, praise, and let them gain their own confidence, it won't be long before we can watch them run on with heartwarming delight.

Ahead is not better, it simply means we carry the responsibility of leadership, and keeping it age-appropriate, are willing to hand over the controls as our children grow up.

Beside

When *Beside* our children, are we their friend, partner, or support person? If we are the friend, their expectations of us are those of playmate or the one they hang out with. While we can thoroughly enjoy being in each other's company and sharing friendship, it is different from being their friend. I have a remarkably close relationship with my children — we appear as friends — but we are all under no illusion that the parent relationship is primary. They talk about me to their friends, rather than to me as their friend. This is not a limitation of our relationship; it is a subtle difference in respect, expectations, and boundaries while parenting.

The confusion within this friendship is very common inside the Complex Family. We see it in the mother who is so emotionally fused with her child, with their emotional happiness and time schedules, that all other relationships are dependent on the dynamics of the duo. The beauty of friendship is lost and replaced with neediness and emotional manipulation; this is an unhealthy place for both of them.

> Beside is being their support person.

Being *Beside* your children is being their support person. In this manner, your children learn you are reliable and dependable; you are someone for them to lean on when they need assistance. When they stumble and injure themselves and are in need of extra support, whether it be sore of head or heart, you are there. You get beside them, put your arm around them, and walk at their pace, in their time, giving them confidence that you can take their weight for a while. Your children want, and need, you to walk beside them at times, to be willing to carry their load as they hop alongside. This is being a *Beside* parent.

Beside is a temporary position and one not to be confused with closeness in friendship, so there is a difference here in timing and phases. While you can be very close to your children, especially as they get older, you are wise to raise them in the direction of adult independence rather than as your friend. In this way, they are free to stand alone and become independent, and you will be rewarded with the joy of a true friendship as in time your relationship becomes one of two healthy adults, rather than one of disguised neediness.

Behind

Very few parents want to categorise themselves as taking a *Behind* position; it just sounds like they are going to walk in unmentionables. However, this is the most common of the four parenting positions. When life is busy and we find ourselves constantly in a hurry, yelling, demanding, and frazzled as we rush to get to the next place, or buy the next thing, or need to do more with less — this is it, *Behind*. We hear ourselves shoving everyone along in front of us, as we constantly nag and hurriedly prod them up the bum. We feel like tail-end-Charlie who picks up all the pieces everyone else has dropped. If you can relate to this, this is where you are standing, and it is hard slog pushing.

Behind is not to be condemned as wrong, for it also has its place; just don't stay *behind* for long — or you will get dumped on. Have you ever tried moving your furniture around the house? Pulling is useful — very efficient in energy and direction. As you get closer to the wall however, pop out from behind it, and push it into position. This is when pushing is worthwhile. There is strength, focus, and short-term effectiveness.

> Behind is the back up and quick reminders of boundaries ... being the belay.

It is the back up and quick reminders of boundaries. It shows your children you are here to catch them should they fall while you remain as the belay. Being *behind* provides a safety net of confidence, contrary to the lifeline ahead offers. It helps to develop their strength as their natural leadership abilities grow; it gives them the courage to undertake navigational challenges. When you teach, you lead the way, and you do this before you move sideways to allow them to take over; that is why *behind* works best.

When boundaries are forgotten, *behind* is not kicking butt. It lets them turn around to see where they have come from, and brings closure to the route along the already walked path. As you stand looking forwards, constant in your confidence in their ability to take the next courageous steps ahead, you block them from turning back, from giving up on themselves, their dreams, and purpose. *Behind* is sometimes simply being the roadblock to prevent history repeating itself.

Nowhere at All

Nowhere is still reasonably common, but one parent who abdicates all parenting responsibilities in pure abandonment is on the decrease when compared to the numbers of Complex Families. Since it has become more acceptable for us to take on shared parenting, we see fewer willing to relinquish completely.

For some families, *Nowhere* is a blessing. This does not distract from the needs your children will face when dealing with the confusion, anger, and disappointment they feel towards the *Nowhere* parent; however, the time such abandonment can be a blessing is in the case of violence and abuse. In such circumstances, most adult children reflect upon the space between themselves and their estranged parent as having been an asset rather than a curse.

The more concerning aspects of *Nowhere* are twofold; that of Physically Present, and Physically Absent.

1. **Physically Present:** This is the parent who has been overtaken by work commitments during the day, followed by poor priorities at night. This behaviour of *Nowhere* sends strong signals to the child; they have a subtle, constant reminder of the distance because the parent is

physically there, but not engaged. With the parent who has confused priorities, the child subconsciously places him/herself beneath the value of the distracting objects such as work, alcohol, or entertainment.

2. **Physically Absent:** This is the parent who has geographically relocated due to some circumstantial issue such as employment, education, health, or lifestyle. This *Nowhere* of course affects the children with feelings of abandonment and lack of personal worth that is infused by the parent's physical absence. In spite of the physical distance, it is important to do whatever is possible to minimise the toll this will take, and use some practical tools that are helpful to maintain connection and communication.

If choices have forced the Nowhere position to continue for months or years, the communication and contact needs to help bridge the physical gap much as military families do who live within a traditional family structure. There can still be a connection regardless of geographical location; but it takes constant work.

Find ways to overcome the obstacles and develop new methods to stay close. Quickly sending off an e-mail, text, or posting a two-liner on a social-networking Internet site does not equal connection; this may let them know what you are doing, but little heartfelt bridge-building is achieved this way. Many distant parents have found it disheartening to realise they have been disregarded with the slogan *out of sight, out of mind* applied to their relationship; other's are later told of their child secretly sleeping with their photo under their pillow, hoping to relieve their sense of loss. Get creative and put energy into it. Book in time with the children and make sure there are visits, phone calls, e-mails, and so on, but most of all, genuine sharing — your children are worth it.

> When my children were young, taking a trip (business or pleasure) away from them outside our normal routine, I would keep daily connection with them. A fourteen-day business venture to the other side of the world saw me create 42 'Mummy packs' so they could each have one every

morning as they awoke. These packs encouraged them for the day, reminded them that Mum loves them, and as appropriate, included a little fun something. Towards the end of the time away, the notes would start to count down the number of sleeps before we'd see each other again. A major key to the success of these was being mindful, sensible, and respectful of the Ex to ensure this did not compromise his time with them. Neither should it create a hankering for what was absent; it was just a wee reminder of circumstantial changes and allowed our connection to remain consistent. As our children grow in independence, daily touch points become unnecessary because a strong foundation has been created.

It would be easy to assume *Nowhere* is a negative within parenting, or at least, second best, but as children transition into adulthood, indeed *Nowhere* speaks loudest. This is time when parents need to step aside and allow independence to be expressed. Parents first practice *Nowhere* when children start school or childcare arrangements without them. The short bursts of time away and the reliable pickup times builds security and independence at the same time. This expands naturally as mutual separation unfolds. If this is not allowed to occur, differentiating yourself from your children becomes challenging, and as a result, unhealthy dependencies develop. By giving them the space to fly free, you will have the pleasure of warmly welcoming them back as an adult peer.

> As children transition into adulthood, Nowhere speaks loudest ... parents step aside and allow independence to be expressed.

Discipline

Discipline of children post divorce or separation is a challenging topic to find relevant and meaningful discussion. In our modern generation we already see a decline in respect towards parents, and for that matter, for adults in positions of authority. Couple this with the devastation children feel through parental separation and we find strong influencing factors that allow poor behaviour to go on unchecked.

Let's start with understanding discipline and the realisation that what has become *normal* is not *natural*. Discipline comes in two forms, *internal* and *external*. The majority of parenting discipline is focused on external when children are young. This is done by having the external consequences be sufficient to cause the child to make an alternative choice. This uses the *Pain – Pleasure paradigm* that has been taught throughout the years. That is to say, the avoidance of pain will stop us from acting a certain way, or the attainment of pleasure will have us undertake certain other ways.

However, while this achieves some desired outcomes, the most effective form of discipline is that of *inner discipline* that grows with maturity. This inner form is free of the external forces operating as a negative deterrent or positive incentive; instead, it becomes our personal choice to act in a constructive manner for the good of ourselves and others. It is our true intention that carries the creative power.

Taking discipline in its two basic forms, internal or external, we now add a complexity to the external component that is frequently mixed in with the term *discipline*. I would like to separate it out and approach this as a stand-alone issue to be discussed: *punishment*.

Punishment is the external penalty given for poor conduct, and is usually unrelated to the manner of

> The most effective form of discipline is that of inner discipline that may grow with maturity ... our personal choice to act for the good of ourselves and others.

the 'crime' committed. Using the example of robbery, the person is locked away to remove them from being able to do this again; however, this does not solve the problem caused by their act, nor deal with the reason the person made such a seemingly poor choice. Punishment also requires someone to enforce the consequence, and in a family setting, usually it is the parent. This method of control eventually dwindles as the children grow physically bigger, and as they become more independent; they rebel further unless we increase the severity of the punishments.

To adequately discipline within a Complex Family environment, we begin by accepting the difference between the Learning environment and the Performance environment. Discipline lives within a Learning environment where we develop the lesson while in the experiences so the children maintain their power of choice. Punishment, however, is within the Performance environment as it is based on the result of an action.

> Discipline lives in a Learning environment … Punishment in a Performance environment.

Let's take this into the Complex Family environment to help to understand some key differences between traditional family discipline and the new world of complexity. Due to change in authority, time lapses and altered routines, you often have significant challenges when it comes to effectively enforcing external consequences. It is probable that groundings will not be respected at the Ex's house.

Another factor is the play-off between homes that can cause any parent to cringe at the thought of their children threatening to opt to live elsewhere to get their way. If you lack the emotional or physical back-up from another adult at home (when the buck stops with you) sometimes it is just too hard. Adding to this complication, of course, is how things are made worse by your Ex's rules that are usually significantly different.

Traditional forms of discipline can begin to appear a little flimsy and impractical inside a Complex Family, so let's take a closer look at the most common ones:

Smacking:
- This is becoming an unfavoured form of discipline largely due to its misuse.
- This teaches that hitting is a permissible use of violence to control another's behaviour.
- Very few parents who support smacking do so after the younger years, and require an alternative method as their children grow.
- Issues are quickly dealt with, free from dragging it out for weeks as with groundings.
- The older the children grow, the harder you need to hit to have this be effective.
- The hypocritical message you send by smacking your child because they have smacked their sibling makes considerably less sense these days.
- The result may be a change in behaviour in the short-term to avoid further pain; however, it does not affect the beliefs or thoughts that caused the behaviour to occur.

Time Out:
- A technique that separates the child from offending again in the short-term; however, it is largely based on a method of punishment that fails us as a society — the prison system. Historically, the success rates of inmates choosing a constructive life path following their experience behind bars is significantly low.
- A very popular form of discipline that is promoted as the next alternative to smacking.
- When it is used, it is usually very poorly executed due to ignorance.
- Time Out can often be scoffed at by the offending child who is not afraid of being isolated; hence, it is no form of discipline at all but rather provides time for them to emotionally brood or perhaps become distracted from the issue of concern.
- To have Time Out as a form of punishment has the greatest effect on the child who loathes isolation. This child may be very sensitive about being locked in their bedroom or being removed from

others, yet continuing to inflict this upon them due to their poor behaviour, further increases these fears and anxiety, and in turn increases their sense of loss, and their poor or antisocial behaviour.
- When is Time Out best to use? The only time I believe it is effective to use Time Out is when you (as parent) need to separate yourself from your child. It provides you with the time out you need if you have become emotionally or physically too tired to handle the situation in a positive alternative manner.

Removal of Favourite Items:
- This is another very common suggestion in parenting techniques. Take your child's favourite toy, possession, privilege, or outing away from them for a defined time. This threat of loss is meant to entice good behaviour due to the discomfort they will endure by losing their most precious item.
- I strongly advise all parents who are part of a Complex Family to avoid this method. Our children have already experienced loss far more than we could ever reenact; however, the act of taking their most precious object away from them cuts to the very core of their feelings of loss, and leaves them to cope by gradually becoming numb. As tempting as it is due to our frustration, it's best avoided.
- The exception to this rule is if this is part of a natural consequences. Your child losing the use of their mobile phone because they are irresponsible with it is natural and makes sense.

Emotional Manipulation:
- This is a special favourite in the Complex Family. The transference of the parents' feelings of guilt, or obligation, where your children believe they must conform to avoid your negative emotions.
- This is equally so in over-controlling parents and parents who seem to have no rules at all.
- Emotional manipulation is vicious; it robs your children of the opportunity to discover their authentic feelings and beliefs throughout life; it builds anger, paranoia, bitterness, and other negative reactions.

How to Discipline

Having done away with 95 percent of the current parenting techniques dealing with discipline, you may well ask what am I going to suggest to replace them. The method found to be most successful focuses on the type of environment you create for your children to grow up in.

The majority of practice for the first three traditional forms of discipline briefly explored is based in the Performance environment. It is saying your children are judged by their actions and the consequences of nonconformity are set out by the parents. The child will follow what you say or you will inflict a harsher penalty to have them submit. The Performance environment is one where the results are the focus of most parenting decisions. This is to say, attention is directed to modify the child's behaviour to produce the desired outcome.

An alternative is the Learning environment. This is where attention is focused on the process rather than simply the result; a word of warning here: it can feel like a far longer path to reach the most desirable behaviour. This technique is usually so far removed from what you experienced in your childhood, it almost feels as though you let your children get away with things; but when done well, it is the most effective form of discipline.

> Focus on the process rather than the result ...
> Initiative
> Action
> Mistakes

To create a Learning environment three key elements are required: initiative, action, and mistakes.

- Without *initiative*, your children follow you and always look for the external guidance for what they are 'allowed' to do.

- Without *action* there is little opportunity for learning to occur; it's only theory without the practical follow-through of experience to learn from.

- Without *mistakes* little learning occurs because the focus is on being right rather than on accepting how much can be learned from getting it wrong.

This new philosophy applies an ancient principle of truth:

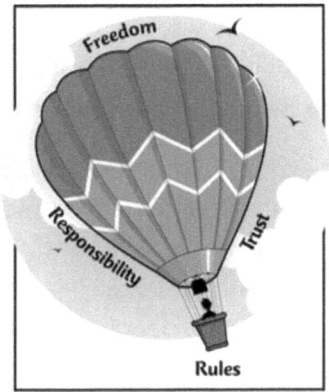

*The more **responsibility** you display,*
*and the more **trust** you develop,*
*the greater **freedom** you will experience.*
The choice is yours!

"Freedom of choice enables the development of character."

This form of discipline turns your attention away from what your children are doing wrong and highlights all they do that is constructive. Instead of their energy and focus being centered on ways of becoming cunning or looking at how to break the rules or push the boundaries, they focus on ways to develop their trust with you while they show responsibility. Their preference for freedom continues to drive their behaviour even while they test boundaries and learn where initiative, action, and mistakes are celebrated — and where they are not. They develop themselves and grow beyond the limits of requiring external rules to regulate their behaviour.

When your family lives this way, there is no need for threats — or for you to become excessively clever in conjuring up suitable consequences. It is simple and clearly defined for everyone, regardless of age or circumstance. The more freedom they want, the more responsibility they will need to display as they continue to develop your trust in them. When your children know these two key principles are their focus, you will be able to create boundaries for them to explore the manner in which this is to be done. Once they get used to this, living in this manner will make sense to them. It calls on the development of commonsense and a rather pragmatic approach to living instead of adhering to some obscure set of house-rules that hold little meaning, and result in threats and promises with unrelated consequences.

Through this simple change, your parenting will take on a new level of maturity where reminders replace nagging, expectations are simple, complexity remains outside of your daily decisions, and natural consistency is evident.

> Freedom of choice enables the development of character.

Ticket or Lecture

This is a common trap for us all. When the natural consequences sometime appear to be inadequate to the crime committed, as parents we tend to adopt the next best thing — lectures!

> A little while ago, a friend relayed a story of a time he had been indulging in driving too quickly as he tested the power of his latest purchase. A traffic officer pulled him over to the side of the road, started the normal procedures to check the car registration, driver license, warrant of fitness, and other items on their mandatory checklist. Our friend, hoping he would be lucky enough to get off with just a warning, was friendly and obliging. Without a change in tone or stance, the officer started writing out a ticket and with it started to tell him about his shortsighted behaviour in breaking the speeding laws. Our friend interrupted, "Are you giving me a ticket?"
>
> "Yes," replied Mr. Officer.
>
> "It's the ticket or the lecture; but not both." our friend retorted.

This is a conversation that frequently jumps to mind as an extremely valuable lesson for us as parents. Let your children have the natural consequence, but don't bore them with the lecture. It is their choice, and they were prepared to live with the consequences, so let them learn. The lecture only adds to your angst and does little to get the message across.

Natural Consequences

Let's outline a few examples of natural consequences, free from traditional parenting punishment and see how you feel about practicing these:

My child does not eat their dinner and is then hungry before bed so I need to give them something else.

If you believe you are serving up healthy wholesome meals that the majority of the family are happy to eat, simply follow through on natural consequences. When your child does not eat with the rest of the family, they go without; however, they still sit with the family at the table and interact with everyone. They will not starve to death and they are unlikely to develop an eating disorder from such a commonsense boundary. This is simple; eat your dinner or there is no food until breakfast. However, do not serve up their dinner for breakfast; this would be punishment. Your child simply goes without dinner, and the natural consequence of this choice is that they are hungry until breakfast.

I've asked and asked for their washing and it still doesn't make it to the laundry; I have to go and get it from them.

Do not touch their dirty clothes. Close the door and leave it. When they run out of clean clothes, it is their problem to solve. You are wise not to do the emergency washing pile either. Their choice has been to reject your offer of doing their washing at a time that suits the family flow, so it is now over to them to solve the problem. If they ruin their clothes, they will learn that it was better to have their parents do the washing, or they will learn very quickly how to do the laundry themselves. This is the art of the Learning environment. If we constantly take steps to avoid the mistakes, we rob them of the opportunity to learn the lessons.

My eldest has come home later than we agreed.

This is simple; the amount of responsibility shown here clearly does not warrant this form of freedom the next time. If you are unable to trust your teen to abide by the prior agreement, freedom is removed and rules imposed. The next time they ask permission to go out, you will either adjust the curfew time significantly, or they don't go at all. If they are late home a second time, it is commonsense to allow no freedom for outings without a parent present. Some parents have left their children locked out on the front porch with sleeping bag and pillow, sending a clear message of their unacceptable behaviour. However, with mobile phones and friends nearby, I'm not sure I would do this; but it is a logical consequence for selfishly disturbing the sleeping household. There are plenty of ramifications, but this issue needs to be handled with the two key principles of responsibility and trust.

My teen storms off to her bedroom and slams her door when upset.

Remove the door. It's easy to explain the acceptable behaviour, give alternatives, and reaffirm the consequences of actions. The next time this is done, simply remove the door. You don't need to say another thing. The drama will teach the lesson itself, and she will learn a new level of respect, as she understands boundaries and the consequences. Most of all, she will know you mean what you say.

Last night's dishes were poorly done before going to bed.

Get them out of bed to do them properly. If you discover it in the morning, drag them out of bed early and have them complete their responsibilities — they won't forget too often. Perhaps you choose to have everyone remain in the kitchen after dinner until the dishes are completed satisfactorily and the trust/responsibility is apparent.

At times, the natural consequences are plainly obvious. They sleep in and are late to catch the bus to school — they catch the next bus. Your children run late in the morning and run out of time to make their lunch — they go hungry until they get home from school. It is only a few hours from lunchtime until home time, and it won't kill them. The children have left their homework on the kitchen bench and they might get a detention if they don't hand it in — they will learn to pack their bags the night before.

Finding the natural consequence can sometimes be challenging. When no easy answer comes to mind, the best way to do this is slow and steady. Take your time and be willing to talk about it in a group or family discussion. We have been amazed by the consequences our children will think up for themselves, and each other, when they are asked well in advance. There is no point to ask for their thoughts on the consequence once they have offended; this opens it up for manipulation, trades, and tantrums. What you have to do is establish the boundaries ahead of time, before negative energy becomes the dominating factor.

Family Meetings

To introduce this new form of discipline, family meetings seem to work best; however, depending on levels of respect, routines, or rules, this will vary. Here are some suggestions you can modify to suit your family; but above all, have some fun and keep it light. Generally, it is about keeping it simple, logical, and very natural. Some people find their family meetings need a little order compared with other families where it's hard to get anyone to speak. If interruptions are an issue, borrow an ancient ritual — take a stick (or a spoon) and whoever is holding the stick has the mandate to speak while all the others listen. This gets passed around depending on who wants to speak next. Of course, this can add laughter to any meeting with the enthusiastic ones diving across the table for it.

1. The first family meeting is to *establish an understanding of the Learning environment*. Discuss what words like freedom, rules, responsibility, and trust mean to your family. Explain the diagram where equal portions of Trust and Responsibility need to be present to continue towards Freedom. There is little point to have one without the other — they go hand in hand. Perhaps, get pens and paper, and give everyone an equal opportunity to express their opinions.

2. *Select three core values* that, as a family, you can agree assist in demonstrating such attributes as Trust and Responsibility. It may be speaking the truth, being punctual, using respectful language, or showing respect in the way chores are completed. The suggestion is that only three be selected; that makes it easier for everyone to remember, and it forces you to focus. These will become the focus of the family's learning and practice for the coming weeks.

3. Next, *establish natural consequences* for when these are not upheld. Start with some of the key routines.

   > TIP: do the ones that will give you the largest improvement and yet are the simplest to tackle. E.g.; when having a shower, respect is about leaving the bathroom as you wish to walk into it next time. One member of your family may not even notice if there are two inches of water all over the bathroom floor, while another finds it irritating that people cannot put their toothbrush back in the holder correctly.

The variances are what adds colour to the family, and these can all be worked through in this forum. Remember, there is always a solution, and you may find it in the most unlikely way; so be creative and try anything at least once. Ideally, everyone needs to agree. In practice, sometimes this is not possible so find a solution to the non-agreement challenge first. Perhaps majority rules would be an option; then focus back to resolving the bathroom issue.

> We have had many occassions to drag our shower culprit out of their cosy warm bed for leaving the bathroom in an undesirable manner. Has it worked? It was Work In Progress for years, and agonisingly slow at times, but it continued to slowly improve to the point where it ceased to be a health-hazard. It is encouraging to watch the development shifts occur, to the point when the lapses do happen, they are genuinely expressed as slip ups of inner discipline, rather than an attempt to break rules and hope to get away with it.

Family Meetings may be quite regular to start, even once a week.

However, the key to their success is that all rules are upheld until the next family meeting. There are no negotiations or changes until then, regardless of the bribery and manipulation techniques employed. This way, meetings remain the powerhouse they need to be; otherwise, we have only conducted another exercise with little point. A perceived injustice for one week (or two) will almost guarantee your children will have some good buy-in next meeting. The 'I'm not interested' attitude from your teen displayed at the last family meeting, quite quickly disappears when replaced with the natural consequences of not caring for the week (or weeks) to come. The simplicity of open communication in the form of family meetings is very powerful when practiced.

> Key to success … all rules are upheld until the next family meeting.

Changing Position

There are those times, however structured and organised we get, that we have an exception. As a parent, you can change position when you know that it is your time to be Beside them instead of in front or behind. This is when you recognise that it is worth the dash up to school to help them out, and that the human kindness of parenting is simply adding support. Keep a watchful eye as such instances should occur no more than once or twice a year, rather than once or twice a month.

When children are going between houses, it is often difficult to uphold the natural consequence, and therefore, it takes a lot of giving, and a little taking, along the way. The difference is, *you make allowances, but not excuses.* You can clearly see when the attitude is there but the slip happens — let it go and be on their team. When the attitude reeks and the slip happens, perhaps a wake-up call is coming, and this is your turn to become coach rather than team player.

Eventually, family meetings are called by the children, and they have the agenda. When this happens, you will become part of the unit, rather than judge and jury — with the rewards well worth the discipline.

FAQs:

My Ex will not use this discipline; can I still use it?

That's okay, they don't need too. The difference between the two homes is highlighted significantly through this point with agreement on forms of discipline not being necessary for it to work effectively. As a parent, you only need to explain the principles to your children, since they are the ones making the choices and living with the natural consequences.

Sometimes it can take a little while for the initial changes in style to sink in and show signs of effectiveness, but it is surprising how quickly your children will feel the difference, although often they are unable to verbalise what it is. Regardless of which form, or combination of forms, your Ex is using as punishment or discipline with your children, the creation of inner discipline through using this method will benefit them in the long run. Their growing maturity and expansion of commonsense will also assist them while living in the Ex's home.

> Creation of inner discipline will benefit them in the long run ... and assist them while living in the Ex's home.

The natural consequences happen once they're at the Ex's house.

This is very common, so if you can live with it, leave it until they return so that the natural consequences are still there when they get back. If you can't do this, it becomes part of accepting life and the Complex Family structure. Let's say your children were meant to have done the dishes before the Ex arrives to collect them. They have wasted time and they are still not done — granted, it can be very frustrating. You have many options to choose from, but here are a few to start: you can invite the Ex to come inside and have a cup of coffee while you wait for the children to do the dishes; you can leave the dishes for when they return if you can live without that particular set of dishes; or, you can arrange a routine where this time constraint is not a common occurrence. One-offs are going to happen, and that's just part of the complexity; however, when an issue becomes repetitious, you will need to become more creative with your solutions. The dominating factor here is the difference between *reason* and *excuse*. If the reason they have not done the dishes is because they have genuinely run out of time given their back and forth routines, you may decide to do them even though it can be frustrating. If they are using their family complexity as an excuse to avoid the dishes, you need to become aware of this and adjust the consequences.

Reason or excuse?

What age can we start to use this discipline?

The earlier the better. Your infant learns behaviour through natural consequences. They scream; we come. Although your children do not have the ability to articulate much of what they feel, it does not mean they are not learning. Natural consequences make sense to your children far more than being smacked because they said no, or being put in Time Out because they drew on the wall with a felt marker. So while getting your toddler to help clean and remove the marker from the wall is not much of a consequence, the removal of access to this form of creative expression is.

When your preschool child throws a tantrum inside the supermarket, timeout, smacking, removal of their favourite item, and emotional manipulation are not the greatest tools to use. In a Performance environment, our focus is usually on the result; therefore, getting the shopping done irrespective of the manner in which this is achieved — this is normal. You have timeframes and deadlines to meet and your poorly behaved child needs to put up with it and just behave; so you attempt to ignore the outburst or bribe good behaviour and hurry through the rest of it quickly, red-faced or bulletproof.

In a Learning environment the point is to learn while in the process of achieving the result. Natural consequences would mean you temporarily remove yourselves from the supermarket. Although it is inconvenient, you would firmly explain (without emotional overtones) that you are returning to the car because of their poor behaviour. At the car, you would calm them down, and in a firm tone remind them of what the appropriate behaviour is. When your child is calm, you can then deliberately reenter the supermarket to continue your shopping. This way, your toddler learns their way is not successful, and you both preserve the dignity of all involved, complete the task at hand, and still maintain the Learning environment. You are fostering initiative, action, and mistakes — with the consequences of these being determined by their choices. If you say you are going to do something if they continue their poor behaviour — do it. There are no threats, and only one warning.

> The earlier the better. Your infant learns behaviour through natural consequences.

One parenting technique I have always found pointless is watching parents count to three. Have you noticed the children always wait until two and a half or three? It always seemed to me that it quickly became a game; so why start playing it for them, to then get so frustrated by it? They already know what the expectations are, so allow them to have their consequences after the warning.

Toddlers are meant to be learning boundaries and power. They are in the stage of discovering how to play with power, and it is your job as parents to teach them *power with* rather than *power over*. Although you may be bigger, plenty of toddlers are seen to *power over* their parents — do not be fooled. Your toddlers however, will learn a healthy form of power if you teach them within a Learning environment.

My children don't listen. Help!

A snippet from many parents ... *"I get up each morning and start thinking today will be different, but before 8:30 a.m., I'm yelling and we're still late. I've tried star-charts, bribes, and large rewards; it doesn't work any longer than a week, and then we're back to the chaos."*

While star-charts, bribes, and rewards will modify their actions in the short-term as they strive to receive the benefit, this does little to change their thoughts and beliefs about the situations they are surrounded by.

External incentives are short-lived solutions which is why we focus on the development of inner discipline and allow maturity to naturally grow.

Parenting is leading by example, and yelling at your children to get out the door on time may be considered normal, but it is not great leadership. The morning routine is often chaotic with parents and children attempting to gain their own momentum for the day, so this is a great time to begin your leadership practice. A benefit of starting with the mornings is that the time is only a couple of hours; it has defined tasks that need to be completed; and it sets the tone for the rest of the day. Once you have the morning routine sorted, the same principles can apply throughout. So here are a few pointers to help get things flowing:

- **Plan:** To help the morning go smoothly, start with a little planning. If you have five people to get through showers in the morning, and you only have one shower, to avoid the yelling, knocking on doors and running out of hot water, you need to get into a routine where people understand expectations. Work it out the night before, and try a few alternatives. It may be that some people prefer to shower at night before bed, while others want to shower in the morning — five showers may quickly become two or three instead. The point is to work out a plan, communicate it, and then give it a go. When there are still some shortcomings, don't give up on it, just refine it; work with the strengths, and find ways to resolve the issues. Work out what is best and develop it from there.

- **One Step Ahead:** Whatever the routine, as the parent, get up earlier and be at least one step ahead. If you stay one step ahead, you have the opportunity to remind without feeling flustered. When things start to head off track, you can alter the course or bring the children back to the agreed path simply and calmly.

- **Individual Responsibility:** This means the routine moves along with reminders or suggestions, but without you doing everything for them. Get your children to make their lunches, pack their school bags, make their beds, put their washing in the basket, stack the dishwasher, etc. Work together as a team with everyone individually responsible for their piece of the action.

- **Reminders:** A firm statement of "Five minutes and we're leaving," is a good start. Often the tone of what you say (the strength in delivery) is enough to have your children realise 'she's serious' this time. Avoid the nagging and stick to reminders only. Make up lists if your children find it difficult to remember what is expected of them before they leave for school in the morning. Provide the Learning environment where your children learn to take responsibility for their own start to the day without relying on you to make it happen.

This principle applies regardless of the timeframe; mornings just happen to be a good place to measure the level of healthy personal responsibility inside the family home, but this can be seen equally at nights, after-school, weekends, and holiday routines as well.

A further point to note when speaking of communication, examples, and discipline with your children: If you want your children to speak to you respectfully during the teen years, it is best to practice leading by example, and give up yelling now. If you object to hearing children of any age swear at their parents, refrain from swearing in front of yours. If you are disappointed by the level of alcohol consumption and drunken behaviour in young people, show your teens an alternative. If you want your young people to drive safely, be careful how you drive. Also, it is important to consider the material you promote as fun, entertaining, or stimulating when watching movies or TV. Think about the messages you send from your position of leadership in all areas of your life.

> Parenting is leading by example ... consider the messages you send from all areas of your life.

My teen lashes out — it's hard to know the natural consequence.

If your teen or children constantly cause issues in your home, they need to be constantly reminded of your discipline model. For them to deliberately hurt someone indicates they are feeling poorly about themselves, so hurting them in return is going to do little to break the vicious cycle. This being said, you must protect other family members from their toxic behaviour and remove the power their control dramas have over the family environment.

> Teens deliberately hurt when they are feeling poorly about themselves, so hurting them in return is going to do little to break the vicious cycle.

Many times teens continue their poor behaviour because they enjoy the control they feel when they spoil the family's good times. Your teen will find it easier to control a situation through the negative than influence it through the positive; eventually this practice becomes very comfortable to them. If you can step out of this negative form of control, they may initially protest by trying harder, but eventually they surrender and realise they can have more of what they want through cooperation than through conflict.

Conversations should be held in private with your teen first and frequently. Talk with them. Take the time to understand them and be willing to listen twice as much as you talk. It is very easy, as parents, to forget the difference between *talking with* and *talking at* your children. They will have some very strong ideas and great responses for you if you can stay quiet long enough for them to speak. If you are struggling to find a way to start a conversation with your teen, don't be afraid to connect with them by using text or e-mail as an icebreaker. It's not a substitute for conversation, but it can be a start; they may feel safer and more relaxed hiding behind technology in the first stage of building a better connection.

Highlighting the control drama in the presence of all family members may appear confrontational, but is a very strong way to have the family step out from living under their negative power. Do it gently, without making your teen wrong, while pointing out their attitude will no longer control. This example is best said with your teen present. Allow no interruptions, niggles, or sarcastic comments to be passed by others. Always pull up the offenders equally because it needs to be done in an open and honest forum where people feel safe. This is family in practice.

Example: *"As you all know, Jenny's behaviour can be difficult and is causing a few issues for us all right now. You also know, we love Jenny very much and value so many positives about her like her spontaneity, love of music, creativity, and her strength of friendships. So, although she has been very capable of making some feel intimidated by her actions — and sometimes her words are cruel — we need to continue to accept and love her, remembering we only ever hurt another because we feel hurt and unloved ourselves. If Jenny felt good about herself right now, she wouldn't be acting this way. Jenny has been given the opportunity to think about what she is doing, and as you know, her freedoms are restricted until trust and responsibility are displayed to us all. So, let's pull together as a team and continue to support someone we love, and one who is obviously hurting at the moment."*

The keys to discipline are communication, consistency, and the courage to continue leading by example. Your teens need you, but not the nagging or groundings. What they are looking for is your example, to both respect and rebel against. It is like a piece of elastic; discipline pushes them away and then draws them back to you. The question is, does the elastic hold firm or is it so flexible that it is hardly worthwhile? If the boundary is defined and the consequences are understood, while it is real, they still want to know how far it can be stretched. If it is firm and fair, they will respect it even when they disagree. If it is weak, they will continue to find the next area of wear and tear, and continue to push to reach break-point.

> The keys to discipline are communication, consistency, and the courage to continue leading by example.

My 8-year-old son hit me; help please.

We don't need to know any more detail than this single line; and don't be fooled into thinking that this is a result of solo parenting; many parents in traditional families face this issue as well. This issue, however, is more often between boys and mothers than with girls or fathers. Boys are more physical in early development, and hence are slower to learn how to deal with their frustrations and disappointments in other ways. Within the Complex Family, children have experienced deep disappointments, and boys definitely need some extra help to not resort to physical outbursts.

One of the benefits of a healthy Complex Family is that fathers often become far more involved in their children's lives than before the separation, and the children benefit enormously. Fathers and sons have the opportunity to spend days hanging out together, rough and tumbling without being told off or nagged about the next item to be mistakenly broken. What appeared to be an initial mistake becomes the next adventure as they set off to the hardware store and together father and son repair it. This is quite different to the usual inside workings of Mum's home, that's for sure.

The way Father deals with a son who hits him is quite different from Mother's way. Fathers are likely to firmly show him he's still got some growing to do. A wise father takes the time to teach his son that physical violence does not resolve issues, although temporarily he may think it does. It is for Dad to start teaching a boy to feel his frustration and make wise choices, rather than physically taking it out on people or things. If, as a Dad, you fall short of being able to help your son in this area, you must begin to learn how to handle this in yourself because it is this behaviour that is mimicked by your son. Your son looks to you for guidance, to see how he ought to be living, and it is as he watches how you handle situations that he will learn far more than your words can ever teach.

As for mothers, you instantly see 10 years ahead to the time your then towering 18-year-old is ready to deck you and anyone else nearby because you have said no to something they deem important. Fear immediately enters the picture, because while you may have been able to restrain your 8-year-old, you know when they reach 18, you stand little chance.

Mothers — as much as you love your boys, stop being their friend and start being their parent. Your boys need to learn to develop healthy relationships with women and the relationship with you is their training ground. It is your wake-up call to realise your son currently holds little respect for you and views the limited boundaries you set with no fear of consequences. Boys do not pick fights with the tough boys in school unless they believe they have a chance of winning. When your boy believes he has a great chance of winning against you, only then will he have the nerve to take the first swing. It is serious, it needs to be taken seriously, and it needs real consequences to avoid the creation of habitual patterns of disrespect that will play out on women in the future.

> Mothers — stop being your son's friend and start being their parent.

The consequences do not include grounding, yelling, emotional fallout, or smacking back. What must be done is to place yourself back into the role of the *parent* who guides their children through their developmental years.

This is best done by sitting down with the offending child for a conversation that explains that the dynamic between you has become toxic, is totally unacceptable, and must be changed. Remind the child that there are boundaries and this line between parent and child has become blurred. Make it clear that this is in no way acceptable or appropriate behaviour, and that as *parent*, your role is to guide their development and teach them to respect boundaries.

The delineation between mother and son is the point of focus here so the conversation could go like this:

"To help you learn and appreciate what Mother actually adds to your life and well-being, from now on there are two big changes; 1) you are no longer to come into my bed when it suits you. 2) you will be required to take further responsibility for yourself and do some things I have previously done for you. You will be the one who makes your own lunch, packs your own school bag, hangs up your towel, and keeps your bedroom tidy."

Start having some simple firm rules for them to follow, and stop doing everything for them — stop the nagging.

These simple steps will help to place you at the head of the pack, and help your son to learn that women are to be respected as valuable contributors in life, and not to be regarded as their servant. This doesn't mean you're not able to help out and be fun and friendly, but it does mean you are to break the emotional entanglement that is causing confusion in your son's mind. If you do this during their developmental years, you will have the opportunity to welcome them back in adult years as your peer.

> My son had just turned six when I realised he was ready for the next step of independence. We were on summer holiday and had been down at the beach snorkeling and swimming. Time came to head back and as we came up the path towards the house, I asked him to pick up his belongings and carry them. He said with all the cuteness his age afforded "That's your job Mum!" It was about then that he gained a new perspective on what his Mum's job really was.

There comes a time in our sons' lives when they have to learn healthy respect for those in their life, their own physical strength, and the choices they make. To take responsibility for their actions we teach them to learn to express feelings and frustration appropriately rather than by swinging fists inappropriately. If your young son gets away with breaking items or threatening physical harm when he's angry, he will carry that pattern into adulthood when the consequences can be life-changing in a few seconds. Do yourself and your son a favour by correcting the responses while he is young enough to learn the gentle way.

Daughters are different; they're not better, just different. It is normal for girls to share emotions and feelings with parents and friends. There is a stronger acceptance of support offered and received; and while girls have issues of their own to contend with, it is the minority who resort to physical violence in the hope of solving a problem.

Sibling Rivalry

If there is one thing that gets most parents down, it is sibling rivalry. As much as you try to ignore it, eventually it becomes exhausting — especially when you are a solo parent. The more children there are, the greater the constant cacophony of noise and increased opportunities for these issues to arise. It is clear to all who have more than one child; sibling rivalry is going to happen. As parents, it is best to accept its inevitability; however, this is far from condoning this behaviour or allowing it to become normal inside our homes.

Rivalry has a Job

If you can understand the learning opportunities sibling rivalry can offer, it will help you to accept it and then work with it to the benefit of you and your children rather than allowing it to become increasingly toxic. Inside the Complex Family there are two subtle differences; many children have been affected by years of parental fighting, so to battle it out between themselves is normal. Also, an acceptable conclusion to fighting is to separate — an established pattern of avoidance — that does not teach them to deal with the issues.

> Sibling rivalry handled well allows your children to develop their strategies for handling conflict throughout life.

The tension between your children can work in their favour, although it's a challenge to see. What you need is not ways to squash it, but the strategies to build the positives that outweigh any negatives. When handled well, it can create strength, courage, teamwork, and responsibility, while it adds a great deal of camaraderie, fun, and laughter along with ongoing entertainment. When not — it's a nightmare.

Conflict Resolution

Sibling rivalry handled well allows your children to develop their strategies for handling conflict throughout their life. As we all know, disagreements are inevitable, but conflict is our choice. When ill-equipped to handle such conflict, your children react with a loss of passion for life; they become numb and apathetic, or alternatively, they bottle up a sea of rage that awaits the scratch on the surface to dramatically explode. Sometimes, it leaves parents in a bewildered state wondering how their quietest children end up so violent.

Sibling rivalry is not to be ignored; it is natural family dynamics; your children must learn that it helps to shape their outlook on life. What it does need, however, is to be harnessed and used as an opportunity to learn healthy conflict resolution.

FAQs:

Between fighting the Ex and the children's fighting, I'm stuck in a nightmare.

Your children will follow your lead. More often than not, those parents who are struggling with their Ex will also struggle with out-of-control sibling rivalry. Although largely unnoticed, it is rather hypocritical for parents to tell their children off for their child-sized banter when they are taking the other parent to court for an adult-sized issue. Although we like to deem it real and our children's as not real, it all points towards poor conflict resolution strategies.

If you are to become a leader within your family, the art of resolving conflict is one area you need to practice, and there is no better training ground than with your Ex.

If you are free from issues and arguments with your Ex, but still your children are constantly fighting, examine what they are reading and watching as sources of entertainment. You may find it intriguing to start to understand what they believe is funny, and allow that to open the doorway for further conversations surrounding appropriate and inappropriate behaviour and expectations.

I'm tired of being asked to solve their petty problems all the time.

Part of parenthood is solving seemingly petty problems because children learn with the small things first. However, this being said, it is also about assisting them to learn while you offer possible solutions for them.

Here is a simple question to use to start teaching your children to respond rather than react. Ask: *Is it Tattling or Telling?* Tattling is getting someone into trouble; Telling is getting someone out of trouble. Herein lies a great secret for reducing parental ping-pong. It does not solve sibling rivalry, but it does go a long way towards educating your children about how to handle it with you. Your children will learn to identify worthy problems and those that are likely to backfire.

> Ask:
> Is it Tattling
> or Telling?

If your child is doing something that they should not be doing, and it is life-threatening, dangerous, or emotionally damaging, would you want a sibling to let you know? Yes — and quickly. If your children have been schooled in the difference between Tattling and Telling, they will have more chance of making a wise choice when they need too. They understand that sometimes, to get someone out of trouble, they first need to land them in temporary trouble. They learn how to manage the dilemma of keeping a secret; when is it the best option?

> My inventive 8-year-old daughter decided to light a fire under the house. My 7-year-old decided it was worth Telling, to get her out of real trouble later. In a similar way, many siblings have assisted their parents with issues of substance abuse, addiction, or petty crimes before those parents were otherwise aware of the problem.

When you are about to be dragged into another judge and jury session with your children, make sure you have first asked one question — *Tattling or Telling?* If they are tattling, ask them to rephrase their question to only tell. They do this through leaving out the drama and whining and sincerely tell; otherwise, you don't want to hear.

To some parents this may seem as though they are invalidating their child's feelings and freedom of expression. This is not about invalidating the expression of authentic feelings, rather it is sorting out those issues that feed drama and promote blame. As your children begin to understand the difference between Tattling and Telling, your requirement for stepping in diminishes, so when you do, it becomes far more meaningful.

Once you have established that your child is sincerely Telling, if the situation allows, *ask them to give at least one solution to the problem*. In the event of my eight-year-old's fire lighting exercise, this was clearly a time for the parent to drop everything and run, but then most situations are not as serious as house fires. When free of the need for immediate intervention, ask and wait for an answer. Although it's not necessary to take their suggested approach, it will encourage proactive solution thinking to become as usual as the corrective Telling.

I have children who fight saying it is fun, how do I stop them?

It is not uncommon for siblings to gain a great sense of camaraderie through ganging up on one another, and for some siblings, this may be the only time they feel close to their brother or sister. In a strange way, the conflict forces a closeness that otherwise is not recognisable, so the conflict itself becomes addictive to stimulate this sense of belonging. For the one being picked on, it is usually feeding their victimised thinking, so it all becomes a self-fulfiling spiral.

Instead of wearing yourself out with techniques to try to stop the fighting, spend the majority of your energy focused on ways to increase the opportunities for camaraderie to be felt in a positive setting. If your children can gain the sense of belonging they are in search of through creative and constructive pastimes, the addiction to the fighting will diminish. You can do this through changes such as swapping hours of playing games based on command and conquer for building a tree hut, or doing some baking together.

For the child who is usually the one picked on, you will need to do more than just defend them or tell the others to leave them alone. You will need to focus on building their sense of self worth so the dynamics can change naturally. As they become more empowered with who they are and the choices they make, you will see the change shift to the point where the picking on becomes meaningless.

To solve the issues, you need to take your focus off the problems and turn your attention towards the solutions. Your children won't stop fighting because you tell them to — you know this, and yet isn't it what you most commonly resort to doing? They will stop when there are greater reasons for their attention to be elsewhere.

> Your children will stop when there is greater reason for their attention to be elsewhere.

I have two children who constantly compete for everything.

Competition, unfortunately, has become somewhat of an accolade, acclaimed as the hallmark of success in our society through our preoccupation with sports and wealth. The desire to win at all costs has become generally acceptable in most modern thinking, and leaves behind disastrous consequences.

Children at some stage will compete, but the question here is about what and to what level. The point of competition has been lost because we celebrate winners as victorious heroes, while those who lose are downtrodden losers. We have forgotten that to have a competition, we must have first have had participation. We have lost respect for those who provide the challenge, and instead, focus on the result and not the process. Overall, our society has become a Performance-centred culture rather than one that celebrates continual learning. If you speak to our greatest champions, they will tell you that they learn a great deal when they lose, sometimes even more than when they win; it challenges them to make different choices the next time.

When you examine your parenting, if you see issues of favouritism or possible comparisons between your children, then you must first resolve to end such divisive techniques in your parenting. There is no place for favouritism in parenting. Although you may go through phases where one child may be easier to relate to or parent, this will do little to help you develop a healthy relationship with them or them with their siblings. You need to be genuine and authentic about equal love and care for each child; otherwise, competition between siblings is inevitable. Your children may never hear or see evidence to support their suspicion, but if it's there, they'll feel it, and this is enough to cement their belief of personal inadequacy.

If you hear yourself saying "Why aren't you like ... ?" you are fueling your children's competitive discord. Avoid all temptation to use such phrases, even if it is praising one while expecting another to live up to this example; it will not produce the desired result. Comparisons are a natural, healthy part of life; however, it is from this attachment to *better* that comes with such comparisons that the issues of inadequacy stem. If you, as parent, are going to compare your children, be sure there is no hint of a suggested better, only *different*. This can often be difficult to achieve, so it's best avoided if there's any doubt.

> Comparisons are a healthy part of life ... it is the attachment to 'better' where issues start.

Here are three tips to help with competition:

- Give up trying to eliminate competition, **dilute** it instead. Take the power of needing to be better and grow different instead. It is okay to win — it is not okay to win and not support and promote those who allowed the opportunity through their participation.

- To dilute the level of competition, **expose** it for what it is and discuss it openly. Discuss the shortcomings of our modern addiction to competition. Show that as a society, we live from one fix of winning to the next, and believe we have gained significantly because someone else has lost.

- To further dilute competition, **celebrate** the uniqueness of those who compete. If one of your children is academically brilliant and another is intellectually witty, enjoy the difference this brings. One is not better than the other, they will both add variety and stimulation to your dinnertime conversations. Instead of having your son or daughter focus on what they wish they had, expand the strength they already possess to refine their talent even further. Allow your children to consider their uniqueness as a strength by encouraging their differences as important, valid, and equal.

Do we split the children up between houses because they fight?

This may seem to be a solution in the first instance, but it's a band-aid with little upside. The family, whether traditional or Complex in structure, is your children's foremost educational centre where they form their beliefs of how life will treat them in adulthood. As part of this learning, your children learn acceptable behaviour, how to relate to others, and the consequences of choices they make. If you attempt to avoid conflict by separating them, you will merely teach them avoidance rather than healthy conflict resolution strategies. This could follow through into adulthood where poor skills that were established through avoidance techniques can destroy their own personal relationships.

> If you attempt to avoid conflict by separating them, you will merely teach them avoidance rather than healthy conflict resolution strategies.

Although you may prefer that your children not argue or fight, when it does occur, it can become a valuable tool to teach them how to handle life's complications. As your children mature, they will come across people who seem to get a kick out of arguing and fighting. The more prepared your children are to handle such situations, the less likely they are to be dragged into the physically damaging, demoralising, and energy sapping sagas these circumstances provide.

Sexuality

This is an equally hot topic when debated or practiced, with one commonality all parents share; we have experienced the wonder this physical act produces through the creation of new life. Human sexuality is both poorly understood by the masses and grossly distorted through the media. The freedom of expression brought about during the 'sexual revolution' of the 60s and 70s, saw us step out from under the prohibitions of religious doctrine and begin to participation in open experimentation and conversation. The more common this has become, the less power our cultural or religious beliefs have been able to maintain over the most natural form of pleasurable physical expression that can be shared between two people.

Although I realise the subject of sexuality is so vast that this small section within a chapter cannot not do it justice, I will endeavour to speak primarily of sexuality as it is met in raising your children within a Complex Family.

Sexual Energy

> Sexual energy is irrespective of gender ... masculine and feminine energy ... the primary driver behind the physical act of sex is to balance these two energies within ourselves.

To understand sexuality, we need to begin with a basic understanding of sexual energy and the force behind both its power and pleasure. Sexual energy is irrespective of gender; although for simplicity's sake, it is divided by name into the two established labels: masculine and feminine energy. We may see a man function with more feminine sexual energy, and likewise women who function with higher levels of masculine sexual energy. The primary driver behind the physical act of sex is to balance these two energies within ourselves; therefore, the majority of us search for a way to share our sexuality with the opposite gender, male or female — however this is not always the case.

Masculine energy is the driving and doing action, forward momentum and the explosion of energy. It is raw and powerful, built from an insatiable force that is constantly trying to find fulfilment. Masculine energy is looking for sex hoping to feel love.

Feminine energy is the open, nurturing, and responsive energy that embraces and draws in. It is an energy that fluctuates in intensity and moves between the slow simmer or rapid boil that is enhanced through fulfilment. Feminine energy experiences sex as a result of feeling love.

From these paragraphs alone, it is very easy to see why there is confusion surrounding sexuality.

Sex or Making Love

Sex and Making Love are frequently used interchangeably; yet they are dramatically different in both act and essence. Some professionals will categorically state the importance of both inside a healthy sexual relationship; others will place *making love* as the only valid form of sexuality. I am here to debate neither one nor the other, but rather to ensure you understand they are different and therefore leave you with the choice. If you can educate and empower your children with the same knowledge, you will give them a better chance to make good choices for themselves when it really matters.

Sex is the physical act. It is best described as the animalistic urges we have that ensure the repopulation of our species. It is dominated by the male energy, and as such it requires constant feeding. The pleasure received is derived from the fulfilment in the *Need, Sensation, and Desire cycle*, spoken of in the development of this phase in Chapter 3. However, in relationships where this cycle is only fulfiled through the repetition of this rather raw and simplistic act, it can leave the participants longing for stronger stimulation to produce an increased level of sensing required to fulfil this desire. Left unchecked, it can mimic, on a smaller scale, the rather extreme animalistic urges of large male cats that have been known to mate an astonishing 150 times in one weekend.

Making love however is using the same physical act as it melds with *love*. It is in the melding of *love* with *sex* that one begins to attain a mutual fulfilment that fully satisfies. It is in this experience that sexual energy shifts, and an overflowing feeling of love connects the two through the unspoken. It is then that there is a special look in the eyes and a touch that transcends the physical pleasure and wraps both in bliss.

> It is in the melding of Love with Sex that one begins to attain a fulfilment that fully satisfies.

Naturally, for *making love* to be so fulfiling it must be developed through equal involvement and connection. One cannot gain such pinnacles of satisfaction without sharing.

If you do not, or have not, experienced the dramatic difference between these two forms of sexuality, it will be challenging to uphold the intrinsic value of an intimate physical relationship. It is fair to say, given the vast majority of sexual propaganda our media is perpetuating, *making love* is sadly rare. Perhaps this is because, it is the former control that has kept both guilt and grief as a dominating force in our bedrooms, rather than a true understanding of *making love* that brings fulfilment.

Intimacy and Sacredness

It's very easy to become cynical at the mention of the sacredness of sexuality given the horrific suffering millions have experienced throughout lifetimes of sexual abuse and inappropriate conduct. As the pendulum has swung in the direction of open, frank conversation, sexual acts in our entertainment media, and generally accepted sexually explicit dress and behavioural societal norms, we have praised many of the advantages this has provided. I certainly do not want the pendulum to swing back to the previous control, secrecy, domination, or prohibition; however, I do think it would be advantageous to reach a healthy middle ground. The disadvantage of extreme openness is a loss of intimacy and sacredness that can be experienced between a loving couple.

We have become so consumed with concern for safe sex physically that we have forgotten to protect ourselves emotionally and spiritually. While many sexual issues have arisen from the inappropriate manner in which religions or cultures have attempted to curb our natural act of physical pleasure, the core message buried deep underneath such distortion, was and is, still sound.

This core message is not so much that we should abstain, or restrict, but rather that we should choose wisely. It is to recognise the power of the physical act and treat it with respect, not careless abandon. To develop and maintain ongoing intimacy with our beloved is to treasure and nurture our sexuality rather than expose and flaunt it for external judgement and influence to dilute its specialness.

Safe Sex

Safe Sex physically is one portion of sexuality — and an important one; however, it has only become critical because we have become so ignorant of the other two aspects of sexual activity that we have lost perspective. It is much like taking a three-legged structure, ripping two legs away, and expecting it to perform the same function it did when whole. If we can build an understanding of the other two critical areas of *safe sex*, the physical aspect will naturally be held in balance. These other two factors are *emotional* and *spiritual*.

The only safe sex is *sex with love*. Sex without love will most certainly damage the emotional and spiritual relationship experience; therefore, it has a higher chance of causing physical damage as well.

> The only Safe Sex is Sex with Love.

Let's look at the *emotional* aspects first, as this is undoubtedly more commonly recognised and far easier for us to understand. If sex is had without love it causes the resenting of the physical act, can heighten guilt, and inflict grief. It is the nagging conversations inside your mind that try to replay how you might have avoided the encounter, or perhaps the numbing of your senses to the point you believe you are not worthy to receive love. Sex without love can produce the blaming conversation where physical satisfaction is not frequent enough and therefore personal tension or doubts surface. The absence of love within sex that continues habitually will build a resentful wall of death between the couple; this is one of the reasons most relationships based on sexual activity die within 6–36 months of the first encounter.

When love is present within the sexual expression, the emotional involvement is healthy in both the giving and receiving of pleasure and love. Continuing this in a constructive manner will increase intimacy and strengthen the relationship between two people as it builds a strong foundation that allows life's situations to remain outside of the relationship's sacred centre.

Spiritual safety with sex is a little more intangible, and therefore, a little less likely to be accepted as natural; however, I will briefly discuss the main essence of it and those interested can investigate this aspect further.

There are three times in our lives when we are completely open to the transference of subtle forces into our lives: one is when we are born, one when we die, and the other is during a sexual orgasm. Given that this is usually the desired outcome of a sexual encounter, we open ourselves to transference from our partner, as reflected in our physical exchange. The matter being transferred, however, is not bodily fluids but the very essence of the beliefs that rule our choices throughout life. The transference is so subtle, especially as the emotional and physical intensity is so strong, that it goes unnoticed; however, this level of exchange comes with a difference. If we look at the physical connection, it is broken after an appropriate time and we who were one, become two people again; our emotional connection, however, remains. This emotional connection can last for days until another encounter is experienced and rekindles this emotional tie. Spiritually, however, this tie is unique; it remains constant, and we forever carry a tiny bit of the other person with us, as we, in exchange, have given them a bit of ourselves. This being the case, it is easy to see why a person who has shared their sexual energy with many partners, may begin to look and feel fragmented and often seem to carry an uncomfortable sense of being continually shared.

> Physical
> Emotional
> Spiritual

This is the primary reason our religious teachings have attempted to curb sexual expression although this great truth was long ago lost within dogma and traditions, losing the wisdom it was originally designed to instill. Instead, it became a pointless exercise of abstinence, in constant conflict with growing natural desires.

Education and Experience

Increasingly, educational campaigns are run in schools and institutions around the world with the intention to help young people make informed choices. These choices will be based on the information they are given; while much of it is relevant, this is primarily concerned with the physical aspects of sexuality, with perhaps a little of the emotional experience included, but the very existence of the core essence of what our sexuality involves is omitted.

For sexual education to be meaningful, it needs to be relevant to the stages of physical development, but not exclude the future implications of the pathway ahead. For pre-teens, their greatest need is to understand that their body is changing and that sexual organ development will begin to take place. For teens, an understanding of the development of their hormones and the effect this has on their choices and emotions is critical. They need to understand the importance and sacredness of sexuality, but until they are sexually involved, it is premature for them to develop an understanding of techniques, positions, and rules of engagement. This only rushes the future into the present.

Their ability to handle the complexities of emotions, hormones, changes, and peer pressure, is topped off with confusion, vulnerability, and expectations. They soon become unable to identify what is best, and choose to participate in what has become acceptably normal.

I am not advocating draconian stances on sexuality, but neither am I waving the flag of teenage freedom. I am saying that we give them the true time and space to develop their firm Yes or No to be said between consenting adults. That we help them avoid the pressure of peers, media, and society, and avoid selling themselves short of *making love* through sheer ignorance, as they practice unsafe sex. Sexuality is *natural*; *sex is normal*; and *making love* is the *natural*, intended experience through which we have been designed to reach pinnacles of physical, emotional, and spiritual bliss.

FAQs:

How do I talk with my children about sexuality?

For many of our generation, at best, we were handed a book and left to sort the rest out for ourselves. We gleaned information from our friends or snippets from movies and magazines to fill in the gaps, and we hoped the rest would all follow quite naturally. Obviously, as you are a parent, you have at least experienced sexual intimacy — however it may or may not automatically follow that you are comfortable to talk about it.

It is important to talk with your children (especially teens) about sexuality — and to do this regularly. It's a real mistake to think that a one-off fact talk on the 'birds and bees' will give your physically maturing teen enough perspective and the emotional maturity to make wise choices. If you constantly talk to them about sexuality and their 'love lives', you can overdo it, place undue pressure on them, or send signals of overprotective parents lurking in their intimate domain. Strive for balance; this will be different for each family, and for each child within the family, so here are a few pointers to help you along.

- *Does your child talk about sex (or sexuality in some form) frequently (daily or weekly)?*
  If they do, they need to feel free to communicate with you about their questions, concerns, and intrigues. If not, this doesn't necessarily mean they don't want to know about sexuality; more likely, they want the security that you are able to create a safe or accessible zone for them when they are ready to discuss something so intimate.

- *What type of movies, books, or media does your child choose?*
  If they are exposed to adult sexual acts while they are pre-

adolescent, you are wise to direct their attention elsewhere. If they are teens and overly pursuing this, you need to add balance and turn their attention to broader horizons.

- *Does your teen show unusual levels of embarrassment or disengagement with sexuality?*
  This may mean they have insufficient confidence in their relationship with you to communicate with you about sex when they need too. If this is the case, they will turn to alternative sources.

Talking with your children about sexuality can sometimes call on you, as parent, to take a deep breath and keep a poker face — to avoid blurting out *"You What?"* on the impulse to call a full-scale emergency. It's worth it; if you struggle with awkwardness, find a way to talk while you are doing something that does not take your concentration, but allows you to keep your eyes and energy focused elsewhere. You could go for a long drive, roast marshmallows over an open fire, or simply walk along a beach or park together. It is about creating an environment where steps of trust and respect can be shared.

Your children only need to know what is appropriate for their stage of development and experience. If they are not physically involved in sex, you do not need to explore the intricacies of sexual encounters or positions; however, you can expand on their concepts of sexuality to include both the emotional and spiritual components, and give them a more balanced and complete picture.

> Your children only need to know what is appropriate for their stage of development and experience.

Some things to avoid.

- Avoid trying to scare them into abstaining — it will come back to bite you as their own experience may well contradict the scaring tactics; you will have lost credibility and damaged the potential for important communication in the future. Consider too, don't you want your adult children to have healthy and harmonious sexual relationships? Lies now can deeply affect their experiences later.

- Avoid being overly protective — this is their choice, their life, and their bodies. While you want to give them all the good reasons to make wise choices, sometimes the only way they realise what you are saying makes sense is to try it for themselves. Your reaction to this will determine how far you will be included when they have future problems to solve.

- Avoid living a poor example for them to follow. Sometimes this period of a child's development collides with your release from the unhappy marital relationship, and you can be tempted to make up for lost time. While this is entirely your own choice, make sure your children do not become the innocent watchers of a bedroom's revolving door. This does not foster physical, emotional, and spiritual sexual intimacy, but rather downgrades it to a display of fulfiling our simplistic animalistic urges.

Talking with your children about sexuality needs to be kept comfortable and respectful. They need to know very little of your own life story — as most children would rather believe they too came from a virgin birth than imagine their parents 'doing it'. When they feel comfortable to talk with you about their experiences, you will probably know more than you really wanted to; but consider the alternatives, and be grateful you have the opportunity to openly influence them.

What is the right age for sex?

This is a question frequently asked, and one with no simple answer because appropriate age and sexuality are different in our society than in others, and different again in our generation than in others. Simplistically, I would say to teens, "The older you are the better." There is nothing wrong with being a virgin — it is to be treasured. While I'm not promoting that we all stay virgins until we're into our late 30's, I feel that there is far too much pressure put on today's teens (and younger) when they are emotionally unprepared to deal with it. They have such a limited context in which to understand relationships, let alone sexuality.

As an example, if you have a 16-year-old, it can be helpful to speak with your teen about how grown up they felt at age 13, believing they knew all there was to know. Compare that to how they feel when they see a 13-year-old now. This will help them to realise how much this 13-year-old doesn't yet know. The same will be true when they are 18 and look back at the 16-year-old. This gap, of course, will change considerably when they reach their twenties — and again with each decade right through their golden years. However, while young, perspective is key.

> "Teens ... the older you are the better." There is nothing wrong with being a virgin — it is to be treasured.

Let's give our teens a chance to safely explore their own opinions and feelings about sexuality without it being ruled by peer expectations and programming. Relationships, hormones, and academic education are complex enough, and your teen can really benefit from the perspective you provide. Sure, generations have changed, but issues surrounding sexuality have been with us for millennia; so give your children full information, appropriately protect where you can, and support them as their experiences unfold.

My teen is promiscuous, what can I do?

Promiscuity in the teen years has unfortunately become rather normal; this is not too surprising given how much is done to seduce us in our quest to find happiness. Simply put, we have confused the beauty of sexual intimacy with an overpowering focus on the masculine side of its energy and look for sex in an attempt to feel love. This approach is insatiable, and our raw selves respond to its very core energy. Advertising companies have long understood its power and use it to sell every conceivable item from ice-cream to cars, body products to careers — all of which distorts our understanding of the essence of sexual energy. Sadly, for this driving force, the moment it reaches the state of perceived 'love' it will be on the lookout for the next encounter to feel loved again, and much like an addiction, this energy when out of control, rules our decisions. Remember, this energy is irrespective of gender; this is sexual energy, and a large portion of today's rather self-assertive and liberated young women embrace masculine energy without fully understanding the implication of this for their own sexuality. Women are now free to initiate encounters with the same enthusiasm as men; and most men are going to respond equally.

The answer to the question asked by parents throughout the world, "What can I do?", is again more complicated. Usually, you have very little control over your children's choices by the time they reach this stage, as they are beginning to step into independence. If you attempt to impose a ban on their sexual activity, you are likely to be shut out of conversations, and inadvertently encourage deceit. If you condone the behaviour, it does little to help them understand the value of the most precious physical expression they can share with another. You can talk reason; you can talk logic; but in the end, you can only be a guide and let them experience the consequences for themselves. If you have neither practiced boundaries and discipline, nor helped them develop the art of making wise choices during their younger years, you may find it is simply best to live your own best example, and talk wisdom with them when each opportunity presents itself.

Taking a firm and fair line may work, and there is no problem with being the parent who steps in to provide a much-needed safety net. Regardless of how liberal or conservative you believe you are, they will always have a desire to push the boundaries you set. So, if you are going to draw some lines, be sure to give yourself some leeway. The use of commonsense rules for things like practical times to be back home, group outings, responsibility/trust/discipline, and reaffirming the importance of their own choices, works. However, a word of caution when taking a firm and fair line — it requires *prior* conversation and agreement — not reaction in the moment of transgression.

There is also great benefit to be gained from exploring the developmental stage discussed in Chapter 3: Stage 2, 6–24 months. This area of life affects our sexuality because it is about Pleasure and the Need, Desire and Sensation cycle. If a strong imbalance is displayed through promiscuity, Chapter 3 has some helpful tips that may assist.

My Ex and I contradict each other on sexuality; please help.

When parenting with an Ex, contradictions are normal; the challenge lies in how we convey an alternative perspective without making the Ex 'wrong'. The simple, yet not easy, answer is that you take the opportunity to add balance (or another side) to the story they have told.

When this principle is applied to issues surrounding sexuality and your teen, you will quickly see that regardless of what your opinion is, or how strongly you hold this view, your teen is going to make their own decisions — with or without your knowledge. As sexuality is such a strong natural urge in developing young adults, the way that you go about adding balance by your own example, to an otherwise one-sided perspective speaks far more loudly than any words.

Instead of contradicting your Ex's opinion, it's useful to agree with what they are saying and then explain that while this path is valid, it's good to consider the consequences that may arise. Once you have fully explored this avenue, expand on another aspect of sexuality that the Ex has not discussed. Remember to consider age-appropriateness and the consequences of choice. The good thing is that there is plenty of material to be discussed, and the principles of a great, healthy, sexual relationship can be highlighted in many ways.

Pornography: what about it?

While access to pornography has never been easier for young folks, this availability does not make it appropriate for them. It is not uncommon for prepubescent boys to explore Internet porn sites to satisfy their natural curiosity about sex.

If you happen to find pornographic material belonging to your child or teen, resist the impulse to shame or scold them for curious exploration as this will damage an important line of communication between you. On the other hand, this is not the time to either praise or encourage as that will hinder your teen's understanding of the intimate difference between *making love* and *sex*.

Take a deep breath, and have an open conversation about the wisest choices one can make. Present those points raised in the beginning of this section. Explain that adults find sexuality a large and confusing issue, and one that often causes great tension in long-term relationships. You can offer time and abstinence as very valid options — and make sure your child always believe their 'no' is a legitimate response.

Let your young ones know that one's sexuality is the greatest physical gift they can give to another; and whilst is has become very common, they would do well to avoid partaking in the commonness of it, and instead, treasure it as a great gift of intimacy to be shared when truly appropriate. It is up to them, and to no one else, to protect this aspect of themselves — and to do it with a sense of inner pride. Also, it is only sensible that they accept they do not know it all at the age of 16 or 18; one beautiful aspect of sexuality is that it is a lifetime journey, and when embraced in its fullness, dull repetition, hollowness, or boredom are simply not part of the picture; this is one of the many rewards for wise personal choices.

The Super Parent

The modern parent in the Complex Family carries the expectations of a Super Parent. They are expected to be Provider and Nurturer, Counsellor and Constable, Entertainer and Oracle. It is these feelings that tear at our heart and produce feelings of divided loyalties, overwhelming inadequacy, and our own frailty when considering the responsibility we carry for creating another's life view that they will carry for most of their adult years. We find ourselves trying to be all things to our little people, all the time; and frequently, we feel as though we are failing miserably.

Stepping out of this perceived rat race becomes our gift of freedom, not just for ourselves, but our family also. When we escape our self-imposed prison and become comfortable with our parenting style, unique and valuable as it is, we fulfil our original parenting quest with greater authenticity.

> The key to being a super parent is to stop being the Super Parent.

> Sitting in the lounge, with baby in arms, you could find me reading quantities of parenting books as I attempted to understand the best way of doing things. I quickly established there was no single methodology that would ensure my child succeeds in this world; there were contradictory opinions about everything — natural or otherwise — from breast to bottle, routine to demand feeding. There is the "spare the rod, spoil the child," or freedom of expression is the holy grail for raising your toddlers. It didn't matter which topic I picked, contradiction confronted me.
>
> In the same manner, contradiction begged me to ask more questions of myself, becoming part of the Complex Family invited a great deepening of understanding into the choices I made surrounding parenting. I started to write some questions, searched for my own answers, hoped to break the struggle, and ease the tension. It was tension that was stealing the beauty of parenting from within our family, and I needed to grow beyond it.

Here are some of those questions I asked myself — and have subsequently worked through with other parents who have felt equally overwhelmed. With a little explanation for each, take the time, maybe weeks or months to consider the answers and continue to refine them as needed.

1. **As a parent, what do I do well?**

    Take a pen and paper and write down at least 10 things you enjoy doing and you know you do well. It may be little things like the drop offs and pick ups, the meals, making the birthday cakes, watching sports, music lessons, teaching, making the children laugh, bedtime stories, etc. It is the parts you enjoy in being a parent, and the things you feel more energised doing in place of the things you put off.

2. **What do I believe is good parenting?**

    This is the time to expose your preconceived ideals and beliefs. These might include such statements of "Men provide, women are best at home." "A real family is one that is traditional in structure." "We can never give the children enough." "Life is a compromise once we have children." Many of these are outdated and damaging beliefs, yet if you can highlight them, you have a chance to make a choice instead of allowing them to subconsciously rule your emotions. If you still believe these are true after your evaluation, you can build on them; if not, then you let them go and feel the freedom your chisel of choice provides.

3. **What do I see in other parents that makes me feel inadequate?**

    This helps to highlight your hidden beliefs. If you do not feel either superior or inferior when watching other parents in action you are without obvious judgement. However, if you do have feelings of either superiority or inferiority, you are holding judgement around it and this becomes your clue, leading you to reevaluate what you believe or what you feel you want to hold as true in that matter. It doesn't mean you need to change; it is just a way to highlight a belief.

4. **What does my Ex do well in parenting?**
   This may be a little harder, but this is a step in enhancing your Parenting Team. Even if you don't like your Ex right now, through writing down the things they do well, you recognise them clearly; this sometimes opens a door for help rather than spreading yourself too thin. Some people find their Ex wants to do more because they are given the opportunity to do what they thrive at naturally instead of feeling equally overwhelmed by the Super Parent pressure. Sometimes it doesn't help the Ex at all, but it can help you celebrate their strengths which is better for you and your children.

5. **Can I build a Parenting Team that enhances our strengths and supports our dislikes or areas of development?**
   If you can cooperatively find a balance between parents, you can enjoy parenting more by doing what you enjoy while being good at it, and your Ex is given the freedom to do likewise. It does not replace your responsibilities, but can enhance your Team by focusing on your strengths rather than on rigid expectations.

Once you answer these questions, you can identify those areas where you might be tormenting yourself instead of celebrating your strengths.

We all have aspects of parenting we could improve upon, likewise, we have aspects with which we can equally become an expert. It is simply the fact that parenting is a journey; continually changing and because it is unique to your family, this makes it so challenging.

Mechanical

To cope, the same old strategies used by parents world-over become normal to you too. A common technique used by many fathers is to throw themselves into work, sports, technology, or perhaps find relief in the bottom of a bottle.

For mothers it is to deny themselves and give to their children instead. With passion dwindling, and the freedom of choice slowly eroding through unending demands, life becomes intently serious. Just beyond serious, they then fall into the trap of numb — it doesn't take long. It somehow happens between baby one and baby two, and quietly they submit to the forces of parenthood without even knowing how much they've changed.

Not too far down the road, perhaps someone comes and takes your children for an afternoon so you can do what you would like to do. It sounds great but then comes the question — what will you do? It is either, "I no longer even remember what that might be, or which of the 45 things on my list will I do whilst I have the time without the children."

This is the beginning of waking up to realise that although we are splendid, we are not made to be a Super Parent who has become mechanical — deadened to the beauty of raising children.

> It is hard for me to describe those early years of parenting, being quite a blur of sleepless nights, chaotic days, and the myriad of things that needed my attention. Three children in under three years, with little support, saw me become highly organised and nearly passionless about the undertaking. Loving my children was not the issue, being responsible and conscientious was easy; it was the life-giving enthusiasm I was missing. Through all the tiredness and demands I took on, I had forgotten how to laugh at those special moments that are priceless. The one's we can tell tales about as the years tick by, but at the time they spelled more work — and that was too much.

Maintaining the Adult

In the Complex Family, as a parent sometimes you have more opportunity to stay alive than in a traditional family. Often you have the opportunity to gain a routine adult-time where your children are with the Ex. This of course assumes you are not breeding again with a new partner. If you are, you will simulate part of the traditional family structure, and make the complex a touch more complicated.

The freedom that is on offer through a Complex Family environment is of great benefit to both children and parents. The weekends you are free from child responsibilities can be carried out discovering and experimenting with your pleasures, hobbies, interests, and self-development. During the weekends with the children, you make the most of meaningful family time and the balance of the two creates a structure where powerful parenting becomes natural.

> Recognising very early in my divorced life that I could choose to enjoy my weekends with children as much as those without children, gave me another key towards full freedom. It was through embracing this power that I juggled my own businesses, grieved my lost marriage, made new friendships, discovered new interests, read books, kept house, booked facials, trained for an IronMan, discovered new love, and so on, while I learned to became content with living each moment to its fullest.

FAQs:

I feel very alone in my parenting; there is no back-up or support.

It can sometimes feel very lonely, a common feeling shared by all parents, but none more so than when parenting partnerless, with every decision and demand resting upon your shoulders alone.

It is those times when your children push and push, and there is no one to hand over to say, "your turn", to mercifully give you the time to regain strength to continue. It is the time when you would love to share in the beauty of the moment with an adult who can delight in the same cute or precious phrase, and yet when you turn, there is no one there. The moment has passed and its essence is somehow lost when later retold.

> Find others and be there for them as their back-up so they can be yours.

These are the times when you feel it most, but these are also the times when you can remind yourself of your independence. Remember, you do not have to negotiate with another adult about how things might be — you make the call, and you live with the consequences — good or otherwise.

During times of sustained lack of support and back-up, look at ways to provide this through alternative structures. Find others in similar situations and be there for them as their back-up so they can be yours. Tackle some of the smaller challenges that can be exhausting once you are living in the Complex Family; start to build bonds where you can share in each other's highs and lows and accept your own vulnerabilities that are very normal in parenting. Give to another what you yourself are lacking and see if it solves your initial wanting. If you need someone to take care of your most precious children, take care of someone else's most precious — and it may not even be their children; it will help you to step outside of what you lack and turn your attention towards what you have.

My children miss out because some things I just cannot do.

We are all unique and to young children, parents are idols. Mothers fall from this pedestal usually more quickly than fathers, but this is related to familiarity, not who we are. Since mothers still hold the majority of the action of nurturing the youngest for the initial years of their lives, they are removed from the pedestal early.

If you have passed this stage, you can probably remember the time the teacher suddenly took top spot — and of course, this faded too. Fathers fall also, and if it hasn't happened before the teens, it will most likely happen during the teens' process of reevaluating their personal values. This being said, the high regard often returns but it is somewhat changed — it grows to being a healthy respect instead of an unrealistic idolisation.

> As a parent, part of what I thrive on with my children is projects. We create things — sometimes from virtually nothing, and sometimes a little more is needed; but there is always the lesson my constant intensity delivers. We have built models, inventions, numerous crafts, bedrooms have been redecorated in themes, play houses built, camping adventures, simulated safaris, weeks of Around the World cuisine, and all manner of projects to stimulate and teach the children. Usually, I gain as much from it as they do, perhaps more, with the need to remind myself

of the intention that it is to be a family project, so I don't take over in the desire to have it exactly right.

However, as adventurous and fun as the above may sound, I accept I am not a mother who gets in and plays imaginary play. I do not spend hours telling fantastic stories before bedtime, and I am not the parent who is found just goofing off with my children. That's just not me. For many years, I felt I was falling short as a parent because I would marvel at those who could continue a bedtime story, evolving nightly with the unique voices, animated caricatures, and ever-increasing plots to delight their children. I loved watching the parent who was happy just playing silly things and seeing the thrill the child received from their pure enchantment with innocent laughter. It made me realise I didn't do this with my children, and it tugged at my chords of inadequacy.

It took me a while to become comfortable in my own parenting skin. I realised it's okay; I don't do all these other things, but my children will gain experiences with me that will carry them in their own unique way. I'm me and I have my unique style, in just the same way someone else has theirs. This continual comparison made me focus my attention on the things I was not doing instead of the magnificent things I was.

Find what you are good at and enhance these. You have your own unique gifts and things you enjoy doing. Make more time for these, while balanced with your other responsibilities, and your children will not miss out; instead, they will have full-flavoured parenting with your unique fingerprint being the watermark.

> Find what you are good at and enhance these.

I resent the restriction the children cause in my life.

A snippet from many parents' letters: *"Since the divorce, I'm constantly frustrated because of the compromises I have to make, and the lack of support."*

Getting comfortable with the divorce will greatly assist in releasing the resentment you feel towards the restrictions your children place on your life. Regardless of your marital status, having children has an impact on your pre-child freedom. You will need to reach the place where you accept the position you're in and cease to argue with the reality of it. Your inner resentment and your constant state of frustration that sits just beneath the surface festering will be felt — and reacted to — by your children. These feelings of discontent wait for something to scratch your surface so they can remind you of the resentment that's still there; this will usually mean you overreact to circumstances, and as a result, affect your children's Learning environment.

In my experience, I found it useful to use a tool called "reframing." With this, when you find yourself restricted in your activities because of your children, you can review the limitations of your situation. You can see yourself as being so committed to their development, education, and well-being that you decide not to participate in activities that would be inconsistent with this commitment. This may sound like semantics or playing with words, but it is a very powerful process. The reframing, expresses your freedom to choose.

Your routine with the Ex may mean that you do not have a great deal of time away from your children. When this is the case, you can feel like you're suffocating; however, when you reframe this, spending so much time with them could be the reason you have built such a strong relationship. It may have given you the opportunity to become a positive leader, influence their beliefs, and limit the external interference that counters this. Also, when you have your children with you for longer, there is more time for 'natural consequences' in discipline to be effective. When you have consistency of routine, you have the opportunity to plan.

Although these may all seem as cliched as looking at the glass half-full, it is the full acceptance of your choices that brings an inner peace and joy to an otherwise endless sentence of frustration.

Special Events

People want to know what to do about the biggies — Christmas Day, Birthdays, Graduations, Weddings, and all the other special events that happen during our lifetimes. These are meant to celebrate successes, fulfil rituals, and to enhance the bonds we share as a family. They can provide the greatest of highlights — and yet for many families, these bring formidable nightmares.

The knot in the stomach as you approach the door before stepping into your son's wedding — to be met again with the unforgiving angry glare of a non-accepting Ex and family; the tarnish of a day with family photo objections or simply refusing to cooperate; the complexity of seating plans to avoid an unnecessary scene — all because petty aches have turned into emotional boils that have never been truly lanced and given the opportunity to heal.

Making these events special means keeping the reason for them in focus. Birthdays are to celebrate the life of the one whose birthday it is. Christmas is the occasion for giving and receiving mutually as a family. Weddings are for the couple who are making their lifelong commitment; Graduations honour the graduating student; Mother's Day shows respect for the Mother; Father's Day shows respect for the Father; all these were celebrated or observed free of hinderance before the divorce — and can be after.

> Making these events special means keeping the reason for them in focus.

Annual Celebrations

A common cause of conflict inside the Complex Family is what to do on Christmas Day. Families travel from afar carrying expectations and hopes of further family bonds being extended through great memories yet to be created. For many, the excitement of advent calendars, shopping, food preparation, and the tree being decorated leads up to the 25th of December, a childhood memory we cherish. This fondness becomes our wish for the fairy-tale to be continued in our children's lives and we are eager to protect the opportunity to celebrate together. It should be a time when hardships and disagreements that may have occurred throughout the year are put aside and the focus turns to the bond that brings us together. So if our children are not able to participate in the way we intend, we feel robbed and this sets another tone.

Regardless of whether it is Christmas Day, Mother's Day, New Year's, or any other annual celebration, it is the repetitive nature that offers both the conflict and the resolution. If you can agree upon the importance of the Day, perhaps you will have more chance of resolving the tension. Some simple things to start resolving the conflict:

- You can alternate years — taking turns where the children will be — Christmas Eve with Mum one year, Christmas Eve with Dad the next.

- You may choose an alternative date to avoid conflicting celebrations resulting in your children receiving a double bonus.

- You may need to stay nearby ensuring ease of swapping over during the day if your family celebrations call for it.

- You play to your strengths: some prefer mornings, others evenings, and if these are at opposites with your Ex, try for a compromise solution.

There are many ways to resolve the issue provided the focus is on the intention of the celebration and the attachment to it definitely happening your way is loosened.

It is helpful to remember

- Respect: this naturally highlights family togetherness.

- Timetables: keep an eye on these and do your part to drop-off or pick-up on time rather than when it suits you, leaving your Ex to deal with the chaos.

- To avoid competitive responses or probing questions when

discussing celebrations with your children concerning the Ex.

- To keep the celebration focused on building a constructive experience and give up feeling responsible for happenings inside your Ex's home.

One-Off Events

These are the Weddings, Graduations, and other important milestone times in our lives; usually their significance deserves to have both parents share equally in the celebration. Unfortunately, these events are often tainted by former conflict, and an undercurrent of tension can be felt by those family members who have taken sides.

Focusing on the event's *purpose* and avoiding the temptation to indulge in your own sense of self-importance will go a long way to resolve any conflict that may arise on the day. Observing *boundaries* and the appropriate timing of conversations will enhance the comfort levels for all during shared family events. If your Ex knows you can be trusted not to bring up challenging conversation at inappropriate times, they are more likely to relax and enjoy the event, adding to the milestone you are there to celebrate.

TIPS:

- Avoid games that attempt to 'out do' someone or have them feel inferior, in an attempt to boost your own self-satisfaction.

- If making a speech, and your Ex is included in any way, (implied or otherwise) make sure you construct your words to hold your Ex in a positive light. *To diminish your Ex is to diminish yourself* — especially if it is an event for your child.

- If you cannot be sure of your emotions, avoid alcohol; this has become a social lubricant and inevitably weakens personal resolve and boundaries.

The Special Events and celebrations throughout our lives are numerous — this is especially so in a Complex family. We want to look forward to the beauty these events offer without any of the emotional overtones or stomach churning that so many people experience. Through shifting attention away from ourselves to focus on the experience we are there to share in and celebrate, we enhance a strong Parenting Team, and find the specialness will remain. This will allow it to become a time of genuine sharing and laughter between families where our Parenting Team can lead by example for the greater whole.

Chapter Six
Stepparents

How to practically embrace the inclusion of stepparents ...

The stepparent relationship is one of the most challenging we have inside the Complex Family, perhaps even inside the broader category of Personal Relationships. Done well, it is a selfless act of giving through a love held for another — the biological parent.

Further Change

Stepparent relationships are similar to any relationship — what we put in is what we get out; however, the foundation of this relationship is unique. It is not built upon mutual desire, but rather on initial mutual tolerance, that one day may grow into genuine love. The relationship of the stepparent can be one of enormous value inside our families; it is one relationship that is not to be confused with that of parent, but rather accepted as an enhancement of the Parenting Team.

I am a parent, not a stepparent, as my beloved is without children. I have been involved with stepparents throughout my entire divorced life, adding to this is the learning from years of friendship, coaching, and counselling with those involved in the stepparent relationship. It is a relationship I hold with utmost respect, and as such I would like to applaud my children's marvellous stepfather, and their much-loved stepmother, for all they have been, and are today, inside our family.

Although unique, the stepparent inside the Parenting Team is powerful. There is a blessing to be gained personally where love that is grown from being within the family enhances the life of the parent, stepparent, and the children involved. The daring and courageous stepparent who accepts the journey ahead, gains rewards unable to be touched by biological-parents: the receiving of love which is both given and gifted, not from a position of birthright, but rather because of the beauty of who they are.

For children who have lost a parent through death, they can testify to the powerful bond cemented when their life was created; regardless of their parent's poor or stunning parenting techniques, they carry a longing to know and understand their parent. It is an inherent longing in us all, yet in the stepparent relationship, this thirst is not present. Not because there is limited love, but because the inherent searching we deeply feel is generated by our inner desire to know ourselves, masked in believing we need to know our parent — the seemingly elusive part we gained from our parents, not our stepparent. A stepparent who understands this, recognises the inner search is a natural urge, and therefore chooses to embrace the freedom this provides rather than compete for position, is a stepparent who can add the most to themselves and their family.

> Unfolding this relationship can make or break family cultures and dreams.

The unfolding of this delicate relationship, however, can make or break family cultures and dreams. To assume, as biological parents, that the stepparent relationship will just happen because we deem it to, is rather naïve. The invitation for an adult to become a stepparent is normally recklessly stumbled upon rather than appropriately arrived at. In this invitation, further family cultures collide with more unexpressed parental expectations intersecting at every turn. Options and opinions that were neither apparent, nor previously worthy of consideration suddenly become central to another relationship quarrel or another well-positioned brick being laid in the stony wall of silence built between us and them.

It is wise to consider this invitation as a choice — a choice made by two adults, the implication of which has an impact on our children's lives forever — and therefore to be taken very seriously.

Leavee

As a Leavee, you are usually not the one who has a new partner. It is more normal for you instead to leap into the arms of another to ease your hurting heart, without necessarily considering this person to be your significant other. It is during this tender time that you will begin to understand the added complications of post-married life.

One feeling that is normal for you to experience can be the desire to make right your broken home or split family. The inner ache of damaging your children through the hopeless statistics and powerlessness you feel compels you to seek out another person who may be able to fill this void. Subconsciously, it can draw you to begin living this contradictory external persona — on one hand, you are a capable, together, fun-loving person ready to begin life afresh, and on the other, you are the vulnerable adult who is often lacking in discernment.

Another normal reaction as a Leavee is to parade your facade where life is blooming, and keep up staunch appearances, especially to the Ex as you try to prove you are capable of living without them. To appease your inner feelings of rejection and betrayal, you mask this through outward abandonment, and leave yourself feeling hollow and empty. This further bruising may last months or years, depending on your how authentic you are when feeling your inner pain.

Sometimes it's hard to believe, but if you sit inside a bar and people watch for a moment, it's interesting to guess the Leavers and Leavees. They will often gravitate towards each other without even knowing it as they listen to life stories which simply dovetail with their own experience, and before long, the emotional scars begin to speak. After the retelling of tales, you can see the point of connection where the bond of being understood is interpreted as newfound love.

This delicate warren of emotions is where the line needs to be drawn between child and adult, regardless of the age. To be rather draconian in approach, and as a precautionary tip, I strongly advise any Leavee to refrain from introducing a potential new partner to their children until conversations of significant commitment are at least on the table within the adult discussions. Give yourselves time — and plenty of it.

> Give yourself time — plenty of it.

Although time in itself does not heal, through the combination of time and healing, your choices of those you attract into your life will change significantly. It is not that you shouldn't have relationships, as these are often very useful in the process of healing, it is however to keep your children free from those entanglements.

Leaver

Many Leavers leave because they have found new love. Some do not; however, it is believed the majority do, albeit the same majority most likely do not have the original new lover in their life beyond the first year or two of change.

This is enough of a reality-check to cause one to be careful about the introduction of a new love to your children. Although there are no guarantees of relationship success, significant pressure is felt during the first year or so of a divorcee's life, and therefore a relationship worth leaving over is one worth waiting for too. This is not to say it is wrong to set up home together, but rather to make sure there are equal levels of commitment towards what this means for your children before such a step is taken.

The fairy-tale impressions of stepmothers are less than inspiring; this is equalled by the mass media's paintings of toxic stepfathers interfering with children and other despicable behaviour. All of this has children cautioned about interaction with stepparents; added to this includes the cases of emotional manipulation when one parent leaves to be with a future stepparent. The irrational and angry influence a Leavee often extends, causes the foundations of the child/stepparent relationship to be placed on a shaky footing before it's given a chance to bloom.

Being involved with a possible stepparent at the conclusion of the marriage, adds to the complexity your children feel as they are torn between loving the leaving parent and struggling with their own feelings of anger, rejection, or betrayal for the changes being forced upon them.

Ensure equal levels of commitment in your relationship before you set up home together.

Perhaps your children's father may be leaving, and therefore by default, it may be implied to an innocent mind that mother *is no longer 'good enough' for Dad*, thereby leaving them to (incorrectly) conclude this other person must be better. As your children find it near impossible to reject both parents, they will immediately see a solution to this subconscious quandary — *if the 'other person' was not around, this problem would go away*, and they instantly begin to look for any sign of validation from us, as parents, to justify this limited perspective. Hence, we begin to understand the child's justified reasoning and motivation to vent anger and frustration towards the perceived intruder. In most cases, the desire to get to know the new stepparent is nonexistent. Through feelings of betrayed loyalties, confusion, anger, guilt, and a raft of negative emotions, the beauty of a blooming relationship is kept away from those who may benefit the most.

Your Children

For most, a beautiful moment arrives when you find new love worthy of your family's involvement. Feeling excited and slightly anxious at the possibilities of long-term success, you tempt fate and introduce your children to your new partner — their stepparent. It is only natural to want your children to like your choice in partner — after all, there is a lot at stake here. Likewise, it is equally natural for your partner to want your children to like them, as they realise it will make the path ahead less complicated.

Make no mistake, your children understand the only reason this possible-stepparent is in their lives is because of a desire to be with their parent. While most children understand the loyalty and commitment the parent/child bond holds, it is bound to be questioned when competition appears on the radar screen.

> The complexity is the balance between your children's power and their belief in this power.

The complexity here then is the delicate balance between your children's power and their belief in this power. If your children believe they hold the power to either accept or reject the incoming member of this family unit, you may begin to expose them to responsibility beyond their years. Likewise, if you disregard or invalidate their opinions and feelings on this matter, you will greatly impact their sense of belonging inside your home.

Although many blooming relationships that involve children promise to take things slowly with introducing a stepparent, most do not. As you have been married previously, many stepparent relationships are conducted free from formal decisions surrounding longevity while you face the reality of juggling your daily lives. Often, the children are introduced before long-term commitments are discussed; you want to test the waters to gauge reactions and suitability.

Your children have no guarantee this relationship is going to last, and there are times indeed when your children may believe they have the power to effect its duration. While your children may influence the harmony within the relationship, it is inappropriate to let them believe they have the power to affect its lifespan. If they do, you may need to consider your boundaries and priorities.

Building an intimate relationship inside your home with this special someone, requires a union between parent and stepparent that extends well beyond the involvement of your children. It needs to be independent of them yet accommodating at the same time. It needs to celebrate the highs and support the lows that come with relationships and parenting. It needs time and investment, and an appreciation of the enormity of the journey ahead. If your children become the central focus of the parent/stepparent relationship, you will have restricted the advantages your new relationship offers, and unconsciously burdened your children with more power than they deserve.

In the event the relationship terminates and your children have held central power, they will experience divorce again — this time with guilt. If the relationship remains independent of the children's power, if they witness separation it is without reliving the trauma associated with divorce. This being said, sometimes in the early stages of a new relationship, your children are great little detectives and innately feel duplicity without being able to verbalise or interpret their inner hunch. It pays to listen, but respond as a responsible, mature adult.

Inside the Mind of Your Partner

Previously, we have looked inside the mind of our Leavee, Leaver and our children. Now is the time to look inside the mind of the Stepparent. They will have their own history, and it may include divorce; one thing for sure though, stepparents enter into a world they are completely unprepared for, and yet they come with their own view of how they see the family dynamics panning out, even if only with blurry vision.

If stepparents were likened to a coin, the two sides of understanding are those who take this position with intense responsibility and commitment — and those who do not. Although there will be variations between these two extremes, it is easier to demonstrate the tensions and delights that occur when we look at distinct differences rather than fuzzy similarities.

The stepparent who is intensely responsible understands the package deal aspect of the relationship from the onset, and they hope they can overcome whatever obstacles present themselves. They are usually highly committed individuals with a high level of personal sensitivity. This stepparent will often have the best of intentions, so when the times of inevitable conflict occur, it is usually because of expression, not because of the intention itself. Because they possess such strong feelings of responsibility, they are often highly dependable people who immediately ease the burden of the parent. Seeing such a weight lifted and the corresponding positive response it produces from the parent, the stepparent's desire to take on more parental functions is increased, and immediately heightens the levels of expectations and hopes in both. This stepparent will find it difficult to compromise inside the Complex Family Parenting Team environment, but with time and practice, they have a strong possibility of becoming a substantially strong asset to your family.

In contrast to the first stepparent, we have the other side of the coin. This stepparent knows the children are there and accepts the limitations they place on their partner's life; however, they keep their distance believing it is the parents' job to raise the children, and they will not interfere — not much anyway. This person is normally focused on their life being fulfiled outside of the family constraints, maybe inside a career, sport, or hobby, so we frequently see them protect a boundary of personal space and time, to the exclusion of both partner and child. Although often generous and obliging, these people are best described as more aloof than anything with the children, almost holding the presence that there is a life for them waiting beyond the walls of this current confined family. Occasionally this changes, more often than not coinciding with the arrival of their own child, or some major life crisis that causes them to reevaluate priorities. Until that point, however, this stepparent is not usually interested in strong participation in parenting, and therefore even less willing to assist in Complex Family Parenting Teams.

Mutual Feeding through Sharing

Regardless which side of the stepparent coin you live with, highly involved or aloof, the facts are your stepparent is in the family because of you. Naturally, in the bloom of new love, you find it difficult to differentiate warning bells, intuition, and blissful contentment. But after the initial haze has settled, it is normal for tension to rise where the stepparent wants time with you, and you alone, to build the relationship. They want to unbundle the package they agreed to and have their piece to themselves. Often coming from adult freedom, they step into the whirlwind of family life and are forcibly awakened when the ouch-moment strikes, as they find the balance between time with and time without children very challenging to navigate.

In joint parenting with both biological parents, there is a camaraderie that is shared with glowing pride and intimacy when dealing with your children, even if it can be wearying. You normally see the child as an extension of yourselves that you created and birthed into this world, so the gift bought and given to your child, feels like a gift given and received by you as parents, with great pleasure arising as you watch them respond with such excitement and delight. This feeds you while it feeds your child — a mutual moment of joy. Now that you are with your partner, the stepparent, they do not have this intimacy with your child, and although they delight and share in the enthusiasm, they do not gain the same mutual feeding. They require this feeding from the relationship's development with you, and not yet from the relationship with the children.

> Gifts bought and given to your child, feel like gifts given and received by you ... a mutual moment of joy.

The implication of this in the family can see the stepparent appear less willing to celebrate expenditure because it is frequently perceived as indulgent. This can cause immediate tension between the parent who wants to buy and the stepparent who wants to avoid spoiling the children, or perhaps a more practical reason — to stop the spending.

In our family this became very real when setting up home together. Birthday celebrations always held significance in our family culture; my beloved barely remembered his own birthday one year to the next. To him an excessive amount of time, energy and money was spent. To me it was one day each year when a person was given the focus of affection and celebration by all — and while I kept to a budget, my energy and effort was lavishly applied. It didn't occur to me that it was an effort — it was a pleasure. I gained as much delight from my giving to the children as they did in receiving — sometimes more I'm sure!

The mutual feeding grew for my beloved over time through fostering a strengthened sense of belonging in our family.

If this difference is healthily respected in the early stages, a stepparent will grow into this intimate camaraderie and thereby develop the same mutual feeding that comes from your children's success — but if the relationship is not given the time and effort to develop, this will forever elude you.

So while you, as parents, enthusiastically want to share, recognise that much like all young life forms, your relationship will require nurturing, protecting, and concentrated time to ensure it keeps growing free from too much pressure that can ultimately cause premature death.

It is Different

When stepparents first step into the family, the magnitude of the differences to be experienced are seldom understood by all involved; yet over time, most of these different bubbles do rise to the surface and we begin to see that many do not resolve themselves naturally. As parents, we need to accept there are fundamental differences at the very core of this that are so significant they will not change. This does not sentence us to conflict or substandard relationships, but should we decide not accept these and work with them, we will find they frequently trip us up.

One aspect of being a parent may be described as fluid, in that we mould and develop along with our children — perhaps learning as we go. We have the advantage of birthright, and we know that regardless of the highs and lows ahead, we are forever linked with our child. The stepparent does not have this *forever-linked* assurance, and therefore comes with a certain lack of fluidity. This is not to say they are rigid, but rather that they constantly look for clarity when changes occur so they can determine how their parenting partnership will be affected.

> Stepparents look for sign-posts of definition from parents ... discovering the surprise unspoken boundary shift.

This difference perhaps is as blatant as saying that much of parenting is inherently intuitive, and the stepparents are without this natural birthed advantage. So, while stepparents may develop intuition as a personal skill, it is not delivered to them as a gift when they choose to become stepparents. The outcome of this difference sees stepparents who constantly look for sign-posts of definition from you as parent. Even the most communicative and open parent/stepparent relationship will discover the unspoken boundary shift that catches us all by surprise.

> Your teen asks for the keys to the car. The stepparent remembers an agreement decided on two days ago and begins to say, "No." You, as parent, forget the agreement that was made and automatically say, "Sure" as you absent-mindedly hand them the keys. You have completely contradicted the parental pact and leave the stepparent feeling slapped in the face for standing up for what had been a strong signpost previously agreed upon.
>
> What happens as a consequence is that instead of their being able to stand up and fulfil their role in the Parenting Team, they have immediately become the enemy of the teen, and bewildered by the contradiction of the parent.
>
> As parent, you can see the oversight and correct it, as you take back the keys, apologise to your partner, while your teen walks off muttering under their breath. For you, it's almost case closed,

but not for your stepparent. They are left with a hollow, gut-wrenching feeling because they know the reason there is tension in the air tonight is because they made the call — and your teen knows this too. Regardless of what is said to make good of the slip-up, a raft of other emotions continue to simmer and feeds your stepparent's feelings of being an outsider, while being ripped off and losing points through no fault of their own.

The effects of this genuine slip-up have completely contrary feelings for the parent. This difference is subtle because while you can understand the contradiction, and see it as a slip-up, you may also be able to feel the stepparent's vulnerability. This places pressure on you to make sure you don't do it again and inadvertently place your stepparent into this position. This temporary moment of recognition and resolve for what you did is then replaced with a feeling that your parenting is being monitored and critiqued, and thus, a rather simplistic oversight turns into a full family debacle. This is a prime example of the fact that the support you so often rely on — and benefit from — can backfire, and it reminds you of the power of their involvement since you decided to share family and home.

The Score Card

The introduction of stepparents into the family is only the beginning; and sure, first impressions last, however, it is in the ongoing, unspoken code that is developed between stepparent and child where we see another large difference between parents and stepparents. Most stepparents agree they believe they work on points with their stepchildren, and to a lesser degree, their partner when parenting. What this means is your partner feels they must constantly earn their place in the home; this is completely contrary to the position you hold as parent. Even if your children do not understand this concept, they do, however, start living by it within the first few moments of meeting their stepparent. You will see stepparents start the process to win favour with special attention, gifts, overlooking of rotten behaviour, and so on, all in the hope of building a relationship between themselves and the child that will enhance the relationship they share with you, the parent. Although this is of course how a relationship develops, it is also a foundation that is fragile — hence the belief it is built upon a points scoring system.

Your stepparent lends the car for a term and earns a few points. They ground the teen for a month and lose more than the year's worth of points they gained from lending the car. Your stepparent takes your child shopping and buys ice-creams on the way home; once home, a tantrum is thrown so the child misses out on the next thing and the stepparent has now become their enemy. Sure, as parents, you may see the same cycles, but there is an unwavering consistency where your children know you are their parent, and the biological family is one we cannot argue with. The choice of stepparents, however, seems able to be influenced.

To deal with the feelings of needing to constantly score points, the best solution is to build relationships with the children independently — free from parental influence. If the stepparent and child have any chance of changing the push and pull scoring that is inherent in the "step" relationship, they need to define their interactions between themselves.

> To change the score they need to build relationships between themselves.

The more mature stepparent will be able to have conversations with the child or teen, and at least highlight some genuine trade agreements that can be made; this will allow time to invest in learning the art of unconditional love, while they grow in their understanding of appropriate discipline and the variety of parenting positions that are required.

The Outsider

As much as parents roll their eyes in the common understanding that comes from having an Ex and parenting, stepparents roll their eyes in the common understanding of being made to feel like an outsider the moment there is a disagreement between parent, child, and stepparent. The *Pack is back* — and in full force. Much like we see lions be king, even when solo, the stepparent realises that parents quickly become the lion, and there is simply no point to argue with the laws of nature. Even if the parent is obviously wrong, if they believe they are right, the children will side with the parent and leave the stepparent high and dry.

This *outsider* mentality is highly damaging to the development of the stepparent's identity and position inside the family dynamics. It is not that stepparents seek to be king, but they do want to be treated as equals. To avoid all such occurrences is nearly impossible, but to reduce the number of times it happens is the important focus. To do this, openly talk about it with your partner, and then do your best to avoid future situations where such choices need to be made.

Much in the same way you learned to deal with conflicts and disagreements with your Ex, you do the same here. The stepparent's position will become more firm and robust as time and energy are poured into the relationship with the children; however, sometimes you need to let things flow naturally without arranging or bending circumstances or opinions in your favour. There are times you will simply encourage the Learning environment, even when you can see it may be a sore lesson for all involved. The stronger feelings of camaraderie and acceptance the stepparent and children will feel through having to pull together in the face of short-term catastrophe may well be worth the inconvenience to you. This being said, commonsense says this is only in situations that are neither emotionally or physically damaging, nor life threatening.

> A stepparent was telling of her experiences — some humourous and some not so — while she and her stepchildren took the time to learn what it meant to be living together reducing her Outsider experiences. Through the numerous pre-stepparent reminiscing tales, the school events, exclusion in doctors waiting rooms, Ex's conversations, dismissive relatives and so on; the largest 'Outsider' feeling for her was evident in names.
>
> As simple as it was, there is Mum, Dad and then Abby. It wasn't Stepmum, neither is it Stepdad (and practically speaking, no stepparent I've met would want that title), but it is a subtle influence in feeling as an outsider — a constant reminder that you came into the family somewhere down the road.

Exposure to Double Loss

An aspect of stepparenting that parents do not have to contend with is the ramifications that birthright gives. Stepparents know they are with your children for as long as they are with you, and should some relationship fatality occur, they will lose the relationship with their stepchildren. There are instances where stepchildren and stepparent continue to see one another after relationship splits; however, over the years, this frequently dwindles to being almost nonexistent.

When an argument breaks out between parent and stepparent, irrespective of it involving children or parenting, the immediate feelings of loss can cause exaggerated emotions to surface. An almost irrational fear overtakes the most together stepparent because they sense monumental heartbreak — especially if they have developed a healthy, loving relationship with the children. Regardless of the promises and ongoing personal commitment the parent makes towards the stepparent, this fundamental difference in the relationship dynamics haunts the stepparent, and rears its ugly head when under pressure.

> When an argument breaks out ... exaggerated emotions emerge.

The feelings of vulnerability are usually triggered by an insecurity carried deep within the stepparent, and therefore, the new relationship provides an opportune environment in which to develop personally, rather than to constantly rely on the parent to reinforce the relationship's stability.

One powerful point the stepparent usually fails to understand, perhaps not even acknowledge, is that the parent's commitment towards the children will sometimes be the overriding force in the resolution of adult relationship issues. Rather than being tempted to wander off to find greener pastures, most parents will look for solutions with a stronger desire to spare their children from the turmoil of another parental separation, especially since having been through significant relationship upheavals.

Inviting the Stepparent

Whenever the stepparent relationship is introduced, the change in dynamics is significant. For those who have been parenting alone, you have developed your methods, routines, and opinions, and you have become comfortable with your way of doing things just as your children have. Volunteering to invite another's opinion to challenge and influence these established patterns may sound straightforward at the beginning, but sadly, it is a common catalyst for the cessation of your new romance. The conflicts between parent, stepparent, and children can become so demanding they have you, as biological parent, dealing with divided loyalties and further confusion, while your stepparent feels invalidated and at times inadequate in their attempts to feel they belonging, and so the relationship blows apart.

The dynamics of having a partner in your life should not automatically mean they are suddenly in your children's lives. This decision requires that choices be made, so below are some prompters to help you consider your best solution ahead of time. When discussing these, it is helpful to seek as much understanding as possible from your partner so areas of difference can be highlighted before they are encountered.

Points to Consider and Discuss:

- Both of you accept that embarking upon a relationship with someone who has dependent children is a package deal, so implications for the children will be handled responsibly.

- The invitation to a stepparent to join your family is not made by the children, but affects the children significantly, and therefore requires appropriate wisdom.

- Discuss how to assure that adequate time is given to develop the relationship between parent and stepparent without the children being involved.

- Discuss expectations surrounding involvement in the Parenting Team, and do not assume it will happen smoothly. Place some definitions around this and be prepared for them to change as the relationship changes.

- Stepparents may perform parenting functions as part of assisting in the new family dynamic; this is not to be confused with an attempt to replace a parent (your Ex) in the children's eyes.

- Extend the invitation to your stepparent to meet your children.

- Extend the invitation to your stepparent to meet your Ex and their partner if they have one.

- Avoid placing biological parents into situations where the parent believes they have to choose between loving their children or loving their new relationship.

- Avoid placing stepparents into situations where they feel invalidated or detached from the family they have chosen.

- Lead by example: your children will watch you to learn if the boundaries have moved, and what the relationship will be like.

- Give children and stepparents time and space to form their own unique bonds.

- As a stepparent, remember how much you love your partner and how much your partner loves their children; never do something that will hurt your partner by the way you treat their children.

How To; When Your Partner is Stepparent

Forming the Bond

When you invite your partner to share in the home and the lives of your children, you embark upon a sea of uncharted waters. You cannot be adequately prepared for the highs and lows of what is ahead as nature has made us unable to detect our futures; however, you can make a fairly good estimation if you look at how you are either responding or reacting currently. For as true as it is that the sun will rise in the morning, it is true that when there is a stepparent in your home, it changes almost everything inside the current family dynamics.

As part of this change, you as parent, need to be willing to gradually have your children form a bond with your partner that is independent of you. This is not to say you will abdicate parental responsibility, nor is it that you will recklessly place expectations on either party, but rather that you naturally allow, encourage, and watch, as a bond forms between your children and your partner as stepparent that allows them to rise and fall with the consequences of their own decisions. To truly do this, you must be courageous yet vulnerable, gentle yet strong, determined yet flexible. You will live your leadership, while opening a space for another to share the lead.

Sharing the Pleasure, not the Pain

Parents know that for all the pleasure they receive in parenting, there is a certain level of contrasting pain. You love your children — that's unquestioned — but through the years, there are definite sacrifices and compromises you make because you hold this love.

When your partner enters this equation as stepparent, it is hoped that the pleasures of the package will outweigh any pain of the burden. In many instances though, you may feel you want to shelter your partner from perceiving pain for fear that may drive them away. Your levels of organisation, resolve, and time-management routines will dictate how long it will be before your partner begins to feel the pain-pinch in their new role. One thing for sure, however, they will feel it. Your children will refuse to oblige; your Ex can screw up a routine; you have a mini-meltdown as you feel caught by divided loyalties; or your finances are stretched because the children cost more than expected. At some stage, there will be something that will trigger an 'ouch' moment.

> We hope that the pleasures of the package will outweigh any pain of the burden.

Part of parenting with your partner as stepparent is learning how to handle these moments rather than prevent them from occurring. To attempt to protect causes your behaviour to become more controlling, neurotic, and meddlesome inside your own family. It disempowers your partner while it builds a wedge between them and your children. If you trusted your partner to enter into your home and become part of your family, you need to allow the subsequent step relationships to develop without you being involved.

Your pleasure comes from a deepening partnership that grows out of resolving the issues your partner's efforts may spark as they do what they need to to feel they belong — in good times and tough. Indeed, this is where the pleasure/pain points become real and you gain true benefit.

> This one caught me — and took a while to understand why it hurt so much. I had opened my life and home to include my beloved in my family; I believed to share children with him would not be too hard. What I hadn't realised in my naïvety however was the intense pressure I felt to protect him from the children's shadow side. I wanted him to enjoy them and gain the love my children so freely gave, especially to a fun-loving extravert adult. I didn't want him to feel the pressure that came with children, or witness the meltdowns, nor feel the pinch — only the good stuff please! Of course that didn't work and neither should it.
>
> When they'd do something I knew he would disapprove of, I would instantly be on guard and sometimes with an over-corrective measure instead of at the appropriate level. I found myself beginning to think

through every detail in the hope of avoiding any unnecessary pressures — I planned — I second-guessed — I controlled — I was exhausted; this wasn't good for any of us. I took my hands off and watched, coached, supported, laughed, cried, and stood strong through it all; today we enjoy equality and relish in our unique offering to each child.

Learning on the Job

The sacrifices you make as parent can at times test your partner who comes from a life of adult singleness. The freedom to do what they want, when they want, without needing to organise much more than themselves, contrasts sharply from their new situation.

It is easy to forget the emotional upheaval we felt as our newborn turned the simple task of getting out the door to visit a friend into an hour and half's ordeal of planning and preparation. We forget how we walked around in a state of shock for the first few months wondering where the end of our little tike's transforming power was. Your partner is learning all this and more, without the advantage of the ignorant bliss your newborn provided for you. This time there is an audience: you, your children, and possibly the watchful eye of your Ex.

> Stepparents need to be given permission to screw up and to learn the parenting lessons just as you have.

When your partner takes on the role of stepparent, they need to be given permission to screw up and to learn parenting lessons just as you have. Many of you can recall how your newborn wriggled between your hands while you learned to wash them for the first time; you wondered how they could end up half-drowned so quickly — but they survived. If there had been someone watching over your shoulder to evaluate you or comment every time you did something dumb, you would never have been able to develop the confidence you have today. For your No to mean No, and your Yes to mean Yes, it has taken time, practice, and a few hard lessons for both you and your children.

Does this mean your children provide a training ground for your partner to practice parenting skills? Effectively, yes; however, a naturally wise stepparent is one who seeks to learn from those with a little more experience. It does not mean your children ever need to tolerate emotional or physical harm or life-threatening or compromising situations; you would not do that to your children and neither would a valuable and worthy stepparent.

It is, however, the autonomy you grant to your partner to make decisions, choices, and judgements without you; when these fail, you encourage them to learn through their own experience. A lesson many parents have learned the hard way is that whilst you may have parented longer, there is no guarantee that you will have the best understanding in all situations with a particular child. Inside the heart of parenting you know principles work, yet each child, in each stage, requires evaluation to determine the best strategy for any given situation; your partner may have the objective perspective that helps you to make a better decision.

Sharing Treasures

The African proverb *Niyimpa kor ntsetse ba; "It takes an entire village to raise a child"* is usually met with dialogue of wishful agreement, followed by stories of contrasting hardship encapsulating our isolated lives. We highlight how fewer extended families are able to support the raising of their children with the increasing demands on time and resources for all, and complain about the breakdown of the family unit. Some scoff and claim it is outdated; yet for most, it's a remote ideal, a distant fantasy we wish for; dismissed as too hard. Very few take the time to explore its meaning, with even fewer willing to contemplate its significance. Sadly however, it is the failure to embrace its principle, even when it is understood, which most quickly destroys its potential power.

> As part of my transition into divorced life, I met my children's stepmother early. My choice came from my belief that the village has changed in the 21st century; it begins in our homes through inviting stepparents to share in the raising of our children. I chose to turn my back on conventions and beliefs that I as parent, had the monopoly on my children's best interest.

The gift of stepparenthood is the greatest one we, as parents, can give to our new love — to enable them to truly become a stepparent rather than merely an additional adult inside our homes. The greatest gift our partner can give our children is the uniqueness of who they are. It is in the blend of these two gifts that the foundation for a strengthened family culture is created.

The opening of children's lives to a stepparent's enhancement brings with it a level of vulnerability. It is this dynamic duo that when balanced well builds the healthy long-term structure of shared parenting. This *village* is not without complexity, but the power to create a fulfilling Parenting Team exists within our homes; it is here our children gain through the extension of greater resources, much needed time, and enhanced love.

> The gift of stepparenthood is the greatest one we can give to our new love — to truly become a stepparent.

To share our children with stepparents takes courage and trust; it also takes constant communication and strong commitment. In doing so, I believe the risk of introducing contradictions into our children's lives will help create a higher level of discernment and attained wisdom that far outweighs the protection of ideals through sheltered isolation. It offers an opportunity for diversity within unity on a daily basis within your home. Your children can see an example of *different not better* and *appropriate not right*, in action that enables them to be free to choose — and in turn, grant this freedom to others. This is why sharing your children is your greatest pleasure and at times, your greatest conflict.

Emotionally Torn

From time to time, these contradictions can result in emotional pulls which outstrip any surviving logic and cut straight to the heart with confusion or reaction that enters at the speed of light. This instant clamp around head and heart takes hold the moment your child conflicts with your partner — and especially if you disagree with their perspective. Instantly, you want to dive in and solve, settle, or remove the problem.

You want your child to be understood or protected, as the emotional intricacies of adult love catapult you headfirst into either judgement or confusion. At least three people have engaged in a game of tug-of-war here; as the parent, you have become the knot in the middle, helplessly waiting to see which side will drag you over the line first.

To prevent these situations from occurring is almost impossible; however, you can transcend your reactions to them and cause your family to grow instead. To do this you need to take a look inside the emotional maze your relationships naturally create. Your children are used to your moods and sensitivities and they are adept at navigating their way through your subconscious to find the levers and triggers they need to push or pull so they can get what they want.

> To prevent these situations from occurring is almost impossible; however, you can transcend your reactions to them.

When your partner becomes the stepparent, some of these well-travelled pathways are instantly adjusted and force your children to re-navigate their way through a now extended maze. Your children also now need to work out the maze inside the stepparent. The more time they spend together, the more your children begin to understand their uniqueness and idiosyncrasies, and with this the positions of the levers and triggers inside their life. While this occurs invisibly, it forms preprogrammed responses for the near future.

The best way to deal with this tangled maze of subconscious thinking is through good communication between you and your partner. Your objective here is to remove the points inside both your mazes where your tunnels cross but do not connect. You want them to connect, but in a healthy, supportive, and nondependent way. If your partner feels disconnected because they hold a different opinion or belief about a particular situation, they will feel threatened every time this occurs.

When this occurs, the argument between you is then not about the situation (although it still looks as though it is) but rather it could be about their feelings of threatened abandonment which may mean they believe they could lose their family or some other such treasure, such as power or respect. Likewise, if you, as the parent, feel inadequate or criticised every time you do something your partner doesn't agree with, you will begin to resent their interference with your parenting. It is these strong, disconnected, inadequate, or criticised feelings that need to be addressed and worked through; it is not about the circumstantial difference of opinion that highlights them.

Untangling the Maze

To identify the feelings that lie beneath the circumstantial difference of opinion, you first need to create a safe haven for understanding. When situations arise, you need to be alert to your own reactions and catch yourself if you become defensive, hurt, or agitated; in that moment, you need to step away from the issue without trying to resolve it.

If your children are also involved, Time Out for everyone is a useful technique — releasing any harsh judgements. This can release the tension much like letting fizz out of a carbonated drink bottle. The issue is not resolved, but you can accept that you need time to reevaluate what is happening — to make a wise choice rather than spontaneously react. You may not talk about the issue with your partner or child for a few days, but you need to continue the conversation at some stage to conclude the subject; otherwise, you will continue to build crossing tunnels, rather than connecting ones, and over the long-term, this will cause great division.

The safe haven is the space you create for yourself where you can acknowledge the feelings of insecurity, inadequacy, or other negative emotions you hold about yourself (not any other person) — feelings that cause you to become defensive, hurt, or agitated. When you acknowledge this, you have the opportunity to do something with it and eventually affect the circumstantial issue. Chapter 9 addresses tools for change and how to use them. Until this transforming takes place, you will continue to see similar situations occur and cause the same emotional pull — much like the pebble, boulder, mountainside analogy.

For this to be effective, your partner does not need to be involved; you only need to focus on *your* reactions, not those of your children or partner because it is through the change that occurs in you that, eventually, the circumstances change for all. This being said, if your partner values personal development and vulnerability, they will benefit from understanding the deeper feelings you experienced that caused the discord.

If your partner can understand that you feel trapped between your love for your children and the love you have for them — that although unique, both are extremely special — they can begin to be aware of the times when they may inadvertently place you in such a position.

It does not serve your relationship to feel torn; therefore, unnecessary heartache can be avoided through mutual understanding of the cause of such feelings. Remember, it is solely your responsibility to transcend your points of emotional pain.

> Focus on your reactions ... it is through the change that occurs in you that, eventually, the circumstances change for all.

As you become practiced in recognising and acknowledging your deeper feelings, you will develop a freedom from the torn emotions and begin to see the misunderstandings between stepparent and child for what they are. This freedom expands opportunities where you can add wisdom to the circumstantial confusion and thereby create a more harmonious family environment.

Creating a Unit Uniquely

The art of creating a unit between parent, stepparent, and children involves similar principles to building a traditional family; however, this time it is with the subtle influence of history and the ever-present Ex. Choices which otherwise might be considered are often discounted before they have a chance to penetrate the walls of imagination or expansion — possibilities such as an extended overseas adventure, a move geographically, options of alternative schooling, and so on. These are the realities your Complex Family becomes used to considering before progressing such life-altering decisions, and yet still inside these considerations, there is the opportunity for a close-knit bonded family unit to be born.

The understanding that your partner is not to replace your Ex's position inside the family gives them the freedom to decide what role or position they want to fulfil. Lacking in constructive traditional pictures held for stepparents, you have a blank canvas on which your partner and children can form their own masterpiece — with the occasional added dimension of the biological parent's touch.

While some professionals recommend that parents tell the stepparent what you want them to do, or who they are to be inside the home, I strongly suggest an alternative. If you are to give your partner the freedom to form their position within the home, they need to be fully free from your wants and needs, and be able to tap into their own reservoir of uniqueness. It is only when they are free to explore this that they will carry the confidence and mandate required to become a meaningful contributor. The flip side is a situation where they are always subtly overshadowed and controlled by the biological parent.

> Give your partner the freedom to form their position ... they need to be free to tap into their own reservoir of uniqueness.

You may have a partner who excels in fun and they may do this through a love of outdoor adventure, or perhaps, the infinitesimal detail of craftsmanship on a model ship or plane. The strengths your partner possess naturally are those that when fully embraced will strengthen the Parenting Team, and fulfil a vital role in your children's upbringing.

Sometimes, these may appear to overlap with others inside your Parenting Team — and that's okay. When you express your unique talents with your own style, this becomes another opportunity for children to gain greater understanding, unique techniques, and further tips in an area they may not have otherwise encountered.

They will discover the joy of multiple methods that can be used to create enhanced outcomes. Through this you may begin to demonstrate how compatibility does not mean sameness, and dispel the greater fear of difference being shrouded in wrong — just as the false security within sameness breeds right.

It is through these powerful real-life issues inside a Complex Family that you remove the need to define roles, and see the family structure expanded as the responsibility of parenting is shared more fully.

> My beloved went on school camp with my son — and they both loved it. It's not that I couldn't go but the bond between them is masculine, bold, and fatherly. Stepdad looks at life differently to me and my son thrives with this; their humour, physicalness, love of technology, and more, is a bond developed that I as mother have no desire to emulate. Likewise it does not diminish my son's time with his biological father, it adds to it by the reinforcement of healthy, strong masculine role models in his life — free from feminine influence. When Dad was unavailable, Stepdad's attendance was a request from my son because he knew they'd have a marvellous time doing all the boy things together — and they did!

Support Irrespective

A key principle that helps to create a healthy unit, rather than a home environment that is divisible, is constant support. Support your partner — irrespective. This support does not imply agreement and neither does it condone poor decisions; it simply means you support and respect your partner's presence in the family unit. The support may mean you watch some less-than-ideal situations play out and provide an opportunity for all to learn boundaries and consequences. Sometimes, the best way for others to learn is through unconditional support while the experiences are gained — painful as they may be. It enhances the Learning environment in both demonstration and conversation. If you make the choice not to support your partner when with the children, it will rob them of true belonging and open the reciprocal feeling for yourself to be isolated and bereft of aid when you need it most.

To maintain integrity and authenticity while parenting and supporting can be challenging. The way to do this is through your support being equally respected by your partner through apologies and resolution. This means you, maintain support in the face of apparent unreasonableness, secure in the knowledge the respect held for the child being wronged, and the continued support provided, will result in a genuine apology being made by the stepparent at an appropriate time. Please be reasonable here; the same principle must apply in the reserve situation — where your partner is supporting you!

The adage of 'not in front of the kids' is often appropriate when your children are young. This presents a unified team to set clear definitions of boundaries and consequences; however, as your children become more independent thinkers and the teen years roll around, you may find it no longer feels real to keep all differences away from them; this is when your unified team may appear a little more porous.

When you feel that your teen is being unfairly disciplined by an overreacting stepparent, it is normal to feel it strongly, especially if your name is being yelled out for sudden intervention. While it may be necessary to defuse the situation, it is wise to be sure you are unquestionably needed, or if perhaps, more can be learned once the intense emotions have been dispelled.

> Tip: Be mindful not to be hypocritical as you judge what you hear from your partner's lips when you know you have done the same thing and chose to condone it.
>
> This has been a challenge to my commitment in the shared parenting of my darlings. It is easy to say support irrespective, but when put to the test I had to learn to bite my tongue — and hard!
>
> Sometimes I strongly disagreed with what was being said and yet I would support, but only by a thread, and called for a private conversation. There were however times I would be so hurt (or perhaps fuming) too much to talk immediately so a day or two would have to pass before I'd worked out a constructive way to deal with the perceived

wrong. I learned the wisdom to 'seek to understand before being understood' realising that these issues genuinely stemmed from best intentions, faulted by relatively poor execution. A little time spent hearing the reasons, even if it was limited by my judgement, at least gave us a starting place for a positive path forward.

My beloved has been extraordinary in his commitment to apologies and resolution with both me and the children; a mutual respect that builds confidence in the desire to support.

Contradictions

In a situation where you are about to contradict your partner, remember to *praise the person and reprimand the behaviour or attitude*. To contradict your partner occasionally is not bad parenting; it is real. To contradict your partner constantly invalidates their opportunity to create respect and presence inside the family and diminishes true confidence and well-being. Always support both your partner and child, while you refuse to take sides; discuss the situation, behaviour, or attitude, while boundaries of respect and constructive communication are maintained, you will then teach positive conflict resolution.

To shy away from situations teaches denial; to fight, teaches aggression; to lead by example, with the opportunity to call Time Out if necessary, empowers all to constantly look at themselves first.

The use of these techniques puts power in its place. It brings life into the principle of *power with* rather than *power over*, and brings resolution without stripping the people who are involved of dignity and choice. This is fundamental to the success of the family; to operate with feelings of strength and power; to confidently build towards adult maturity rather than foster the controlling and demeaning alternatives, where short-term individual advantages may result, but immaturity remains overall.

> To shy away teaches denial; to fight, teaches aggression; to lead by example, empowers all.

The Ex

It is fair to say the topic of your Ex will come up in conversations with your partner, and depending on relationship dynamics with your Ex, this could become toxic to your budding new romance. Your Ex has little or no influence over your new partner-relationship unless you allow them to. It is simply your choice. Although, due to circumstances, such as impending court proceedings or constant requests for further payments, you may not feel this to be so, it is. The pressure felt may appear to be a wedge, but this can only happen if you stay emotionally entangled with your Ex, or have an attachment to a specific outcome.

Inside your new relationship, keep the Ex in perspective. They have been, and in a reduced way, still are, an important part of your life; they will always be a very important part of your children's lives. To pretend this bond does not exist is not being real; even though for many, as they reflect upon the time spent with their Ex, it is described as being more like an alternative lifetime, than just a memory.

Ideally, inside the Complex Family, it is most beneficial for the children if the parents and stepparents can cooperate; however, personal choices to hold grudges and resentment may prevent this from being the case. In situations such as these, the stepparent is advised to do little more than support the parent towards personal resolution first, rather than inflame the carnage through an added opinion.

> Avoid poisoning your partner's picture of your Ex — they will see them soon.

Regardless of how tempting it may be, be careful to avoid the impulse to poison your partner's picture of your Ex — they will see this person for themselves soon enough. Instead, start to build towards a constructive relationship that needs to be formed in the new Parenting Team, and stay clear of comparisons and critiquing in which the Ex is judged.

When there is tension between you and your Ex, your partner is wise to remain as a neutral sounding board; this gives you a secure zone, and grants you time to consider your own choices. Your partner may have an alternative perspective that can help you move towards a solution, or not; but simply by being supportive and willing to listen, they can take the sting out of the conflict. Alternatively, if your partner says or does something to fuel the fire of unrest, solutions are almost never found, and the result can be significant ill feeling in a poor Parenting Team.

In a Parenting Team, there will be occasions when your partner agrees with an opinion held by your Ex and that can leave you flummoxed, as any trace of betrayal and isolation you might have felt during divorce instantly resurfaces. Usually this happens because your partner is free from the long-term, ongoing, emotional entanglement between parents and children, so the alternative perspective seems to make sense, it's not because they are attacking you personally.

While agreement over a particular point is not in your favour, this does not automatically infer joint opinion must mean right decision either — but it is a good time to reevaluate your stance. See if you are resisting due to hidden motives, or if indeed, you have not fully explained yourself nor fully understood. Either way, freedom of thought, alternative perspective, and conflicting choices are all part of being real — especially when parenting with an Ex and a new partner.

If you always lead by example in treating your Ex (and their partner) with respect, being mindful of their position within the family unit regardless of sustained tension to date, you can begin the transformation towards creating a Parenting Team.

Discipline

Most people who enter into a relationship with a parent have their own ideas about raising children, and their beliefs of what constitutes proper discipline. For the first little while, the responsibility of discipline remains with you as parent, but before long, the boundary moves and your partner steps out and creates a new line. Depending on how it is done, it will affect the response your children have; most likely, the first time it happens there will be a slight look of disbelief, quickly followed by Test II to see if they misinterpreted it — now it is *Game On!*

Although other professionals have believed and spoken out that stepparents cannot, nor should they discipline unless they enter into the children's lives at a very young age, I believe they must participate. It is important for a stepparent to become involved in discipline in the family because if you do not allow your partner to undertake disciplining actions, you disempower the position of stepparent to little more than an adult body, stripped of initiative, opinion, and strength, and lacking in identity and intrinsic value. This being said, it is also important for your partner to develop a positive and meaningful relationship with the children individually before discipline becomes appropriate. If this bond is not built, discipline becomes the practice of *power over* causing more division than benefit.

Any criticism from a stepparent can be intensely hurtful because your children's feelings are especially vulnerable when they share their home and parent. Some children have incredulously believed that because their parents have allowed the stepparent to live within the family, it means automatic agreement with the stepparent's statements or opinions, and thereby equates agreement with the criticism. When using this logic, the child hears any criticism as if it comes directly from the parent. They are too immature to understand that your new partnership does not mean a unity of opinion.

> Criticism from a stepparent can be intensely hurtful ... when they share their home and parent.

When an occasion like this occurs, your children may attempt to dismiss the hurt and try to gain control in order to avoid the vulnerable feeling of sharing home and parent. They may seek to dull the pain by distancing themselves, becoming apathetic, or acting in a manner to gain their parent's attention, in an attempt to mask the inner anger that is brewing. This does not solve the problems though; instead, it sets the stage for further expressions of emotionally torn feelings to surface between parent, stepparent, and child. Resolving this problem comes from simply increasing awareness of disciplining principles and the ongoing development of the stepparent relationship with each child individually. In this way, the stepparent upholds the appropriate right to discipline.

If your parenting styles are dramatically different, a new process to resolve disparities will need to begin. To help keep this in perspective, find the common ground first; build on these areas, and develop a compromise for the conflicting aspects later.

Most of us caught our parenting style from watching our parents. We either do not think about it and therefore continue in the same style during our child-raising years; or we agree with what our parents chose and therefore have an opinion that we want to see followed; or we disagree with what they did and so attempt not to repeat it.

In any of these scenarios, if your partner is interested in reading or learning more about it, suggest reading this book as a starting point of conversation. There does not need to be agreement with all points raised, but rather a perspective put forward from a third person who is then deemed to be neutral; this is to encourage discussion rather than defend a prescribed position. Take the time to understand differing perspectives on discipline and punishment, be willing to challenge the accepted norm, and constantly look to refine your approach given the ever-changing stages of your children.

Acknowledgement

The job of being a parent has often been recognised as being one of the unsung heros of the world — where small tokens of acknowledgment are handed out, but really, the life-altering responsibilities of becoming Mum or Dad, has few other rewards than the relationship with our children and the opportunity to learn so much about ourselves as we walk the path together.

Your partner is in much the same place, but usually without the small tokens of acknowledgement because the children are not theirs. For this reason, it's common for stepparents to require more acknowledgement than you do. While this may sound as though you are pandering to their need, it is possibly more accurate to say you respect this fundamental difference, and therefore, choose to bridge the gap.

One ouch-moment stepparents frequently tolerate is when recognition is given to parents when it ought to be redirected to the stepparent. Sometimes a well intended compliment from family, friends, or those who witness change in your children's lives, is meant to be a blessing and instead it has the opposite effect. This is when the compliment is in response to a particular aspect your partner has brought into the family, and yet as parent, you take it without acknowledging their contribution; you diminish them. Diminished to a point of invalidation, by reminding them they are without birthright — the Outsider resurfaces.

> An amazing stepmother was recently devastated by a well-meaning accolade being directed at the parent without a trace of recognition for her efforts being acknowledged or compliment redirected. For seven years she has driven her stepdaughter to ballet, watched every rehearsal, prepared the costumes, and structured her life around this commitment.
>
> Upon her stepdaughter reaching high levels of regional competition, in which she excelled, the parent turned up and was hence congratulated by generous well-wishes. While the parent and stepparent stood arm in arm, the parent smiled and thanked each for their praise. During this time, not once did the parent redirect the accolade to her diligent Stepmum for all her sacrifice and support.
>
> This parent was not being mean or self-indulgent, it was just assumed the stepparent would hear these words and take the accolade without a need to correct those who passed the compliments.
>
> It was not a large thing for the parent to do — and because of this it was to easy to overlook — assuming our partner does not need the public recognition of their unique effort because we are a team. A parent's overlooking robs them of the mutual feeding that comes through parental giving.

Finances

Finances usually provide a source of irritation inside the stepparent relationship, not because stepparents are not generous, but even the most magnanimous stepparent finds the financial pain-point at some stage. This is because money is a scare resource that has reached pinnacles of control within current societal thinking. As our children have been born into a world driven by consumerism and disposable thinking, any parent, step — or otherwise, has issues surrounding money. The more we have, the more is demanded, and an ever-increasing sense of wanting continues to grow.

To avoid conflicts where divided loyalties meet feelings of inadequacy, talk through financial expectations early. Most parents accept they either pay or receive support because of an Ex. Most stepparents accept this too; even if they do not agree or particularly like it. The questions that usually cause the issues, however, are those relating to life beyond the historical agreements, those that affect the family budget today. Here are two common ouch-points that cause post-marriage relationships issues.

> A mother who has pinched and scrapped together money for years, making personal sacrifices to ensure the provision for her children, finally meets Mr. Right and he is willing to assist financially to release her from such a burden. Initially, it seems delightful; but as time ticks by, unrest occurs between them. He becomes tired in his provider status and begins to believe he has been demoted from the heroic status of saviour to what is now a complacent nobody, someone who is taken for granted. She feels a slowly growing dependency upon this new lifestyle that she and her children enjoy, and strong feelings of obligation are brewing. The trap is set. Either the couple will choose to discuss genuine feelings, or their inner resentment will begin to cause circumstantial conflict, evidencing the inner turmoil brewing just beneath the surface.
>
> or

A father of two children cannot see them unless he saves enough money for airfares and expenses to have them visit. He works long hours every week away from home as does his new bride; they both work full-time trying to save. He wants to spend the several thousand dollars to bring his children out on holiday, and she wants to use the money for renovating the kitchen which desperately needs doing. It's not that the father doesn't understand the need for the kitchen job, nor is it that the stepmother wants to withhold the pleasures of family bonding. It is simply a matter of where the savings are to be spent given that a large portion of father's pay has already been sent in child support payments. The stepmother accepts those and unquestioningly makes sacrifices for them daily.

In much the same way expectations evolve and change in other areas of our lives, so do those inside our finances. Not all couples share in joint financial arrangements; some choose to keep individual living costs much like flat-mates. In situations like this, conflict may occur. With experience as our best teacher, it is fair to say, however, the vast majority of couples share finances; in my Complex Family, the stepparents give purely as they are part of our family.

Giving or Trading

Financial arguments usually highlight the confusion between Trading and Giving rather than reflect a lack of willingness to give or receive.

Trading: we give to receive something in return.

Giving: we give without expectation of return.

There is nothing wrong with trading; however, it becomes a point of contention when we are either ignorant or silent of the trade and it is then not fulfiled.

If we openly trade with our partner or children, it means we can say, "I give you this if you do this for me." Then we have the opportunity to accept, decline, or negotiate for acceptable terms. Once agreed, our trade is clear and all parties live by the consequences of the agreement.

When we are giving, we simply give and anything received is considered a bonus.

If we become clear about agreements made between us, our conflict over financial differences will greatly decrease. When we practice forming trade agreements and begin to be courageous and define them as such, we take personal responsibility for genuine giving, even if it highlights the lack thereof. In this way, we can gain greater transparency inside our relationships.

As discussed in the earlier section titled *'Mutual Feeding through Sharing'*, your partner will grow into more genuine giving if you are willing to acknowledge open trading is valid and equally appropriate. There is nothing wrong with either stance, it is only when they are confused that the issues arise.

Gratitude

Another subtle difference between parent and stepparent is the level and frequency of expressions of gratitude expected from the children. Parents almost take the acts of giving to a child as an unquestioned obligation to be fulfiled and thereby all but ignore the need for constant expressions of gratitude. Typically however, the stepparent often feels that expressions of gratitude are more important; they lack the same innate obligated feeling that birthright gives to parents.

Due to this subtle difference, the stepparent will usually feel justified in wanting to fully educate your children to express gratitude. While it could be argued our partner is trading, the benefits for the family that come about as everyone practices an attitude of gratitude, cannot be faulted. It may be challenging, but it is preferable to encourage the practice and lead by example.

Strategic Positions vs. Rank

Is it possible to transcend typical stereotype prejudices and be free to parent equally? As much as I like to speak of a healthy functioning Parenting Team, where we share and treat each other as equals, there is the reality that at times of great division in opinions, parents become the parents and the stepparents take a small step either sideways or backwards, as they realise the point of difference has come. Although I dislike the term *rank* as it conjures up feelings of dictatorial authority and helpless dependency (which is not part of a healthy functioning team), it can often feel this way to all involved.

Another perspective to help reframe this *rank* is that it is commonly accepted within a great team we have strategic positions to assist in the accomplishment of our overall vision. The parenting partnership is no different; it holds expectations of its members to develop their skills, learn enhanced techniques, and strengthen cohesiveness so that when under pressure, it is not so much a matter of rank, but rather the most appropriate person who makes the final decision.

In a parenting partnership our partner will get hurt the same way we do. When your partner is hurt, it is painfully normal to watch their behaviour stoop below where it usually stands, and at times it may even match that of your children. Sometimes, it can feel like you have given them too much rope and you are about to watch them hang themselves. And for you, as parent, you suddenly have an urge to rescue your children and save your partner. However, what is really being called for is not saving, nor rescuing, but rather the reinforcement of the parenting partnership where the parents step in and adds depth and solidarity through examples of support. This is the moment your partner needs to know you are beside them, much as they have been beside your children in times of need. It is being able to provide that backstop that says "I love you both, and there will not be any choosing between you, so let's resolve this constructively, and overlook any short-fall that may have occurred", as you continue to uphold the true essence of the learning environment.

> "I love you both, and there will not be any choosing between you, so let's resolve this constructively."

The reality is, your partner is in your children's lives because they have a relationship with you. If this ends, you, as parent, will still have obligations.

Although a well-meaning stepparent may want to continue supporting and encouraging your children, they have no obligation to do so. This lifelong commitment to your children is one which, by birth, you agree to undertake and it cannot be replaced by anyone. It is a difference that, while real, does not diminish the importance and value stepparents bring to the Complex Family environment.

The Moment of Change

In all relationships, there is a moment when we cross over the line of participation and now are intimately involved, if not attached. Although we may be unaware of this consciously, it is the point where our life would be derailed (albeit temporarily) without the continuation of the relationship, and grieving would naturally occur.

This moment of change creeps up on stepparents, and the title carries no guarantee that this moment will happen in their lifetime. It is the moment when a stepparent oozes with parental pride, sheds tears of happiness, or has an adrenaline rush because of a child's achievement. Likewise, it is the moment of dread, the inner gut wrench, and the nights of worry. It is when a stepparent becomes connected with a child directly, and no longer requires you, the parent, to be the catalyst.

This is the moment when your partner cherishes the genuine love they feel expressed from your children, and knows it is the result of all they are to your family — that their unselfish giving has been recognised by the very ones it has been gifted upon.

How To; When Your Ex's Partner is Stepparent

The relationship between yourself and your Ex's partner can be fraught with complexity. The number of variations in circumstances that occur for when and how we meet this person gives little room for succinct customised solutions; but then, neither are such individual answers necessary. For some of you, the beginnings have been invasive and traumatic, with your personal preferences not considered. Normally, the Ex's partner is someone you do not know; nevertheless, we have all heard tales of those who find themselves estranged from both best friend and spouse as they take up a very sticky start.

> I have been involved with my Ex's partner (now wife) for over a decade. We have laughed together, cried, supported, disagreed, celebrated, and at times avoided each other — all in the natural course of parenting. In those early days, at times I was unable to be strong enough, so distance seemed fair. Most of the time however, a strong respect has been our code where my unwavering dedication to myself as a mother, has been supported and complemented by her in both actions and words.
>
> Our children do not, and have neither been involved in, nor have they heard negativity towards either their other parent, or stepparent, from either side of our family Parenting Team. Although it has not all been straight forward for any of us involved in the team when jostling for positions, power, identity, and understanding, we have endeavoured to keep our ultimate focus firmly on the commitment to the love we hold for our children.
>
> The five years between being divorced and having my beloved, the children's stepparent, enter our lives set the scene where established patterns and expectations were shaken a little when he entered the equation. My Ex had become used to two women loving and supporting our three children, and when a sudden dose of testosterone came close to home, a little time of adjustment was needed. It is not easy, emotionally nor practically, to have our children influenced heavily by someone we

barely know. It takes maturity, respect, and time to have this new dynamic succeed; and for us, succeed it has.

Leavee and Leaver

From a **Leavee's** perspective: hearing that your Ex is moving on with someone else when your own life is not 'on track' can be difficult to celebrate; this new person is likely to be viewed as an intruder into the family context. This can be further complicated by the feelings that if you allow yourself to *like* the other person, it almost justifies your Ex's actions; it seems to validate their choices, and therefore, invalidates your pain. If others rejoice in this, it may stop the flow of sympathy and condemnation for your Ex's actions, which could then turn the focus towards you as being personally responsible for your own actions and feelings. These real feelings and thoughts are part of what makes your judgement of the Ex's new partner appear so necessary, and believably unescapable.

From a **Leaver's** perspective: finally hearing of your Ex being with someone comes with a certain level of delight; you hope this special someone will bring love and laughter back into their life. When the sigh has ended and this immediate relief response has been felt, it can open a new doorway. This doorway is the one to possible competition, hostility, or emotional manipulation to obscure your children's perspective; however, this is secondary to the last release of guilt as the final strands of emotional entanglement are now severed. The final page has been turned, and with it that book is closed.

Your Children

Giving permission for your children to love both homes equally, but uniquely, includes loving everyone inside these two places. This is achieved through the power of your actions, and then backed up by your words – and not the other way around. You do this because without it your children will feel they still live within a split and broken home, and your children deserve the opportunity to thrive in a Complex Family, not a broken one. They deserve to be given the freedom to decide for themselves if their stepparent is adding, rather than subtracting from their life and the life of their other parent. Your children deserve to be free from the adult complexities, love their stepparent for all they bring, and not have to focus on the could, would, or ought to have been.

For your children to be free to make their own assessment of life between two homes, you need to begin educating them towards *How* to think, rather than *What* to think — a powerful difference their adult years will appreciate, as it will give strength and conviction to their choices. Your children learn this vital process as they observe varying personal values being lived, watch the consequences, and benefit from the experience. If you pollute their minds with tales of woe about their stepparents' influence, you will dilute the power of natural learning.

Welcoming Newness

For most, you will be cautious about this new member, and immediately assume the position of scrutinaire to determine if you approve. Any tidbits of information you can glean from your children helps to cement your initial judgements, and you judge harshly especially if your children are treated poorly. If your Ex increases the complexity with the presence of additional children, it is normal to expect the evaluation to be more severe.

Usually the Ex's partner is the same gender as you are — although this is not always the case — however, you'll be well-rehearsed in the behaviours that emerge when in the presence of your replacement, drawing out attitudes of superiority or inferiority, to their maximum power. Sizing them up, you may mark lines of judgement and draw your picture of who they are; this will now be infused within you and affect your ongoing attitudes and behaviour for all to see.

A more obscure observation discovered in my counselling and coaching of couples over the years is how most Exes pick genuinely okay people for their next serious relationship — different, but great. Sure, they have their issues to contend with, but reality says, who doesn't? So although it's fair to say that often this person is not someone we would want as a close friend, they are someone we could get on with — if given half a chance.

The other part of this observation is that most people simply do not want to give it that chance.

Friend or Foe

Meeting the new stepparent was no easy task in my own life — nor in hers. My husband, yet unsure of his life choice, was met with my uncompromising commitment towards living the best I knew in any given circumstance. A phone call that was unexpectedly answered by me was the first touchpoint of reality. The awkward moment was brief as I asked if we could meet in one hour for a chat while my husband took care of our three children. I am quite certain there was more trepidation felt by her, and possibly my Ex than by me, but I vividly recall the defining acceptance I felt, and the timing of such vital choices. My question: was she friend or foe?

Dreading I would see in her what I know my Ex believed I lacked in myself, I braved my own request. Without prior rehearsal of conversation or time to indulge in wishful thoughts, this seemed the most opportune moment to get real. My logic was strong; I concluded that if she was going to be in my husband's life, she was going to be in mine — and in the lives of my three precious children. I could either make this difficult for us all, or attempt to make the best of what appeared to be a very ugly situation.

For over an hour we walked and talked, discussing the highs and lows of our past, the ideals for our future, and the hurt I was currently experiencing. There was little pretense, and a great deal of vulnerability. Amongst guarded conversation and minimal answers, we birthed a new type of family — a Complex one. We have talked of this moment during the years of growing our Complex Family, as it was the beginnings of a partnership which will last our lifetimes. Some points of conversation I uttered that day became the cornerstone for the culture we now all embrace. It was, in essence, the desire to walk a less-established path, a new way of thinking, by which I believed my children would be able to benefit amidst apparent catastrophe. I believed if I could find the strength, courage, and grace, to look beyond my immediate nightmare, something beautiful would be waiting for them — and hopefully, one day for me too.

Although my very human and fragile side was daunted by my own invitation, the courageous and loving part of me shone through brightly that day, carrying with it all my fears (and tears) and initiating what has become a relationship built on respect, tolerance, and shared parenting.

Treasure Chest

The relationship with your Ex's partner may be infrequently engaged upon; however, it may also be a hidden treasure chest that is full of answers and solutions. Depending on your style of family and the type of relationship that is formed between parents and stepparents, it may provide substantial strength to the family.

In the work that I have done, it has become increasingly common for fathers and stepfathers to form an alliance regarding particular aspects of parenting, ones that add substance and strength to a traditional role that has been diminished. Mothers and stepmothers usually find it easier to arrange daily routines and calendar schedules, as they are the ones who often keep the wheels turning inside the homes. Children certainly learn they have four parents — and that playing one set off against the other really doesn't work.

> Children learn they have four parents — and playing one set off against the other really doesn't work.

To continue building the Parenting Team deliberately rather than crossing fingers and hoping it will work, I suggest following the same principle as with the family meetings, except this time it will be Parenting Team meetings — four parents discussing the happenings of the children, giving opinions, thoughts, and suggestions.

We have meetings on average about three or four times each year. Although the contact may be as often as daily during the course of a busy school term, with e-mails, phone calls, or texts, we routinely get together face to face. At these meetings we have a check-up on how we are all feeling about the children, their progress, attitudes, activities, and general family dynamics. Seldom are there issues that cannot be resolved in one sitting, and frequently these are light-hearted and jovial, but the key is our children know we get together for the well-being of our family.

They understand we talk about them and this lets us continue to demonstrate leadership, respect, teamwork, and conflict resolution in action. When something urgent arises, we can get together and work it out because we have an established platform for doing so.

Our children know we disagree; they also know we are not disagreeable when we do not agree.

Through ongoing commitment towards parenting together it becomes hard for any stepparent to bad-mouth the Ex when this Ex has constantly treated them with respect and understanding. It is harder for a child to invalidate a parent or stepparent when they see authentic teamwork in action.

So while the protection of this relationship from those who are immediately effected is important, this extends to greater protection from external influence as vital. While someone looking in may not understand this bond, or the commitment shared, neither do they need to for your team to work. What is wise, however, is to keep the negative outsider exactly in that outside space, because the delicate bond between all four parents can take a long time to cement and it needs to be nurtured not questioned. As parents, you need to be the first to support either of your stepparents — as you trust they would equally do for you.

Permission and Confiding

The relationships between children, stepparents, and parents change. It moves as circumstances dictate: children get older, new babies are added, and updated routines are required. If we have flexibility within our Parenting Team, it means we have the backup and support when we need it most. Keeping the focus on the children removes the barriers of rigid right and wrong, and relies on the wisdom gained from team experiences to be our true teacher.

Sometimes your children will trial out behaviour with the stepparent before they will with their parents. Sometimes it is the reverse. However, when there are issues such as being granted permission or having them confide in you, you need to be extremely careful. The choice to condone or to keep secrets for children within a Parenting Team can sometimes be tricky to work out. Not everything needs to involve all the parents; naturally, this is part of the freedom we seek in living beyond the bonds of marriage; however, it is unwise to withhold when the others parent's ignorance can cause further complications. To keep yourself in check, answer these two questions:

1. How would I feel if this was withheld from me as parent?
2. Is this building *power with* or *power over*?

Take the time to practice with the small issues so when larger ones strike there is a foundation already laid, where trust, respect, and commitment are unquestioned.

A training ground for appropriate confiding is in the area of permissions themselves. It can be very easy for your children to ask the 'softy' to get their way when they know Mother or Father would disapprove. To avoid playing one set of parents off against the other, you may require children to gain permission from the Parenting Team instead of an individual speaking for the larger whole. This way they begin to understand it is not as easy as asking one parent and hoping they get away with it. Naturally one may be the case in some instances, but it's not taken for granted.

Although you do not want all decisions to be Parenting Team discussions, with a little practice you learn where the boundaries are and yet still with the best of intentions, conflict will still occur and sometimes over the most surprising topics; yet if your children are practiced in the expectations of the Parenting Team, this provides the opportunity for further learning.

Stepparent Influences

While your Ex's partner is influential, the core relationship will still remain with the Ex. It is the recognition of the stepparent's influence which is helpful, however, especially since some prior agreements may now be up for review. These agreements may relate to finances, or changes to routines, geographical shifts, or more children. All sorts of influences occur and you may sometimes find it difficult to deal with such effects upon the Ex's thinking.

To help cushion this, the team environment needs to be developed to the point where these changes can be openly discussed and worked through such influences or you need to develop your own open-mindedness. Ignorance is often a large contributor to perceived negative actions in a Complex Family, so if you can start to build a stronger relationship with your Ex's partner, the other stepparent, you will lead by example in creating a more harmonious family culture and possibly reduce the tension the ignorance once allowed to happen.

Another aspect of influence that is more subtle, yet can be equally intrusive, comes about when your Ex's partner has been in your children's lives for a long time and you see their mannerisms and idiosyncrasies being acted out in your home. Although this may come as a strong reminder of your Complex Family, it is important that you accept your children's mimicking, and neither invalidate them, nor their actions. If you do, you invalidate their stepparent, and thus damage the Learning environment you endeavour to create.

If you find it a struggle to accept, try to take a broader perspective and remember your Ex is more than likely also dealing with the same frustrations, only reversed. They most likely see you in the children, and while it is perfectly natural for this to occur, it has become normal for parents to want to change their children's acting to stop the reminders.

Ouch Points

As with all relationships, this one takes constant refinement. It is the ongoing acceptance of our differences and respect for the boundaries that may, from time to time, inadvertently be crossed. As familiarity grows between you and your routines continue, e-mails and text messages fly around with children coming and going, there are bound to be new 'ouch points' that surface. This is predictable; and once again, it is how you respond that counts.

In the Ouch Point moments, here are a few tips to follow:

- **Recognise** it has occurred. Be real and acknowledge you still feel the resentment and have an ouch-point.

- Give the **benefit-of-the-doubt.** Most often, the stepparent or parent is not trying to hurt you; they have forgotten, misplaced, screwed up, or just been insensitive; it's usually not malicious, vindictive or pre-meditated.

- Have a conversation to **resolve the issue** and take action to make good of what has occurred. If there is something that can be done to avoid it happening again, discuss an alternative option. If it becomes clear it is mainly your over-reaction, consider silence as being your first option; if you decide to hand out too much correction, it only shows your lack of acceptance and the loss of an opportunity to learn.

> Focus on yourself and children, not your Ex or Stepparents.

- **Let it go.** Once it is over, let the situation be closed. Do not raise it again in future interactions; choose to let history remain in its place.

As with any relationship, you want your interactions to be the best you can have; however, this being said, you can only do your part. Create the best environment you can — one that is safe and open, trusting and respectful; this will encourage your Complex Family as a whole.

Give yourself time to practice, and be sure the majority of your focus is on yourself and your children, not on your Ex or stepparents.

The Blended Family

The Blended Family is an aspect of being a Complex Family. The blended family is the family who has children who are brought together from previous relationships, not those born into the new relationship. The complexities are similar to those already discussed, but with the added dimension of further emotional challenges. It is normal for blended families to experience extended sibling rivalry, stepparent/parent guilt when biological children are not living with you and your stepchildren are, and further financial challenges to sort through. However, this being said, the founding principles, tips, and techniques previously discussed, if well practiced, will also assist blended families because the core value of parenting inside a Complex Family, irrespective of structure, is that we are simply *Family*.

Matrimonial Home

It seems a little odd to deal with the matrimonial home inside the chapter relating to stepparents; however, this is typically the time where the matrimonial home causes the greatest unforeseen issues — those that are beyond the obvious financial considerations and agreements that may have been reached for those involved in the separation.

The unforeseen issues are those that arise as your partner becomes part of your family inside the matrimonial home. Despite its value, beauty, exceptional floor plan, precious schooling zones, or any other justifiable reasons, once you have decided to set up a home with your partner and you expect to continue living in the original matrimonial home, you are asking for conflict. Your partner may even want to move into the house; however, to give your new Complex Family a chance of building a meaningful foundation, both adults need to be given the opportunity to be inside *our* home, not one with a history. Although you may not see it, it is too easy to subconsciously replace the spouse who no longer lives there, and continue to abide by the established family customs.

There is a familiarity of environment where the old adage of "possession is nine-tenths of the law" seems to highlight how it wreaks havoc in the confidence, security, and bonding of the most robust committed relationships. There is an established family culture that was formed, and has since reformed, inside this home pre, during, and post divorce years — so to opt for this re-creation to occur again and succeed, you ask yourself, children, and your partner to be attentive to the unexpressed family cultural expectations to which you've become accustomed.

At a time like this, if you are struggling with the choice of moving or not, it is prudent to see that your attachment to — and wanting to live in — the same home devalues the importance of your partner's decision. It could be said that you value your possessions or property more highly than your commitment to your newly forming family. The normality of this issue makes it predictable that in a matter of a year or so, the largest source of argument within your relationship will stem from the inability to create a new family culture, as your partner feels swamped. The subtle force of one life entering into a structure of multiple lives has an invisible, yet intoxicating effect upon the psyche.

Let's explain the difference through a simplistic summary of relationships. First we'll look at relationships without such complexity:

> Two lives walk individual paths, at some moment, they intersect; these two lives decide upon ongoing touch-points, gain in frequency and intensity, and grow their dynamic love. Eventually, the paths travel in parallel for long enough their self-defined boundaries slowly merge to form a single unit for the path ahead.

In the Complex Family, the above story all too often reads something like this instead:

> Two lives walk individual paths, and at some moment, they intersect. Love growing and juggling continuing, to maintain the

required level of comfort, single lane person leaps off their path and lands on the wider, larger path; the path with parent and children. They scramble back occasionally to collect their misplaced items or to catch their breath, but before long the stepparent becomes completely absorbed, being carried away by the demands and responsibilities of family — often without healthy self-defining boundaries.

In the second comparative story, the picture painted shows the lack of coming together and the more familiar derailing or swept up in the Complex Family hustle before the relationship has a chance to develop.

It is a significant decision to have a stepparent take up residence with your family, irrespective of the house. When this decision is made, it needs to be done in a way that allows the primary relationship (being that of the two adults) to form on equal footing.

Irrespective of the house, or who financially supports it, the children are already going to express the coming together as the stepparent moved in with them. So, if this is conducted inside the matrimonial home, it often suggests the following ideas are held by you as the parent:

- There is limited understanding of the stepparent's valuable contribution to the family.

- There is limited acknowledgement for the level of change that is required by everyone to be comfortable with the new dynamics.

- There appears to be an unwillingness to physically demonstrate the breaking of ties with the former life.

All of these need to be carefully considered to nurture and foster the longevity of the parent and partner/stepparent relationship, given the amount of pressure it faces in a Complex Family environment.

Chapter Seven
Legal Matters

How to practically manage the legal process.

The Law

In search of advice, opinions, and confirmations of our position, the letter of the law is one of the first places explored when separation is considered. We seek information and assurance of our share and our right to be protected — after all, we've worked hard for what we have. If we have been either shrewd or suspicious, perhaps legal or financial structures may have been established to protect our interests before any mumblings of departure. If we have not considered the possibility of separation or calamity, we could find ourselves in a position where we wake up with quite a jolt.

Deciding on what aspects of the legal system we should engage in, or when it becomes the best option, is no easy task. Having worked with many parents while going through divorce, and the subsequent years of parenting together, I have yet to see the legal route as being the one that produces the greatest benefit considering the significant implications for families. In many situations, the law helps us to get our way — if the judgements are favourable. Beneath all the situational aspects of why you go to Court, it's important to consider the kind of messages that are subtly fed into your children's world.

A point of clarity: Significant issues relating to criminal activity, mental disorders, or abuse, are not the focus of this writing. Although the principles apply, the interaction in such extreme environments are more than most parents can handle without external assistance. The majority of cases before the courts, however, deal with matters of finance, property, geographical complications, routines, and permissions; therefore, it is to these issues I address this section.

> A few days after coming to grips with the fact our marriage was ending, I sat in the sun at an outdoor table with a mass of Easy-Arch files, books, and papers surrounding me. Attempting to make this task pleasant, the warmth of the sun seemed to provide a cloak of comfort to an otherwise tense and awkward undertaking. Pouring through the precedents, agreements, and judgements, I was curious to see what my legal position was.
>
> First things first; I needed my own lawyer. During our decade together, all matters of legal significance were handled by one lawyer because we were a couple, a team, an entity. Now that battle-lines had been drawn, I needed to build support on my side. This shift in loyalties made me feel a tad insecure, unnerved, and intimidated. The thought of battling for my portion, share, rights, and parenthood, reinforced a dull negative feeling of true separation — us versus them. Our life as a team had truly ended.
>
> On the day I went to introduce myself to the person who was meant to be working in my best interest, I got appropriately dressed, had my papers in order, and went with an open mind. I wanted to learn all I could, and

to fully understand everyone's position: mine, the children's, and my soon-to-be-Ex-husband's.

Going through the facts of my situation in a ten-minute question and answer session seemed to dehumanise the entire ordeal. It turned the death of a marriage into a non-emotional transaction, that while it had life-altering implications for all concerned, would soon be completed with boxes ticked, forms filled, documents dated, signed, and stamped before being filed in a dark closet, adding to the annual statistics.

Feelings of significant isolation overcame me; the sense of responsibility and implications were tangibly frightening.

The professional opinion was sleek and slender — there were only two aspects for me to consider: Property and Custody. While these terms may alter depending on where one lives; the important points (however phrased) are money and children.

Sounded simple enough coming from the lawyer, and this reassurance I bravely took as comfort. Little did I realise how naïve I was. My lack of knowledge and understanding of the rather outdated model our legal system uses to address the important issues failed to prepare me for the rough ride ahead. A more accurate and helpful professional assessment would have included a sincere warning . . . a heads up . . . as to life beyond marriage — especially where children are involved.

The Myth

The words *property* and *custody* are far from useful in reflecting the complexity of the realities ahead. These two factors, while important, offer a very shortsighted perspective considering the vastness of parenting once inside a Complex Family structure.

Before you consider having the court assess your interpretation of *for the best interest of my children*, a careful look at how the legal system actually works may help. Not all those involved in the legal profession may appreciate my perspective, and I'm certainly not here to debate or knock a thriving profession, but this is one establishment I believe needs careful consideration before engaging in the use of its power.

The Power of Precedent

A *precedent* is a legal case that establishes a principle or rule that a court or other judicial body utilises when deciding subsequent cases with similar issues or facts. Once a precedent has been established, it can be very hard to change. In many cases of current marital dissolution, cultural conditions and assumptions from years past fail to adequately satisfy today's requirements.

> In many cases of current marital dissolution, cultural conditions and assumptions from years past fail to adequately satisfy today's requirements.

For decades, with the established precedents, men have found it difficult (if not impossible) to share in the raising of their children beyond marriage. Women, through their natural birthright, frequently carried the responsibility with little or no help from the father. Many men have had to fight an outdated system to even begin to have precedents changed. The fact that fathers are vitally important is not new; it is only the recognition of this importance in the eyes of the law that is slowly changing. The ignorance of this reality has caused tens of thousands of fatherless families to live out a very poor experiment. Occasionally, a man brave enough of heart and finance, has fought for his right to be a father, and initiated the time-consuming and costly process of bringing change to old precedents that insist on reliving the past.

A few questions all disbanding couples would be wise to ask themselves before pursuing Court action and allowing precedents to become the governing voice of their families are:

1. Do I want to relive history?

2. Am I happy with the long-term results these precedents have produced?

3. Am I willing to learn a new way to parent now — beyond marriage?

Parenting with an Ex is the beginning of a new partnership, one where the very best of what you had in your marriage needs to be built upon — and the worst of what you had needs to be acknowledged and given permission to dissolve. Do you really need legal "assistance" to do this?

The Messages

Authority

One area of caution with any form of legal proceedings undertaken is to be keenly aware that the choice is made to hand over the power of final family decisions to an external authority that does not have to live with the consequences of the decisions made. To make matters worse, an unquantifiable and yet indelible message is sent to the children when parental decision-making powers are relinquished to an external party.

With Complex Family parenting, misunderstandings are frequent; inconvenient outcomes go with the territory; there are emotional pulls and confusion over what is best and acceptable; but you retain the opportunity to lead your children as you become a living example of resolution. Conflicting opinions or preferences do not have to mean fighting.

When you engage in legal battles, you cannot realistically expect your Ex to become a great team player during, or after, any such undertaking. To operate as a Parenting Team throughout the years of raising your children, and have both parties participate in future family events and celebrations, after the intimidation, threats, and powerlessness that intrudes into the already altered family structure, is asking for the near impossible. The legal process will take the last threads of choice, dignity, and teamwork and shred them into piles of rubble.

> From the mouths of babes, sometimes we gain great insights.
> Having spent time with his Council for Child after months of

parental disputes, tens of thousands of dollars, and his family in tatters, a young boy quickly established who holds the power — he summarised it beautifully with his one request, "I'd like to meet the judge." Lawyers, council, psychologists, affidavits, parents, bribes, coercion, and the child's personal power all discounted, "Judge, please!"

Two Primary Reasons

To wisely consider the implications of any legal action, you need to understand what you are attempting to gain and the messages that are sent to your children. Given there are primarily two reasons for legal intervention, money or children, you need to separate these to uncover possible intentions before establishing the overall message.

> While there may be a short-term gain, parenthood within the family is diminished.

If you are fighting over property, money, trusts, rights of financial assistance, or anything related to money, you may be sending subtle messages to your children that say, *Money, property, and things are more highly valued than our family itself.*

A fight to demand more time with your children, or to restrict them from being in their other parent's dysfunctional home, could be seen to align with great parenting. The issue is not your well-meaning intention, but the choice of the process you use to gain this end. In such a situation, one parent is inevitably diminished; therefore, while there may be a short-term gain, parenthood within the family is diminished. Your children will not necessarily benefit either because the attitudes and hostility within the Parenting Team are counterproductive. The Learning environment will be in tatters, and the obvious display of the parents' limited conflict resolution skills will fully expose the children to a situation where they feel they are responsible for it. To resort to the court over your right to have your children with you invites severity, judgement, and hard choices into the innocence of childhood; it forces them to give opinions and preferences on matters your child should be protected from.

All too often your children are left feeling they are to be blamed for the angst between their Mum and Dad. Frequently, you hear parents say to their children, "It's not you, it's just Mum, (or Dad) is not making things easy right now, but the court will work it out soon." At this point confusion enters your child's mind. It is obvious to your children the fighting is due to them — because with them out of the equation, there ceases to be any issue. In fact, with separating adults who have no children, they often do not meet again. Children get this — adults don't. Whether parents cover-up in an attempt to soften the blow, or believe that exposing all is necessary, no child deserves to be in the middle of such adult drama and dysfunction.

Rights, Choices, and Power

When we are faced with a situation that is beyond our ability to resolve, we turn to an external party; we seek a specialist, someone who will champion our cause. The focus subtly shifts from the issue in question to finding the best person we can hire to do the job. Here enters the opportunity for distortion — where one party may gain significant advantage through superior resources regardless of the earlier focus on the greater good of the family.

The children are another part of this scenario; so perhaps to relieve apprehension, or maybe sidestep any perception of unfair play they may feel, we attempt to add to their comfort by announcing they have been given their own special person to help them. Enter Council for Child.

A rather simplistically loose interpretation of this could be: *"Things are out-of-control between Mum and Dad; we need you to tell your thoughts to a complete stranger — as nice as they are — so they can speak on your behalf. Don't worry though, there's someone helping Mum and someone helping Dad too, just to make sure it's fair all round."*

> Council for Child becomes the child's place to confide. Albeit these people are fantastic with the children, this stranger is not their parent and is not the one who has to live with the consequences of the outcome.

Council for Child becomes your child's place to confide. Albeit these people are fantastic with the children, this stranger is not their parent and is not the one who has to live with the consequences of the outcome. If you want your children to confide in you in times of need, asking that such a critical question as their living arrangements be sorted by an external party is a signpost for them of your inability to cope with large issues, and that you need someone else to do it for you. As they reach their teens and adulthood when the biggies hit, you may well have set a standard that can undermine their confidence in you as a suitable confidant.

Meeting with Council for Child, children are asked to consider various options, give opinions, and have evaluations performed. They are put in a position where they wonder about the implications of what they have said, and are often left with anxious feelings about whether they have chosen between the halves of their own genetic make-up. No child ever deserves to have to verbalise pro and con, good or bad, high and low, between parents and homes. It's hard enough on children to choose who to sit next to at the dinner table, to say nothing of where to live.

> There has been only one question my children have not liked being asked throughout the years of living in a Complex Family; sadly, it's the most common, and one they accept but have chosen to use as their own chance to educate the asker. It is, "Where do you prefer being, Mum's or Dad's?"
>
> "It's simple," they go on to explain, "we'll never have to choose between them — we enjoy the differences between them, and also put up with the frustrations."

Emotions on the Surface, Principles at the Foundation

Disagreements are inevitable, fighting is optional. We need to begin to teach our children how to handle life's conflicts by providing living examples. A sanitised slugging match inside a courtroom does not equate with great conflict resolution. Our belief that specialisation delivers robust outcomes has seen the demise of commonsense to the point the word itself is almost an oxymoron. Children need to see us in action, and there is no better place to start than with the Ex — their other parent.

> Another typically long day at the office was topped off with the rushed pulling into the drive; a flustered father arrived at the front door hoping to see his little darlings before he finally went home for dinner.

Disagreements are inevitable, fighting is optional.

> Tonight, instead of being met with the usual happy cheerful hugs and kisses from three excited children to make him feel special, it was me. I had kept the children up later than usual in the hope he'd make it in time to fulfil his promise, but as bedtime approached and passed, and feeling frustrated and weary myself after dealing with scratchy children all evening — and the reality of getting them up the next morning, I had put them to bed.
>
> Expressing his exhaustion and disappointment, he proceeded to use threats of legal action for my interferring with his ability to see his children — along with intimidating promises to make my life a living hell. Of course, knowing that with each of us feeling frustrated with the other, it's never a great moment to continue conversations . . . and with a dim glimmer of wisdom, the door closed and he left.
>
> I put my hands over my face and as warm tears fell, I felt my intentions had been completely misunderstood. I had not tried to deny him time with his children; I was attempting to consider the childrens' sleeping routine and give myself a break at the end of my day. Pausing for a few seconds, crying quietly by myself, a noise drew my attention. It was my eldest, peeking from around the corner. I hastily looked away to wipe my eyes, and as I returned my glance, I was greeted with the appearance of child two and child three. Our three children were not asleep after all.

In over a decade of parenting outside the bonds of marriage, our children have witnessed conflict between us only this once. Our argument was disagreeable in both words and tone. Although this may sound sickeningly sweet to most; once is one time too many. Although our children were very young, secure in their routines and home environments, they have never forgotten this one incident. Some, in attempting to appease my disappointment, say, "But what your children saw was real." To me, it was simply not good enough, as we all know there are plenty of things that are real, but we don't want our children to see them. Unless we want fighting to be normal, our children deserve a better example to model their own behaviour on. There are no excuses and no reasons to justify our poor and destructive behaviours.

> We all know there are plenty of things that are real, but we don't want our children to see them.

The Ex and I disagree on most things. To make an obvious statement, we agree on very little — and probably this point included. The requirement to agree is relatively minor, however, because our biggest agreement is simple, *It's all about the children.* They know we constantly contradict each other's ideals, standards, and beliefs, and they accept that the contrast between the two homes is significant. They also see living examples of respect, integrity, acceptance, and tolerance, regardless of a difference of opinion. Although I have been slapped with an occasional desperate threat of court action, we have remained resistant to ever indulging in it; with effort, commonsense has prevailed.

At times, it has felt like compromise. Sometimes it feels like I give up on the principle at stake — yet we deliver in confidence and strength, knowing it is possible to be agreeable in disagreements. Our children know their parents are there for them; even though we may not live together, our responsibility and commitment to our family is strong. This strength is unquestionable and requires no external force to instruct us to behave this way. We have — on our own — chosen to accept our vast differences and embrace the positive aspects this contradiction provides.

Compromise

Compromise has been touched on in Chapter 1; however, when faced with powerless feelings that plague us day and night, and where court seems to be our option of last resort, it is here the ideology behind compromise is truly put to the test. The emotional upheaval that occurs when our children's well being is threatened by our differences, is when we need to put our theory into practice.

> A family of four children, ranging in ages from 16 to four, became yet another statistic in the long line of court battles. For the past four years, Christina had routinely had 11 of 14 nights with the children at her home. Terry decided he wanted to have more time with his children and pursued conversations for the routine to be altered. Christina, unwilling to budge, could not see any good reason for her children to spend more time with Dad; this was topped off with her dislike for their new stepmother.
>
> After months of no progress with Christina, Terry decided to begin the process through the family courts. Enter lawyers, counsellors, council for child, and psychologists. All these professionals were sent in one by one to talk with the children and parents behind closed doors to prepare the best case to present to a judge who would be the one to decide where the children would spend their time.
>
> Terry attempted to persuade the children with bribes of a bigger-and-better house and greater toys if they said they wanted to be with him. Christina took the motherly highroad and said, "Whatever the children want." Month after month, session after session, this family waited for an order to come from the court to say how it would be.
>
> About month ten of this ordeal, the 13-year-old decided to take matters into his own hands. Pleading with his mother, he wrapped it up in the only way he knew how. "In the spirit of Christmas, all I want is for you to decide to agree with Dad and put all this behind us." This child didn't ask for an iPod or the

latest game for his console. He didn't ask for anything materialistic, albeit we live in such a consumer-driven society. He just wanted his parents to stop fighting — not even be together — just end the stalemate.

By now there was more to lose — there was a principle at stake. Christina didn't feel she could back down or she would have set her own precedent for being bullied. Terry, on the other hand, felt that the more unreasonable Christina was, the stronger the reason for his fatherhood, hence his continued fighting.

In the end, 18 months after it all started, Terry got two extra nights with his children, and Christina begrudgingly put up with being alone for what was now five nights in the fourteen. No one won, and yet the entire family suffered. Terry has his children for extra nights, a hollow victory, when all involved know the reason they are there is because the court told them so. For Christina, she doesn't have the opportunity to graciously accept Mike's desire to spend more time with his children; instead, she feels her children have been taken from her.

> The principle you're fighting over is lost; your children usually hear an entirely different story.

The message being sent to the family was neither who has who when, nor was it an attempt to justify fairness and equitable fathering time. The point of Dad's wanting to spend more time with the family at the outset is lost by the time you get 18 months down the track. It's hidden in all the affidavits, meetings, and trials that attempt to justify why the routine ought to be changed and what benefits are stacked in whose favour.

Regardless of how it is wrapped up or what principle we are fighting over, your children usually hear an entirely different story.

The Alternative

There is an alternative. It is one for the courageous and those who have a genuine commitment to creating a family structure that places the welfare of the family before personal gain or attainment. *The Highest Good of All* — being our family. One of the most encouraging factors when embarking upon this route is that it only takes one person to hold this view and act upon it for it to work. It is entirely free of the Ex's power and control.

The Alternative Route may appear longer but this is false perception. A little practice walking this path and you can achieve in two weeks what would take two years through the courts. How can I say this? Living proof — frequently.

> The Highest Good of All — being our family.

To have an alternative route work, you must consider the fundamental reasons for walking this path first. If you are going to dip your toes in the water and hope this quickly resolves your conflicts, you will be greeted with disappointment. There is a cost with either path; however, through following the courts, many people who have been awarded their prize, regret the cost. The costs are recognised as being well beyond financial loss, emotional toll, and the relationship demise. Consider the full price and ask yourself if it is one you are willing to pay?

Collaborative Law

Such is the recognition of mass destruction that has occurred through traditional family courts, Collaborative Law has attempted to resolve these difficulties. Still unavailable in many countries around the world today, Collaborative Law is making progress towards creating workable and harmonious decisions through facilitation.

The critical element involved (as ironic as it sounds) is that both parties commit to not going to Court, nor will they threaten to. This is a major developmental step in our legal system. The lawyers who represent their clients are unable to litigate on their behalf should facilitation fail. At the very heart of this evolving law is trust. In recognition of the ongoing requirement for both parents to be involved in the healthy raising of their children, trust is given as the core value to be upheld.

As expected, there are definitions, rules, and structures placed upon this type of legal advancement to ensure all participants equally understand expectations. Originating in the United States of America, the United Kingdom has since trained 1,250 lawyers in Collaborative Law where it was launched in 2005. There is still a long way to go worldwide, but the celebration of each step towards enhanced alternatives helps to increase their presence and therefore, acceptability.

Moving Beyond Law

"We need not all agree, but if we disagree —
let us not be disagreeable in our disagreements."

While I am warmed by the intention of this facilitation structure, I believe that as parents in Complex Family environments, we can do so much more. Through two parents taking responsibility, we can powerfully lead by example as well-functioning team models with strong conflict resolution skills.

For this to work, you need to become clear on a key conflict constant; where there is no agreement, it means there are two people unable to currently see a solution. This does not imply that you are unwilling, although it does not exempt it either. If there is a disagreement, an attachment to an outcome, or an impasse, it is because two people are either unable, unwilling, or both — not just one of you. Forget about pointing fingers and laying blame; instead, you have to look at your own lack of willingness to put aside preferences, judgements, and best intentions, and ask yourselves what price are you willing to pay and why? The ultimate price being further parental dysfunction during your child's developmental years.

More often than not, the justifications flow thick and fast. I hear the same lines over and over. "My Ex is unreasonably difficult, so we have no choice but to use Court." Most Complex Family parents find it difficult; indeed, very few do not find it extremely difficult at times. Usually women feel they make all the compromises for the good of the children to keep it workable with the Ex. The peculiar thing is, if you speak with the fathers, they will tell you they make the all compromises. Proven with hundreds, if not thousands of couples, this works. Even asking the *luckiest couple*, either party will confess to feeling they are the peacekeeper.

Only two commitments are required to make this path work — both parties deciding it will. It may sound like a big ask since the ultimate life promise of 'together forever' has not worked, but take heart, this is considerably easier than the alternatives.

> We need not all agree, but if we disagree — let us not be disagreeable in our disagreements.

Changing Perspective

If both parties can commit to keeping family out of the courts, it closes the door on all future threats and intimidation. The common mindset, the belief that we only have two options, melts away and in its place comes a willingness to entertain possibilities so that we move from an *Either/Or* into an *And* thinking. The *either/or* focuses our attention on division, possible winning or losing, and carries a threatening tone. *And* is the opposite, it embraces while giving the opportunity for a solution to appear.

Likewise, following the traditional path of parenting structures, our attention is channelled towards the question of our choice in Parent-centric or Child-centric Parenting? Which would you choose? This is where parenting is focused on A) parents welfare and requirements are central, with welfare and well-being for the child considered; or B) child welfare and well-being, with consideration of parents, but ultimately about the child. This question begs an alternative option: Why choose? Why not both? Wisdom would choose *and*. This is where your parenting moves to the point where you embrace the unit as a whole, take your eyes off your way, and turn them to see our way.

To do this requires five principles:

1. All decisions are made *for the highest good of the family*.
2. We can and will resolve issues respectfully (face-to-face whenever possible).
3. Compromise — reaching a mutually acceptable agreement.
4. Trust and trustworthiness.
5. The past is history — use today to build tomorrow.

For the Highest Good of the Family:
This phrase targets the core principle for interaction and discussions with your Ex on the family; not themselves, you, nor the children — it is kept on the family. All suggestions and agreements move away from personal agendas, neither being *parent-centric* or *child-centric*, and become *family-centric* instead.

Solve it Respectfully:
Solution Thinking most certainly requires extra effort, means both parties keep focused on resolution, and avoid adopting a *my way or no way* stance. To do this, we choose not to look at our history and a discussion of shortcomings, but instead, ask the only meaningful question, How? Focus on solutions so that all obstacles become circumstances in need of attention, not viewed as hurdles unable to be cleared. It means to turn your attention away from all the reasons and excuses things cannot be done, and look towards answering *how they can be done* instead.

Keep away from distracting circumstances and wandering negative conversation. Keep it simple. Remember to pause and consider what you say. Before you become convinced of your perspective, consider it in reverse and be willing to hear the response. If you are unwilling to drive 30 km every day, twice a day, why would you expect your Ex to do it? If you hear a justification quickly follow, this is not focusing on solutions but rather bullying another into compromise. By this I mean statements such as, "He left, that's his issue" or "I work far longer hours, she's got time."

Throw away the convenience and delusion of using e-mail, phones, or text as this form of contact does not build communication. With issues where there is conflict or tension, only communicate face-to-face. It is well recognised that words convey only a fraction of our communication. The results from various studies place it as between seven and twelve percent. This means that there is a whopping 88–93 percent that is in the nonverbal delivery. Place the appropriate importance on solving these issues and prioritise your time to make sure you get face-to-face.

In a moment of weakness, your agreement may once or twice have an empty legal threat handed out, (intended for effect but totally unwilling to be acted on). While I strongly disagree with threats, I accept they happen. Avoiding them is your focus, so if a stalemate is reached, and a threat gets thrown in, or progress stalls and frustration mounts, take a deep breath and reconvene a week from now. Where there is a willingness, a way will be present.

> Where there is a willingness, a way will be present.

Compromise:
The constant objective of this Alternative Route is to work towards the *Highest Good of All*. In the case of Complex Families, this means children and parents equally. To have a constructive outcome is to have no causalities of war.

Throughout the discussions, if you begin to feel you are making all the compromises, ask yourself, "Compared to what?" If this is compared to my way, then possibly yes, and that's okay. If it is compared to the *Highest Good of All*, this is not compromise; it is upholding the very essence of great parenting. Occasionally, circumstantially, you may feel poorly done by with the best option being more in favour of your Ex's preferences than your own, and this can be challenging to reconcile, but when your commitment is to the Highest Good of All, it creates long-term health and unfathomable advantages, retaining the wealth of happiness inside your family.

Remember to keep personal integrity close. Hear your intentions honestly and be willing to change course when presented with alternatives to produce the Highest Good of All more simplistically or appropriately. To blur the focus will bring compromising circumstances to at least half the parenting equation; whereas upholding this core focus regardless, will allow free-flowing circumstances that enable you to accept unity within your diversity.

Trust and Trustworthy:
The absence of trust will see any alternative route become extremely difficult. Strategies such as 'hidden agendas', 'reveal only when asked', 'string them along', and so on, must all stop here. Trust goes hand-in-hand with respect. If you can respect your Ex as a parent, you can be agreeable while disagreeing. If you can trust yourself, and your Ex, to speak openly and respectfully, you will find solutions. All dialogue and information exchanged during the meetings need to be held in an appropriate sensitive manner, much as would be expected of two respectful adults.

Trust builds on trust. If you wait for proof of trustworthiness, or defend under the guise that trust needs to be earned, trust will always elude. Trust is given, not earned. If it is missing, give it. There are no levels of trust, it is what it is. Some people may prove more trustworthy, simply meaning they are able to handle the power that comes with it; therefore you be trustworthy with this power. Those unwilling to trust fully, trust not at all.

> Trust is given, not earned. If it is missing, give it.

Circumstantial disagreements with your Ex can point to inner conflicts at a deeper level than the obvious surface issues. As an example, there may be a trust issue where you feel a precedent for bullying or intimidation has been set, and you are therefore reluctant to trust. Perhaps, fear of being cut out of a child's world is breeding insecurity and paranoia. So many feelings are highlighted when circumstances change that it gives you a great opportunity for personal resolution and growth. So take time to consider the feelings that emerge when you talk with your Ex; this will help you to understand where your hesitations lie and perhaps you will begin to recognise that some may be more a matter of misperception than reality. In time, it may even open a doorway to discuss these with your Ex.

The Past is Over:
It is simple to say yet hard to do; but with some practice, placing your past behind you is a constructive life lesson regardless of your family structure. However, in this case, leave the relationship circumstances out of parenting. Regardless of the reasons or excuses for the marriage or partnership ending, these are all separate and outside the function of parenting that is ahead of you now. This is often more difficult for the Leavee to do than the Leaver. If the Leaver has moved on, and circumstantially life is appearing prosperous, the Leavee will find it challenging to remain free from the temptation to relive their feelings of injustice through sneered remarks, inflexible demands, or blame.

> Leave the relationship circumstances out of parenting.

As a Leaver, you need to be aware of this, and not speak or act to defend or justify your actions. Whatever the relationship challenges were, deal with what is in front of you now. Circumstances of geographical differences, financial insufficiencies, routine conflicts, creed preferences, and so on, all need to be kept to the here and now. The Leavee will need to find their own freedom from their hurting space, and as a Leaver, you are not the one to provide this.

The more we learn, the more we see it is very rare for the person who cuts, to also heal — in much the same way a surgeon cuts the body, one must leave the body to heal itself.

Ann and Frank

Ann and Frank have one child and live at opposite ends of their city. Their daughter goes to school close to Ann's home. Their current shared-care arrangements mean Frank drives across town many times a week through busy traffic, on top of tight schedules of work and personal commitments. Since Ann is unwilling to participate by being a taxi, Frank has had enough and wants to change schools and routines for his ease and the child's benefit.

Although in initial discussions Ann conceded it would possibly suit better to change the current routine, she was unwilling to do so. Frank, overwhelmed with frustration, resorted to Court.

Why? Why would Ann acknowledge it would be better and yet still refuse to agree to a change? Through the majority of practice inside our current legal framework, this question begs for an answer, and is tragically ignored. The dependency upon circumstances to prove our points negates taking the time to understand the beliefs that cause such illogical behaviour in the first place. If we could deal with this belief, the following two years of court battles, sleepless nights, thousands of dollars, and damage to the family's well-being may have been spared.

Ann's irrational unwillingness stemmed from a deep hurt and distrust of Frank. She believed Frank possessed ulterior motives and was gradually taking time away from her, and with this, her ability to be mother to her daughter. Frank, on the other hand, was not attempting to take mother out of the loop, but instead believed he could easily provide what Ann was comparatively struggling to do. While Frank held an equally rigid perspective of what he believed was in the best interest of the child, there remained division, hostility, and dysfunction that was unable to be bridged.

After 20 months, and although the court ruled in favour of Frank's preferences backed up with the screeds of opinions and facts, this did little to foster a healthy relationship between the parents.

Ann continues to struggle with her feelings of inferiority that were heightened through the demise of the marriage and her subsequent paranoia. With her role as mother and confidence undermined, her toxic attitudes towards Frank permeate their daughter's home with confusion, sadness, and inferiority creating a self-defeating cycle.

Chapter 7 — Legal Matters

Frank's focus on his belief of 'best interest for his daughter', wedges the gap between father, mother, and daughter wider than before. He won the battle — he travels less, timetables ease, money is saved, increased consistent social interactions for his daughter's playmates, more structured academic schooling, and greater extracurricular activities — so when all is considered, it seems like he's a winner.

However, from this point forward, Ann feels threatened by Frank in all conversations involving her child or parental responsibilities. She is guarded, suspicious, and the simplest of requests is met with hostility and abruptness. As a result, the parenting of this child is carried out in a strict, formal, and rigid framework with parents still struggling to respect one another.

The circumstances, routines, and difference of opinion in schooling will all be forgotten in adult years, but the disharmony between Mum and Dad will live in her memory forever.

> The differences ... will all be forgotten in adult years, but the disharmony between Mum and Dad will live in her memory forever.

The Alternative for Ann and Frank:

Ann and Frank have a routine that needs to be altered. Having discussed the options, neither one is happy to concede at this point about the best path forward.

Both Ann and Frank are strong believers in resolving the issue. They decide to go away without resolution and meet again next week when both parties will offer suggestions.

Next meeting, suggestions are made by both Ann and Frank. Advantages and disadvantages are equally discussed, with preferences being understood. The atmosphere is comparable to that of a familiar business meeting where there is respect, shared time of talking and listening, and a focus on keeping to the points in question. At the end of the meeting, both Ann and Frank feel frustrated. There has been no progress and no resolution.

Continuing, both Ann and Frank schedule the next meeting. Again, they discuss their options and achieve no further resolution. This routine is repeated a few more times, with each step having options discarded, discussed, and some placed in 'possibility' but there is still no resolution.

As the weeks pass, they begin to ask themselves some key questions: How? Why is this so hard? What am I missing? What is the compromise?

As commitment towards resolution grows, the level of resistance diminishes; as a natural consequence, a solution is found.

The last meeting is opened with a commitment, "We do not get up from this table until we come to a solution." Today it clicks. They have been back and forth enough times now for commonsense to prevail; and now there is not another option. This change forces both people to look at solutions only. How? While removing all periphery information, their focus is on the solution. Before the end of the meeting, an agreement is met. Are they as a family happy with it? Satisfied. Do they feel they have had to compromise? Partially, indeed they needed to, but compromising on circumstances only since the true essence of the family's Highest Good of All has been upheld.

Ongoing Results

The result from this form of conflict resolution sees Mum still warmly welcomed at the door, and invited in for a cup of coffee, while Dad is comfortable enough to spontaneously pop in when dropping something off. There is no remainder of ill-feeling when the focus is kept on the family unit expanded and full.

The cynic suggests the tougher person holds out longer and gets their way. In experience, toughness is irrelevant. When the Alternative Route is executed with respect and follows the same method as that of set expectations, where there is a willingness to listen, and both have fair and equal say, it works. Sure, there may be some occasions where one feels hard-done-by, but no more so than in most negotiations. They may trade — I'll let you have this if you let me have that — that's okay. That is real. That is how disagreements are resolved.

I have heard people say they cannot be bothered with all the meetings, week after week. I point out that regardless of which path you choose, there will still be many meetings, and often more if taking the legal route — only then it will be disguised by being spread out over the next two years of destructive patterns.

Experience shows that following the path of multiple meetings, means an hour or so catching up every few months sorts the rest out. Often, a series of meetings with strong differences in opinion, typically happens when major circumstantial changes occur. Such as a new stepparent, geographical relocation, or if intervention action is needed. Otherwise, flexibility within routines, arrangements of holidays, and other normal day-to-day happenings are all treated with ease because the trust and inner sense of security is not under threat. This is the time when the convenience of e-mail or text messages is best used.

When the relationship is free from nasty 'out of control' feelings, there are no knots in your stomach that spontaneously happen each time discussions about events and children take place. Your children are both welcomed and free to discuss options and opinions with parents in either home, without fear of putting their foot in something. If you are inadvertently called the other parent's name, it's a nonevent because there is no resentment, anger, or brewing hostility that tugs at you, nor a sudden dart that gets thrown at an innocent child.

For the best interest of your children, keep the courts out of the relationship. Parents, let's begin focusing on the value of your homes' diversities and differences. Be living examples for your children to take the goodness from each place as they build their own foundation for adulthood, and come to believe they too can resolve conflicts as and when they occur.

> Keep the courts out of the relationship ... focus on the value of your homes' diversities and differences.

The Courts

Embarked upon as the last resort, believing all else has failed, this is the point when parents come to irreconcilable differences — the same point that led to the relationship ending. Life is full of repetitious cycles; each one holding the gift to gain wisdom from hindsight; yet sadly, this is normally ignored. It's the old pebble versus the boulder scenario; life always throws pebbles, then stones, then rocks, and then boulders, until eventually the whole mountainside comes down on us. How severe do we want the lessons to be? It depends on whether the pebble does it or if we hold off until the whole mountainside comes down, before paying attention. Throughout the years of post-marriage living, the opportunity to learn from history constantly invites us to make changes now. Our courts are crowded because this learning is not taking place, largely because we are still dominated by our interpretation of *right*.

> Our courts are crowded ... largely because we are still dominated by our interpretation of right.

If you have been taken to court by your Ex, although simplistic to revert to blame, it is not entirely honest for you to avoid it that easily. It is wise to consider your actions and your part in the relationship communication that has led you to this point.

If you decide to embark upon the path of using Court assistance to have more of what you want from your Ex, consider the price, and ask, "Am I willing to pay fully?" Although clearly I am not an advocate for taking this form of action, I acknowledge the well-trodden traditional path is still an alternative. As such, I have outlined some points to help during the process of court:

1. **Avoid being critical.**
   Avoid being critical of your Ex as a person or as a parent. To err is human, and parenting brings out the most human in us all. I know great parents, excellent parents, yet I too could write a list of their shortcomings that would make them feel inferior and insignificant in their parenting within minutes — as they could do for me. Focusing

on areas of weakness destroys, and in so doing, diminishes yourself in the process.

2. **Focus on function.**

   What particular aspects of the parenting job are you good at and what part are they good at? Where are your strengths, and what are their strengths?

   Some parents are better weekday parents while others are better weekend ones. I'm not suggesting that ought to be the way courts decide, but there is nothing wrong with acknowledging our strengths in routines, schedules, and academic discipline vs. those of us who love goofing off and playing together, or those who get lost in creative passions and lose all track of time.

   If you have to write affidavits, keep them positive. Remove the war zone, the comparisons, the excuses, and only use words and statements helpful to building a Parenting Team. If you cannot do this, or are greatly challenged when doing it, this reflects the amount of judgement you continue to hold. Remember, while you are carrying relationship baggage, your children are wearing it.

3. **Focus on principles.**

   Circumstantial evidence is seductive, exhausting, and time-consuming. Your attention is drawn to what is or is not happening rather than the intention or principle behind it. It is division, not multiplication. Principles multiply. As an example; a principle helpful to your child's development is that of stability and consistency. For your children to experience this builds reliability, trust, and strength that helps them to feel safe, gain confidence, and to start using their initiative. The effects of the principle ripples through your child's perspective on the world.

   If you focus on principles, clarity arrives while maintaining both parent's dignity, and simply exposing what is lacking. Giving examples of how you create this within your family dynamic, you reinforce the message rather than demean or demote your Ex. When you focus on principles, it may even open the door for this to become a learning experience for your Ex to finally understand something previously missed. Likewise, the reverse is true, it could also open your eyes to a different way a principle is being expressed in an alternative environment.

From this angle, the legal experience can be attended to with a more rare intention for creation rather than normal destruction.

4. **Willingness to Let Go.**
Sometimes the willingness to simply let it all go is all it takes; at other times it will be tested. What are you fighting over? Often your lack of trust in life being kind forces you to hold onto what you currently have in the belief that it is your right to retain it. There comes a point in life where letting go is more rewarding than holding on tightly although it may bring short-term jitters; much like letting go of the rope when swinging from a branch out over water — but the experiences can bring greater freedom than you otherwise dared to dream.

> Diminishing your Ex's parenthood is to diminish your own.

If you do gain what you set out to achieve, be aware of the fallout with the Ex and the ongoing ramifications this will have to the Parenting Team.

If you lost as a result of your court experience, it is time to consider the ongoing hostility and the emotions you feel each time such a loss is talked about or denied the opportunity to be talked about. In these small moments, you are wise to consider taking the time to resolve your inner conflicts and feelings of anger, resentment, or bitterness.

"To diminish someone is to diminish oneself."

Diminishing your Ex's parenthood is to diminish your own. Choose wisely.

Chapter Eight
Money Matters

How to practically manage the finances.

Money

The aspect of *money* I am talking about within these pages has little to do with common tactics heard from the traditional financial planning consultants, or those who wish to train our thinking towards the prosperity mindset. Increasingly, we are lead to believe we need to look out for ourselves, with financial gain being the path to personal success and happiness. There is no argument that money has become a significant controlling force; ironically, as an object itself, it has become nearly valueless. It is only the power we collectively give money that enables it to become one of the most out-of-control-forces on our planet today.

Not to rule out the significance money has in our lives, the objective here is to keep it in perspective. I'm not saying we ought to walk away from all material possessions and allow ourselves to be faced with financial wrack and ruin while our Ex prospers, but rather to observe where we place our priorities. It is to recognise that money will control the areas of our lives we either consciously or unconsciously decide to surrender to its power.

For those of us who have been through separation or divorce, we can be sorely tempted to spend much of our energy arguing over or protecting what we believe to be ours. During this process, we blindly rob ourselves of the ultimate objective; this being the security, comfort, quality, and peace we believe we will gain through acquiring the prosperity. It is not uncommon to see couples fighting over their divorce settlement for years in hope of maintaining their share; meanwhile, the dwindling resources are consumed in the ever-increasing legal bills. Pointless as it seems, a principle is often at stake; that is to say, to stop the other getting more than deserved — and here begins the senselessness.

If we bring children into this world, we have a moral responsibility to provide for their welfare and well-being. Financially is but one aspect of this provision; it is not the whole. To continue discord between mother and father due to disagreements over property ownership, income rights, or any other form of monetary entitlement, highlights a misalignment of priorities regarding the children's welfare and well-being.

"Money makes a great servant — but a terrible master!"

We are wise to consider where wealth resides. Contrary to popular financial educators who challenge us to believe money makes the world turn, this perspective only contains a fraction of the picture. It is the importance we place on money which causes us to be in the spin; our world turns effortlessly. The very essence of what keeps our world turning is free. The air we breathe is free regardless of how much money we have in our bank accounts. The life-giving energy from our sun is free. The warmth felt from a human hug, the joy in an exchange of smiles, the beauty of innocence found within a newborn, the sounds of birds singing, the lapping of waves on a beach; these are all free. The world is full of wonder that has nothing to do with money. If we believe the delusion that money is required to make the world go round, we miss the very essence of living, and in turn, we rip ourselves and our children away from natural birthright.

When major discrepancies occur in lifestyles, financial sustenance, and materialistic possessions in our separate homes, we begin to understand the difference between a house and a home. Our homes may be smaller but they can have more heart. Our cars may be cheaper, but come with less paranoia. Our toys may be older and yet equally loved and valued. Our holidays may be camping, but continue to foster our adventurous nature. Our festivities may be less expensive, yet they can create more favourable memories.

Leaver and Leavee

In our society where divorce law is based on the concept of *No Fault*, we can easily shun responsibility. The Leaver or Leavee position is not taken into account; while in some cases this is understandable, there are those who run from responsibility and it becomes easy for it all to seem a little unfair. Having said this, not much about divorced life is governed by fairness and equality, so it is more advantageous if we turn our attention toward the future and recognise and accept that it is normal to undergo significant changes in lifestyle with a divorce. The variations of financial circumstances are as vast as we are unique, and hence so are our financial situations; however, there are some common aspects we share.

To help keep this easy to understand, we develop from our Leaver and Leavee model, and divide the financial aspects into: *Income and Possessions*. Typically speaking, you attempt to hold on to what you believe is yours from the past (possessions), while you attempt to gain security for your unknown futures (incomes). It is easy to see that your past possessions can be emotionally difficult to divide; your present situations can sometimes be challenging to accept; and yet increasingly, your future feels as though it will be the result of all you decide now.

Income

Let's take a look at your future *Income* because this helps to dictate how strong your attachment to what you currently have is likely to be, and the levels of fear you may feel. If you have large portions of future income, relative to your expenses, you will feel okay about your financial position regardless of who made the decision for the relationship to end. If you do not have an income, or a very reduced one when compared to what you have been living with, this will be an uncomfortable time.

So, while we still have the Leaver and Leavee roles, in a financial sense this difference relates to the emotions experienced by either party, rather than to the physical financial difference.

Beyond this first delineation of Leaver and Leavee, inside *income* we have the following two considering factors:

- Employment – Income Earners and Non-Earners
- Ongoing Money Exchange – Payer and Payee

Employment issues can be significant with some parting parents, especially the at-home parent. For others it is not so troublesome if both parents are working and have equal childcare investment. However, in the case where we have those who are earning and those who are not earning, this can indeed become a rather tense topic of debate. To ensure we do not devalue the importance of being an at-home parent, we will purely look at the factor of money and its realistic controlling influence over decisions ahead, so we have those in Non-Paid Employment and those in Paid Employment. A point worth considering here is that normally the decision to be an-home parent is a sacrifice agreed upon between the couple, dictated by the ages of their children, life-style preferences, and cultural or personal beliefs — all of which provide further complexities to be overcome.

> Money makes a great servant — but a terrible master!

Non-Paid Employment

Leavee: For the Leavee as an at-home parent, this threatened change can be devastating. If you have been habitually reliant upon financial sustenance from your spouse, the loss of that income comes as a shock. Abruptly, your world comes to a halt as you believe the very core of your survival is now under threat. Your pain and anger are so intense that the feelings of betrayal, questioning, and confusion can overtake you and cause you to forget your own sense of personal responsibility in providing for your life.

This is not to say that it is unwise to be an at-home parent (not in paid employment) and to trust in the provision of financial support from our spouse — as the benefits to your children can be considerable. What I want to say is the trade agreement you entered into with your spouse is up for review — regrettable as this may seem. Indeed, your survival may not be under threat at all, only the level of comfort to which you have become accustomed is subject to change. However, it is fair to say, this does not alter the intensity of the emotions you feel. The time to begin to reconsider your options, choices, and beliefs regarding personal responsibility for your own financial sustenance has arrived.

> *Consider your beliefs for your own financial sustenance, and those you are responsible for.*

Leaver: The Leaver who is an at-home parent has usually felt an intense dissatisfaction with their situation that far outweighs any limitations that might be created by restricted finances. This is often the drive for those involved in cases of breaking free from emotional or physical abuse. Thankfully, in the western world where we have a welfare system, basic survival can be provided for until further earning opportunities are found. While welfare is often abused, the intention to provide for parents in this situation proves beneficial for the parent, children, and our society at large. Those in this scenario are often courageous people who genuinely seek a better life for themselves and their children in much the same way pioneers travelled to foreign lands in search of a better lifestyle. This is the recognition of short-term discomfort outweighed by long-term attainment of prosperity, rather than being held captive by financial considerations.

Sometimes the Leaver is not breaking free of abuse, but instead seeking greener pastures. Boredom, control, or unrest pushes them to search for a sense of meaning for life outside of their mundane day-to-day routines; they also hope to attain the final prize of prosperity to validate their choices. While some parents are the exception to the rule, this Leaver is usually driven by a belief in the betterment of their children's life and character, rather than by selfish motives alone. This is however a time for you to recognise your responsibilities and commitments, and review appropriate ways to fulfil these going forward.

Paid Employment

Leavee: If the Leavee has been the one with paid employment, providing for the family is nothing new. However, the levels of disillusionment felt by those who have steadily provided for their family, perhaps for decades, in an apparent self-sacrificing manner are abruptly awakened when they discover they are without a spouse to fulfil the initial trade.

The Leaver is content to opt for uncertain financial stability in exchange for the adventures of self-discovery or self-indulgence once beyond marriage; this action is embarked upon regardless of the Leavee's personal wishes. This Leavee tends to protect and justify their fight for their portion of wealth with their belief in the personal sacrifices they made to acquire it. Although the trade was acceptable at the time, in hindsight with it no longer fully supported, they beg for reconsideration of fair value.

> Recognise where your sense of personal value originates.

The opportunity for the Leavee to recognise where this sense of personal value originates is touched in this moment, although normally they would remain unaware of their inner motivating force. This Leavee gravitates towards rather irrational, unfair, and scathing attitudes and behaviour towards their Ex, largely due to their own beliefs of fairness, trading, scarcity, and sacrifice. This is the time for reconsideration of responsibilities and commitments, and a review of motives, intentions, and sense of purpose.

Leaver: For the Leaver who is the financial provider, their sense of responsibility towards their family is in question. As they struggle with the emotional pendulum that swings between guilt and relief that their choice has brought, they are challenged to know what is fair and reasonable in a financial sense.

Due to feelings of relief, they can become blind to the levels of resistance their Ex is feeling. As they are torn to balance prior commitments with new lifestyle opportunities, they often appear insensitive in the eyes of the judgemental onlooker. At times, they may find isolation within the workforce where personal opinions relating to their marital choices are made public. Contempt, guilt, shame, hope, relief, fun, and an exciting exploration of life all become part of the cocktail of emotions they feel.

Although they have accepted the division of property and possessions to be carried out, the other half of this equation is the ongoing income stream. The Leaver may have strong opinions on this; although they may not be spoken, this could well be the masked feelings that fuel their attitudes and contempt in coming discussions. This is the time for the Leaver to consider how to depart while continuing to provide sustainable essentials until independence is achieved — and thus reduce the Leavee's fear of threatened survival that may ravage future communication.

> Consider how to depart while providing sustainable essentials until independence is achieved.

Leavee and Leaver: When both Leaver and Leavee are earning, this scenario has the possibility to produce an easy resolution. This is, of course, unless the Leavee's income is made significantly less due to parental responsibilities; then the situation becomes much like that of the non-employed at-home parent. A cautionary note here: in the case where both Leaver and Leavee are earning, and where legal council is employed to maintain one's share, sometimes the legals attain the highest portion of the wealth. Again, for two earning adults, their focus tends to be on possessions, and a belief that their earnings provide an established basis for sustainable lifestyles going forward — albeit they maybe different.

Ongoing Money Exchange

By understanding a little of the thoughts and feelings experienced by the various employment and earning personalities, we are ready to look at what the considerations are when income arrangements need to be met. Within the financial agreements you enter into, there is a Payer and a Payee.

The Payer / Payee looks at the future as either an income or expense that is usually closely linked to the amount of time your children spend in either home. There are various calculations that attempt to satisfy particular circumstances: the threshold of numbers of nights in a fortnight, the capping of salary, inclusion of more children resulting from a new relationship, and the difference in earnings — all sorts of factors that effect what is believed to be a reasonable amount of money to be exchanged. Equally so, there are all sorts of tactics undertaken by those who want to avoid paying, followed by those who choose for government intervention, to avoid or prevent further disputes.

Our objectives are to look beyond the accepted norm for our particular country, county, or state, and start to focus on how to enhance the relationship amongst the family as a whole, and keep money in perspective — as our servant, not our master.

Let's look at the story of Sam and Nina:

> Sam has significant financial means through his smart business practices and hard work. Nina was an at-home mother who diligently invested her time and energy into their children for some 10 years before the end of the marriage. The children lived in a routine of 9 nights of 14 with Nina and the balance with Sam. Sam and Nina decided to follow the accepted normal

payments via the state laws. The arrangement was made, and the money continued to be paid for the next few years.

Meanwhile, Sam created a new life. Enter Stepmother, and not long after, Sam's third child. This called for a review of the existing financial arrangement between Sam and Nina even though Nina had nothing to do with Sam's ongoing lifestyle choices. The costs of raising the two older children were not diminished; however, Sam announced he would be reducing the amount he is paying Nina to support their two children.

It is not surprising that Nina is a little miffed; nor is it surprising Sam wants to reduce the amount as he has another mouth to feed and further family to support.

This example is repeated a thousand-fold in Complex Families worldwide. There are ongoing ramifications for our separate lives, even though we believe we have moved on from the divorce. It may not be through an example as cited above, it could be the Payer loses their job and this affects the ongoing money to be paid to the Payee. The Payee may gain a promotion and must let the Payer know so they can alter the amount being paid. The varieties of circumstances are endless; and so are the arguments that follow.

Payer: Regardless of how or why, the Payer is the one with the greater portion of income. Most aspects of regulations surrounding the calculations fall short of assessing wealth; instead, they focus on income differences and ongoing obligations to support children. This is inclusive of children born after the divorce.

Working with many Payers over the years, a frequent cry from them is the double blow: *Pay but No Play*. It erks Payers to pay from their hard-earned cash, especially as they are without the pleasure of their children for the majority of the time. Of course, this is not always the case, as there may be a significant imbalance of earnings; however, in the vast majority of cases the *Pay but No Play* is accurate. It is usual whilst we are

> Pay but No Play.

away from our children, we feel a genuine wanting to be closer, so it exacerbates the Payer's pain of paying an Ex who has the blessing of being with those they're missing.

Payee: Payee's on the other hand, are usually oblivious to the emotional feelings the Payer is experiencing; given expenses of raising children in our modern society, they frequently want more. Often this load of parenting with limited resources is so significant it brings a level of compromise to our possible earning opportunities — especially when solo parenting. The ramifications of agreements made many years earlier suddenly appear as a ball and chain which we struggle against.

> The ramifications of agreements made many years earlier suddenly appear as a ball and chain which we struggle against.

This obvious tension between Payer and Payee festers and is often fueled by outside influences such as new partners or extended family. With previous agreements, lifestyles, obligations, and all prior communication now in tatters, how do we deal with these challenges and find a reasonable resolution? Before answering this in detail, let's look at the other side of the financial equation — Possessions.

Possessions

Possessions for this purpose is what we currently have as personal and household effects, property, cash, cars, and all other items of monetary worth, regardless of the structure of ownership. Although structures may determine ease of access, this is covered in Chapter 7 – Legal Matters.

Significant levels of snatch and grab occur when:

1. We believe what we currently have is as good as it gets; or
2. If the price we paid to get what we have is higher than the pleasure of attaining it.

Point 2 is normal when most who work for a wage don't enjoy what they do and only make enough to get by. The enjoyment derived from fulfiling work evades them; therefore, their primary attention is on the accumulation of possessions to convince themselves of the value of their day-to-day boredom. Through the division of property, an inner fear is ignited; this makes them clutch at things with the fear that life will be worse without those possessions.

Different Motivations

The differences in motivation to hold on to property or possessions can be stark. It can be likened to buying art — some people buy a piece of art because they are enamoured of it and it deeply moves them. Others buy art because it serves their investment portfolio well, and have little regard for their personal feelings about it. Another may buy art because it increases their belief in their sense of self-importance and societal standing — and so it is with the variety of motivations when discussing possessions and who gets what going forward.

> Conflict can occur if the price you paid to get what you have is higher than the pleasure of attaining it.

You may value your home highly; your Ex may not. Not because of its financial worth but because you are attached to the security it provides; it may be the emotional pulls, the little things such your children's heights carefully marked on the kitchen door which cannot be replaced. Perhaps it's the many years of toil poured into the landscaping, or the convenience of the grounds for the pets that have become an integral part of the family. Being blind to or invalidating the emotional reasons normally fools us into discounting the underlying current of discord, and forces the Ex to become difficult. If one takes the time to discover the emotive reasons driving the apparent irrational behaviour, it usually provides a key to finding resolution.

Mine, Yours, or the Children's

It is challenging to imagine the possibilities ahead when beginning to separate. The methods are many. Couples have walked around the house placing coloured dots on all items they want, if two on one item, they negotiate. Some decide to leave everything as is, except personal items such as clothes and toothbrush, and move out to start fresh. Others have lists drawn up, detailing the contents down to the potato peeler, evenly splitting based on monetary value; others use sentimental value division; sometimes couples lose items during their fits of rage, so it diminishes those items they worry themselves over; still others pack for the Leaver with the permitted contents being left on the front lawn. All in all, the method is the easy part; however our focus really must be on the considerations for the children.

The children's home is changing. Although the physical environment is secondary to their emotional well-being, it is not to be handled without great thought. The children are innocent; therefore, keep it this way in their physical world too. They already need to come to terms with their parents living in two houses, so if possible, it is advisable to keep one home consistent. This way, the children's environment is constant and all other financial arrangements can remain in the parents' domain and not involve the children in the resultant discussion or emotional turmoil.

The most important factor here is to keep all issues concerning material possessions as matters of less importance than the relationship with the Ex and with the children themselves. If you show more care and passion about keeping your things, than caring for your children, or respect for their other parent, you need to revisit your priorities. The manner in which you discuss or divide will be the defining characteristic of this, rather than the parent who gains more, equal, or less of the possessions. Therefore, it is important to come to an arrangement that works for the family as a whole, not just a single parent.

> Keep all issues concerning material possessions as matters of less importance than the relationships.

Working It Out

Attachment

There is a core principle that is pivotal to all areas of our life and allows us to achieve our desired levels of quality and peace. Somehow, within the context of finances we seem to find it the most challenging to put into practice. The core principle, the ignorance of which has proved to cause more heartache and chaos inside Complex Families than most is Attachment. What do I mean by Attachment? The term describes the victimised state well. It is where we see ourselves enlarged because of our financial gain. It is the belief that we have added to our life through the attainment of possessions or property, and have thereby become more valuable. In the rawest terms, it is when we believe our financial value equals our personal value.

> Financial attachment is where we see ourselves enlarged because of our financial gain.

Inside our society, which has become distorted by its view of financial wealth, it is normal to believe we are what we own. It is also normal to calculate and speak about Personal Net Worth. These indicators give people a false sense of accomplishment; this is often highlighted as false when calamity strikes in another area of life. Perhaps, when their love life or physical health is affected, they suddenly realise the hollowness of their quest for peace through financial gain. However, holding this entrenched belief, they feel threatened when their financial status changes, and as in the case of many divorce scenarios, it greatly diminishes. This is the reason money has become the source of large legal battles and broken family relationships worldwide, including those in and out of the Complex Family environment.

There are no easy definitions for what is deemed fair and what is not; hence the amount of law that exists to cover as many eventualities as possible. However, release of attachment to one's sense of self-worth being derived from their financial statement will help to place money in its proper place — as servant, not master. It places the family, albeit changed in structure, as top priority. The relationship between all involved is enhanced when financial aspects do not dictate the outcome of the whole but rather are dealt with as a supporting mechanism for the family.

"Sure," I hear the cynic say. "It's much easier to forget the pain when I'm sipping the pina-colada my Ex's extra money has bought." This is momentarily true; unquestionably, it is the reason many people have indulged in this illusion. The question of attachment, however, is not one of *Can I have?* but rather *Can I handle it when I do not have?* This is where we discover how much attachment we hold towards our personal value being derived from our material possessions.

Entitlement

Right now you may be saying, "But I'm entitled to ..." and in the view of those surrounding you, you may have this confirmed, even enhanced. Entitlement highlights the surrounding circumstances of your unique situation. Of course, there may be great merit in why you hold the belief in your entitlement — after all, you may have earned it or made great sacrifices for it. Where both departing individuals agree on this, the matters are more easily solved and the redistribution of wealth is exercised in a relatively calm manner. However, to provide assistance where there is disagreement, is the purpose of this chapter.

> The greatest wealth we can give our children is parents who lead by example in a healthy relationship.

Entitlement. What does it mean? It is the right to something. The belief one is owed or deserving. It is a level of expectation, and here we touch on the source of our demise society-wide — *individual rights at the cost of the sustainable collective*. If we focus our attention solely on individual entitlement, we may well cost our family's sustainability. As parents inside the Complex Family, the greatest wealth we can give our children is parents who lead by example in a healthy functioning relationship. This is to say, we place our family's well-being as more important than financial attainment — especially when it leaves the child's other parent greatly diminished. It also places personal responsibility onto both parents to look fully at what is reasonable, without turning to nasty tactics in an attempt to selfishly gain more.

> I was an at-home-mother with preschool children, almost entirely dependent upon the support of my husband's income. Like most, we were unable to afford two households, and therefore significant change was upon us at the time of separation.
>
> Luck has not been the reason our relationship is free from financial hassles, nor has it been through an abundance of money — at times, the exact opposite was the case. It has only been through a continued focus on choosing priorities and recognising personal attachment and entitlement.
>
> On more than one occasion, I have found it difficult to celebrate in the financial successes my Ex has acquired since moving on from our marriage; the comparative wealth has seemed unfair. I have felt the pinch my choice in priorities has brought as I was forced to sacrifice excellence in income while choosing to raise children. His choice of profession produces lucrative earnings as an accepted byproduct of hard work; he reaps the rewards of the earlier years where my earnings supported the majority of our joint lifestyle.
>
> This perceived injustice could be consuming as I watched his wife living the life we had previously dreamt of together. I have avoided slumping into this trap through my desire to see my life as my responsibility.
>
> I could state the facts, and it would appear compelling for some external force to cast judgement, and demand appropriate money be paid. He could state his facts and have the sum reduced appropriately. Neither option is going to bring either of us our ultimate desire: the sense of security, comfort, quality, and peace promised by financial attainment;

neither would those options encourage our Parenting Team to reach the levels of harmony and support we share for our children today.

Beliefs

When we are in relationships, beliefs and attitudes evolve; they quietly and subtly bend the arm of circumstance and draw towards us what we focus on. Unknown to either ourselves or our partners, we create expectations, position trade-agreements, and accept life-altering consequences without discussion. We are usually entirely free from recognising these trades exist; we live in ignorance until circumstantial changes reveal them, and our raw emotions illuminate their existence.

> In my mind, having children with my Ex meant that for a couple of decades I didn't need to work another day in full-time paid employment — unless I wanted to. This was a powerful point he didn't understand. Not because I didn't tell him, but rather because I hadn't realised the extent of my belief until I was forced to consider my work options. I also believed it was his duty to financially provide, following a very traditional, well-established (if rather outdated) pattern in our Western culture. Our lifestyle was dependent upon his good fortune; I did all I could to free him from all domestic responsibilities. Realising the limitations of our earning capacity when we were in our 20s, I juggled in-home-paid-work with three pre-school children. This busyness masked the extent of my belief that my financial welfare was reliant upon him.
>
> During the separation process, I began scrutinising my beliefs. First, I realised my expectations and dreams of cliff-top properties, boats, and overseas holidays were fantasized about due to his continued diligent hard work. In this dream world, I didn't feature as one who would be capable to provide such luxuries for myself or my children. Since my sole focus was as an at-home-mother, I avoided the need to confront my lack of self-belief, so it went unnoticed.
>
> The second realisation was I valued myself by the acquisition of our possessions and lifestyle that produced a short-term feeling of

satisfaction and accomplishment, as I congratulated myself for our family's achievements. This, of course, was followed with an insatiable appetite for more.

As I struggled to accept the ruthlessness of my own delusion, I began to more thoughtfully choose my priorities. Instead of acting out my habitual trade agreements, I had to allow the past to be history, and accept responsibility for my own life and situation. If I truly believed I could not provide monetary value to my children's life, I would face this. Still believing that I needed someone else to financially support me, I dared to confront this. It was only through my willingness to get real, that I gained the security, comfort, quality, and peace that I had initially sought through my Ex's money.

As a result, he has gained the freedom to give me as much, or as little, money as he chooses.

Our beliefs dictate our choices that become our actions. It is through the recognition of our beliefs that we are able to start evaluating our priorities and begin to determine if we are compromising or upholding what is true for us. Through an understanding of our expectations and cultural standards, we start to turn our attention away from those things which no longer work for our family, and focus instead on those choices that will benefit us all. Therefore, it is through releasing attachment and understanding where our sense of entitlement resides that we are able to establish a healthy Complex Family relationship that extends beyond the pressures of monetary circumstances.

> Our beliefs dictate our choices that cause our actions.

How To Move Forward

Below are the steps to follow to work out the financial arrangements. This being said, regardless how clever the strategies I suggest are, tension will arise in the relationship until you, as an individual, have an understanding of the core principles: Attachment and entitlement, followed by a strong recognition that your beliefs about this are what drive you. This is part of the journey ahead as you put the following strategies into practice.

From this point, a line is drawn; consider what you brought into the relationship, all acquisitions since, and the current agreements in place. For some, this is very complex with pre-nuptials, trusts, and other legal entities that permit access or ownership. For most of us, however, this is rather simplistic; regardless, the dividing line is focused on *past* and *future* or Possession and Payments. Here is a three-step process to make this easier to work though:

Step 1 – First Few Months

The practical considerations of bills to be met, payments made and daily living provided for, are unquestionably important. It is best to continue the financial status quo for a short time — a period of between 4–8 weeks. Within this time, agreements can be made without hasty or rash decisions to cause further complications and unnecessary upheaval for the children. Sometimes longer is needed, but usually couples find that a couple of months is long enough to begin the move towards financial separation. Simple yet time-consuming tasks need to be carried out: open new bank accounts, change power bills, phone accounts, close credit cards, and so on. As much as we hear the horror stories, do this *in best faith* and avoid suddenly stripping bank accounts bare to avoid the other party getting the money; this does little to constructively work on agreements that need to be reached. Keep it reasonable, understand that irrational behaviour comes from hurting people, and thus avoid setting the stage for absurd reactions to follow.

> Continue the financial status quo for a short time ... do this in best faith.

Step 2 – Staging the Process

While it is advisable to get the financials (property and possessions) sorted sooner rather than later, as part of this process it can be wise to agree on staged plans. For those who find it excessively challenging to come to an agreement, it is easier to gain consensus for a shorter period of time on significant life-altering decisions that can be too overwhelming, especially when emotions are so heightened; so do it in bite-size pieces. If you can agree on a solution that eases you into separation, it helps the agreement to come as you have diminished the tone of threats or fear.

> It is easier to gain consensus for a shorter period of time ... so do it in bite-size pieces.

The idea is to have a few stages — Stage I: now; Stage II at 12 months; and Stage III at 24 months. The first 12 months fly past very quickly, and given the lifelong commitment most people make, it is not unreasonable to consider a staged process of unbundling your lives where genuine support is provided for a predefined period. The assumption that all attitudes of goodness will diminish in time is often what drives an inner compulsion to get things sorted quickly. However, as separation is usually an emotionally complicated time, the staged approach allows for growing financial independence to be achieved while sustaining the *best faith* intention to place the power in ongoing personal choices.

The overall objective of the staged approach is two-fold: first, to minimise the resistance to an agreement due to the level of fear caused by uncertainty; second, to keep communications reasonable as you unbundle your lives. A fairly typical scenario is:

> Sally is an at-home-mum who returns to the workforce. Ray, her Ex-husband is prepared to assist a little more in the initial stages to ease her transition back to the workforce. Sally understands the portion of money paid by Ray is going to stop at the end of the first year; therefore, she has a bit of time in which to establish an appropriate lifestyle. At the end of two years, both Ray and Sally agree the matrimonial home will be sold and the

equity split. Regular weekly payments will then continue to support the children. Financial independence is achieved.

Sally is supported for a season for the good of the family as a whole. The children stay in the house, Sally secures employment, and together, the family get used to new routines. The panicky knee-jerk reaction of moving house, finding a job, getting routines flowing, and adjusting to living a single life is greatly reduced.

The willingness you have to openly discuss your beliefs of entitlement and fears of scarcity with your Ex will help the entire family, but above all, you need to be true to yourself. Many times the demise of the relationship does not allow for a supportive environment in which you can be vulnerable, but if there is this platform, you must ensure you are genuine, as the power lies in the intention, not in emotional manipulation in an attempt to gain more from a guilty party.

Step 3 – Payments

> The money is for the benefit of the children, albeit it is paid to the Ex.

Payment is the ongoing exchange of money between the parents — typically on a weekly, fortnightly, or monthly basis. The ongoing payment is meant to share the expenses of raising children and should not be focused on sustaining the Ex's lifestyle. The money is for the benefit of the children, albeit the money is paid to the Ex.

As a great deal of law exists to compensate the mother who has supported the family and is now without career, this payment arrangement is separate from the support of children and can be worked out independently. Although it's rare for these types of agreements to be reached without the engagement of lawyers and court rulings, it is possible if you follow the same principles: non-attachment and an open sharing of beliefs surrounding entitlement.

Whether Leaver or Leavee, it is up to you to avoid over-indulgence in the game of 'making them pay', either monetarily or emotionally, and to expect this to appease your inner guilt or shame. While a previous financial supporter is not obligated to continue supporting their Ex in the lifestyle they lived whilst together, it is reasonable to have a period of financial assistance as new life plans are worked out. The reality of paying the bills next month still exists and just because your living circumstances change, a sense of moral responsibility usually helps both of you work together towards a fair and reasonable plan for eventual non-dependence. The key focus is to take care of the survival level. This enables the smallest of positives to be built upon because fear ceases to be the dominating energy, and while this does not outweigh the emotions of anger, betrayal, and other negatives, it may mean you are likely to form a workable agreement.

In the instance where possessions and ongoing income have been split to disadvantage one parent substantially, your children witness the ruthlessness this duplicity forces on their other parent, whom they love and continue to live with. It does not go unnoticed, albeit the wealthy parent is blind to its obviousness. The inner hardening of the heart within the parent who watches their children struggle whilst living with their former spouse who is unable to financially provide the basics, is self-evident.

Equally so is the parent who wallows in indulgent self-pity, expects handouts to make ends meet, and refuses to take personal responsibility to financially provide for their life and the children. The children see and understand this too. This attitude of taking contradicts the self-reliance inside the other parent's home and eventually they begin to see it for what it is. This may well take time, but provides a valuable life lesson when such contrasts are noted.

Guilt Money

Depending on circumstances, or a desire to protect identity or ego, we introduce the term *Guilt Money*. This is where one pays a certain amount of money to appease the hurting one. The opinions of others are frequently sought in an attempt to justify what one deems the appropriate amount to pay or receive. If the Leavee is shrewd, vindictive, or manipulative, this sum could be significant. If the Leaver is full of remorse, panicky, or emotionally devastated, large amounts of financial wealth can also be handed over.

Guilt money is paid in an attempt to alleviate the emotional struggle — albeit only temporarily. As a Leaver, we believe it hurts us enough to pay the money that we ought to be free from the guilt of hurting someone emotionally — especially when we believed we were able to build lifelong dreams beside them. For the Leavee, it may temporarily appease the sense of betrayal, rejection, or other negative emotion; however, this fades and soon the wanting returns.

The entangled net of emotional baggage begins to have an even stronger hold after the original exchange. The Leaver who has paid out *guilt money* often becomes enraged by increased demands of the Leavee. The chance of having quality communication between these two parties is greatly diminished because the conversation is now fused with a nonverbal trade-agreement whereby the Leaver believes they are free, although the Leavee believes they are still owed. Until there is a change in either party's recognition of their personal responsibility, it is likely that finances will continue to be a source of contention.

The Complex Family couples who are without financial tension between them are that way because one or both people have stepped out of contention. It only takes one to do so; this holds true irrespective of monetary wealth as is so well demonstrated when we watch multi-millionaire celebrities fight over pre- and post-marriage agreements.

So is *guilt money* bad? It is not so much that it is bad as that it does not serve the relationship well. The money itself can be very useful, and in some cases the transfer of funds may be a responsible act for family goodness. It is within the context of the emotional entanglement that *guilt money* is placed into its sinister league. It is best avoided.

As a Leaver, avoid giving money because you feel guilty. Instead, give money to ease the fearful state within your Leavee. Any Leavee can become very ugly in temperament while clutching at what they believe is their survival.

As a Leavee, avoid receiving money where you gain self-serving pleasure from seeing your Ex pay. Your enjoyment of the anticipated pain it will cause to them to part with funds needs to be replaced by an attitude of gratitude for their assistance, and accept it as a gift.

If you, the Leavee, have the majority of the funds in your possession, it is sometimes very tempting to depart with a reasonable portion of wealth and believe the money evens out the Leaver's act.

While we can work out what we believe to be fair, the true test of our attachment to this fairness will come either when we hand it over, or the Ex disputes our belief. In this moment consider, How entitled and attached am I?

Ongoing for Payee

When receiving the agreed money from an Ex, consider your approach. Do you believe you are entitled, or do you believe you are deserving of more? Do you use this money to support your lifestyle, or do you use it directly for the good of the children?

As a Payee, receiving the amount with an *attitude of gratitude*, rather than one of deserving, will assist in the creation of harmony between both parties. Typically, with banking being so automated these days, you receive without contact so your reactions to this are often disguised by convenience; however, you will definitely notice it when it does not appear if you are reliant upon the money to make ends meet.

> Receiving the amount with gratitude, rather than one of deserving, will assist in harmony.

To be fair, for many Payees it is challenging to separate the funding of children's expenses from the general pool of funds they draw from. Even so, a technique that is very beneficial for the Payee to instigate is to have the money paid into a separate account where its use is solely for direct child expenses. Even if one is on the breadline, this method is simple, and will continually remind you to be grateful for your Ex's assistance. When your child has lost another pair of shoes, you buy a new pair from the Ex account. When you need to pay for a school trip, you have the money in the Ex account. This helps to build respect for your Ex; it reminds you of their goodness, which is all too easy to forget once beyond marriage.

Although the method may seem overly simplistic, and usually remains unknown to anyone but you, this genuine act of acknowledgment miraculously keeps the positives flowing, with the result being that your money issues with the Ex diminish. This has been the case for almost all who use this method. The Ex does not need to know you do this for it to be beneficial — although many Exes have said how surprised and pleased they were when they did become aware of it — and in some cases, Exes have paid more, knowing the children benefit directly.

Ongoing for Payer

When paying the agreed money to an Ex, is it given with an expectation of how it is to be spent, or is it given to appease your emotional pain? Do you resent paying and therefore attempt to give as little as you must? Do you doubt the choices your Ex is making with your money? Is the payment eroding the beauty your new life was meant to provide? Are your new relationships influencing your sense of responsibility?

As a Payer, if you make your payments with a positive attitude and a sense of responsibly to the shared expenses of raising your children, you will reduce the frustration you feel as you watch the money disappear from your bank accounts and avoid the temptation to make no payment at all. While it is very common to attempt to get away with paying the lowest amount possible, at the same time, you probably do not want your children to go without. The lack of control over the way the money is used usually becomes the toxic component; however, if you are able to release your attachment to the notion that the money will be used for specific purposes, you will find an inner liberation.

If you are a *Pay, No Play* parent, practice gratitude for your Ex's dedication to caring for your children — even if you disagree with some aspects of how this is done. Perhaps you can be grateful for more time to devote to your demanding career, or it could be that you are grateful to have a little more time to focus on building a new relationship.

Instead of attempting to diminish the amount you pay, you may experience the shift that comes when you move away from obligation and step into genuine giving. Start with an enquiry: How much does it cost to fund the children's activities? How much is needed to purchase the basics? Often one becomes ignorant of the accumulated costs in raising children — not because we don't care, but because we get busy in our world and overlook it. The costs can come as quite a shock on the odd occasion when it is necessary to buy forgotten or lost items because the Ex has been doing this daily; usually compromising their own wishes to fulfil the children's needs first.

> Practice gratitude for your Ex's dedication to caring for your children — even if you disagree with some aspects of how this is done.

One of the first questions a Payer wants to know is *How much do I have to pay?* To answer this, there are calculations and formulas all around the world which vary depending on where you live. These are helpful as guides in some instances, but it is advisable to do a little homework yourself. How much do you spend when you have the children? (A week gives artificial costings — too low usually.) What are the normal costs? What are the regular seasonal costs? What would you estimate you spend annually? These are not difficult calculations, and it is not solely reliant on your income; it is more about your lifestyle and personal choices.

You can estimate what you believe to be fair, check it against what the regulatory authorities demand, and then decide what to pay. This way, if you pay more, you let your Ex know you are paying more because of your calculations. Feel good about it and enjoy the giving. It may be appropriate to even suggest the method described in the Payee section — a separate account — where any surplus money that accumulates could even be suggested for use on a holiday for your Ex and children.

For the issue of ongoing monetary support to become neutral, the grudge between both parties must be removed. The situation where the Payee believes they deserve more and the Payer believes they pay too much must be eliminated. If you can change your attitudes, the results are splendid, and the children receive the greatest benefit of all.

Questions Worth Asking

Below are questions that I've used over the years in counselling and coaching; these are free of all circumstantial facts. They will help you to begin to focus on your intention and beliefs as you sort through the issues of finance with your Ex. If you are hoarding and holding, guilty or blaming, you will produce more negativity within your relationship than any short-term gain of financial benefit may bring. In some instances, while you may endure short-term diminished financial wealth, your children will gain family health.

Through the years ahead, your attitude about this will influence many aspects of your children's future, and is a perspective well worth remembering.

Take a pen and piece of paper and start to answer these quality questions that will help you identify your true beliefs about finances. Remember, there are no right or wrong answers; you are looking to reveal what is there, not judge it. Once you know it's there, you have the chance to change it.

1. Identify the historically formed trade-agreements in your relationship?
    By this I mean, can you write down agreements made between you and your Ex relating to your financial position during your relationship, or did it just happen?
2. Have I been clear in my trades with my Ex?
3. Have I been honest with myself about my lifestyle expectations?
4. Do I accept that I am responsible for my welfare, or do I believe I am reliant upon another to provide for me?

5. What are my priorities in life?
    Rate in order Family, Parenting, Career, Financial, Hobbies, Health, Relationship, etc.?

6. How much do I value my possessions as an extension of my personal value?

7. Do I feel diminished when financially I have less?

8. Do I believe better parenting requires money?

As you start to answer these questions you will begin to open the doorway to your freedom, and reveal the pathway to personal understanding. It will become obvious that it is unnecessary to compromise your family's well-being because you feel broke. This is not to say you just walk away from everything; however, it may be that you need to be willing to do so before you can gain the security, comfort, quality, and peace you seek.

If you can begin to understand your answers to these questions, you will start to see where you have expectations and judgements, and these judgements will be reflected in your decisions of fairness as you form agreements with your Ex. This is a stance that affects your family as a whole — consider it wisely.

Chapter Nine
Refinement

How to continue leading by being.

So far, we have looked at the interactions with your Ex, your children, your partners as stepparents, and others who influence your life once divorce, separation, or some form of family breakdown, is or has, touched you. This chapter will move beyond all the externals: the words you speak, the things you do, and the people you mix with — and instead, look at your internal values: what you think, feel, and believe.

When you start to look within, it can be rather unnerving. As thought-provoking and sometimes confronting as this section may be, I have tried to keep it simple yet effective with proven techniques, tools, and tips 'n tricks, that will help you gain the most from your life in a Complex Family.

"You can only teach what you know — you pass on what you live."

Beyond Leavee and Leaver

The Leavee could remain in a 'victim' mindset for the rest of their life, always pointing a crippled blaming finger at the destruction and devastation caused to their family because the single act of divorce touched it. Likewise, the Leaver may also remain steadfast in their perspective and ignore the lessons to be learned, choosing instead to justify their comments and actions while they accommodate the subsequent fallout as a sad, unavoidable, and rather inconvenient occurrence.

> Leaver and Leaver are neither worse, nor better ... they are two lives being lived in parallel ... equal opportunity to move beyond their pain.

The Leavee and Leaver are two sides of the same coin — both are participants in a relationship that ended with hurt. Neither are worse, nor better; these are two lives being lived in parallel, held by the common bond of their children; they have equal opportunities to move beyond the pain and simply become neutrally free.

That is the purpose of this chapter — to map out the pathway ahead, to lead you to a place where you can live free from the emotional scars and deep feelings that plague your current life.

Both the Leavee and Leaver have experienced times of disappointment hurt, betrayal, loss, hopelessness, misunderstanding, anger, bitterness, resentment, arrogance, inferiority, blame, judgement, numbness, control, apathy, powerlessness, and so on. Although we all experience these from time to time, at varying levels of strength, and in our own unique ways, when we do, they feel very real. However, it is not the mere presence of any of these feelings or emotions that damages you, it is the attachment to them that harms both you and your children and holds you in a place of perpetual suffering. When these are left to fester, consciously or otherwise, we see people deaden; they lose their inner flame, and take from, rather than give to the world around them.

Crossroads

We all come to crossroads in our lives, and usually more than once; these are the times where we have to make choices — choices that are not always easy. Typically, it is not because they are complex in themselves, but rather it is the reactions, emotions, and feelings that surface and cause conflict, or even numbness.

The crossroad choice here is rather simple: do you want to be free or not? Using the Complex Family continuum, do you want to come to the centre point of neutrality, where you are neither the Leavee, nor the Leaver? You may have been tagged a divorcee, however this label as you see means you've gained life experience; you've reach the point where you give up your story, your justification, your blame, and accept your life for what it is. You choose to build on the strengths you have, learn the lessons presented, and grow yourself and your family as a result.

> For the first few years of my divorced life, I bravely soldiered on, juggling my new life of responsibility, work, children, friendships, and adult living, with attempted new love, broken-hearted vulnerable spaces, and shattered dreams. I frantically did all the right things, made the best choices, and held myself and family together as much as possible; it was a lot like a theme-park roller-coaster ride, with all the tension, drama, thrills, and excitement we are used to witnessing. It was punctuated with frequent screams of horror, occasional squeals of delight, and the much-anticipated pause — if only long enough for me to catch my breath or perhaps jump off for a rest. At times, I had family and friends who would ride along with me, but most often it was a solo trip. It was I who shed the tears, carried the heartache, the responsibility, and the search for courage to rebuild my life and my family.
>
> While in full-time employment, as part of further training, we were asked to write down goals for the year ahead — both business and personal. I had found goals to be relatively easy in my life as there was always something I was building towards, dreaming of, or looking forward to, but not now. I remember quietly saying to the man who employed me, "I

simply cannot do this exercise. It is not that I don't want to — I do — I just cannot." Everything I had understood, held true, or believed in had shattered when my marriage ended. For me, goals had become another casualty of lost hope, lost future, and lost meaning in my life; the requirement to carry out a simple exercise became the realisation of the depth of my personal pain. The crossroads had become very real for me.

Likewise, for you. It will be when you acknowledge that your life is not as joyous, spontaneous, or abundant as you deserve that you may finally awaken. If you feel an inner deadening numbness, the apathetic dismissal of hope, and the resigned sense of life's humdrum existence, you need to face your crossroad, and begin to ask: do I want to live a hollow existence, or do I want more out of life? If you want more out of life, here is a way to start making it happen.

How To Heal Your Ache

It Takes One with Two

To start getting more out of life, you need to put more into it so you have something to draw from; much like a bank account, you must save to have money available when appropriate. In this way, you turn your attention away from your Ex, your children, and your partner, and start to invest in yourself. Realise that *you cannot change anyone else*, you can only effect change in their environment and the way you relate to them, *you must begin by looking inside and changing yourself*.

So far, we have discussed many useful principles, some tools, suggestions, and tip 'n tricks. In this chapter, we will look a bit deeper and look at principles. From the multitudes available I have selected only five that I believe hold consistently throughout life with a particularly strong relevance to the Complex Family environment.

Following the selected principles, are four tools that can be applied to everyday living. These are simple and effective in creating change, and have the added advantage that you can use them without the external assistance of another; although sometimes discussion with someone who understands them maybe useful. With these tools you can work to reshape your beliefs, and thereby adjust your attitudes. Your attitudes are covered in the final section of the chapter, as they define your responses and in so doing, profoundly affect your Ex and your children.

In our current instant-answer society, we have become addicted to quick fixes, so I would like to add a word of reality regarding the application of these principles and tools. This is NOT a quick fix; it needs practice. It's easy to continue to look at external circumstances, or others in your life, and want them to change first; but since you have no control over another's choices, (without using manipulation or force of some kind) it shows you there needs to be an alternative. The alternative I speak of is personal transformation. This process takes only one person with two things to have the transformation take place. So before we get started, here's a simple exercise to evaluate where you currently stand on the two basic requirements you will need for change to occur:

Evaluate the level of *willingness* you have towards making changes, following new principles, and applying new tools and attitudes to your everyday life?

Low									High
1	2	3	4	5	6	7	8	9	10

Evaluate the level of *commitment* you have towards making changes, following new principles, and applying new tools and attitudes to your everyday life?

Low									High
1	2	3	4	5	6	7	8	9	10

If your scores are high, and show that you are both willing and committed, go for it, and let's start making changes!

If your scores are low, write down what is stopping you. This is not a measure of right or wrong, it's only asking if you are *willing* or *committed*. It is far better to be honest here than to set yourself up for some form of perceived failure in the future when really it was only a lack of *willingness* and/or *commitment*. Take the time to consider the implication of not being *willing* or *committed*, and if the choice of moving towards pleasure, or away from pain, is not yet strong enough, continue as you are. When either the drive towards pleasure or the shift away from pain strikes again, reconsider evaluating your levels in both.

A wise man once said to me, "Never care for someone else's problem more than they care about it themselves." This is a statement that has assisted me to assess where the best use of my time is to be spent as I work with people. At times I found myself more passionate about seeing change in someone's life than they were. They had neither the *willingness* nor *commitment* to see the same change. I was reminded one more time that we cannot change another; it is up to them; all we can do is support, encourage, guide, and love throughout the process; primarily, this life journey is an individual one.

> "Never care for someone else's problem more than they care about it themselves."

Outlined over the course of this chapter are the principles, tools, and attitudes that work when applied with equal levels of *willingness* and *commitment* towards personal transformation.

Five Principles

Principle 1 – Life's Mirror

What I have come to know as true for me and those I have loved, assisted, and worked with over the years, is that Life is a Mirror. That is to say, *Life reflects what we hold as a belief;* albeit limited through people, circumstances, and things, life reflects back to us what we currently believe to be true. In other words, "you see it because you believe it." If you believe life to be hard and people hostile, you will have difficult circumstances and aggressive people in your life who will constantly reconfirm this belief for you. However, if you believe that life is gentle and prosperous, you will experience life to be this; it is by changing your beliefs that you change your experience.

> You see it because you believe it.

To fully appreciate the significance of life being a mirror, we first need to understand how to look at our reflection. Although this sounds rather easy, it is amazing how we are genuinely unable to see our own reality. A particularly visual example of this is observing someone who suffers with anorexia; while we see them as desperately thin, they see themselves as overweight. While we see it as an obvious contradiction, the person who is suffering is genuinely unable to see the reality of their ill health, such is the level of their delusion. Likewise, both Leavee and Leaver cannot see their own delusions, and hence they assign levels of responsibility outside of themselves. Their perceptions become those of a Leaver who failed to stay with a commitment, and the Leavee who has failed to fulfil initial expectations; either way, it justifies the emotions they experience now.

To use Life's Mirror as a constructive principle to move yourself towards the central point of neutral, neither Leavee nor Leaver, you have to begin to observe what is actually in your life — free from the story that justifies or blames its existence. You will come to recognise and acknowledge simply what *is* and that you have the power to change it. That 'power' is *choice* and the choice is yours.

Principle 2 – Resistance

There is a little saying, *"What we resist, persists."* It has proved to be true throughout circumstances, attitudes, and time, and is tied into the principle of Life's Mirror. By recognising *what we resist, persists,* we can begin to understand that whatever our focus is locked on, will expand; whatever we pay attention to, we get more of. Resistance is a force; it is a force applied against something else, and therefore, it builds strength much like resistance training builds muscle. If we do not apply force against our opponent our strength does not grow, and neither does their strength. However, if we continue to push against an opponent, their resistance must continue to grow to allow us to fulfil the 'mirrored' function.

> What you resist, persists.

This concept being a little more abstract, can be challenging to understand fully, so let's look at it this way: If I say "do not think of Shrek," it is impossible not to have an image of Shrek instantly appear in your mind. If I say, "think of a landscape, a beautiful, lush, dense, and thick green native bush which touches the edges of the most serene and picturesque lake, while enticing smells and gentle sounds soothe your senses," you will find it difficult to think of Shrek. It's the same with resistance. When you shift your focus away from what you don't want, it will begin to diminish — much like an untrained muscle without use; it will eventually cease to be powerful or often to exist at all. In other words, as you stop pushing or struggling against something you ultimately do not want, it ceases to be a problem.

Once you understand the principle of resistance, the next step is to apply it. As it is often challenging to see the situation you are resisting, here is a clue: *the only thing that causes pain in your life is resistance;* if you are experiencing a lot of pain, a high level of resistance is present.

The antidote to resistance, is *acceptance*. Acceptance neither condones, is resigned to, nor makes the acts that caused the pain right — instead, it simply surrenders to the reality of the deep hurt, disappointment, betrayal, guilt and so on that you feel. It says what is is, and I accept it is. When full acceptance is gained, you release all judgement held about it. This is usually a process rather than an overnight transformation; however, I am not ruling those out either.

When one moves towards acceptance, it is sometimes described as leaning into the intention to accept, and little by little, greater acceptance is felt. You will find that the gaps between the surges of resistance get further apart, and the depth or strength of the resistance becomes shallower or weaker. When this happens, celebrate your growing acceptance; don't beat yourself up for how far you are from full acceptance.

> The only thing that causes pain in your life is resistance.

If you are reeling with negativity at the thought of accepting the cause of our pain, this is normal. The fear of making the event or person okay, or being perceived as condoning the behaviour you originally judged, can often be immense, hence the practice of acceptance is such a key principle that needs to be delicately nurtured in the initial stages of learning.

To recap the story of the Mariner; the acceptance of the storm does not stop the storm from coming, but it keeps him safe and enables him to make wise choices while in it. It is easy to see the futility of someone fighting Mother Nature in a storm, but when you look at yourself, trapped by your emotions as you continue to resist what your *Life Mirror* is reflecting, you often cannot see that you are using the same futile behaviour.

Movement along the continuum of Leaver or Leavee towards central neutral means that you will cease resisting the complications of life since your marriage or relationship ended, and begin to lean in the direction of accepting your life as it is — complete with all the ups and downs. This way you can begin to make the most appropriate choices for yourself and your children, given your current circumstances and the new direction you wish to head.

Principle 3 – Personal Power

Misguided power is dangerous. Many of us have experienced first hand the reality of an external authority welding power as we witness the carnage; if we have not seen this in our own personal life, we can see it through entire nations or races fighting one another using power that has lost the benefit it was intended to create. Our society gives us numerous examples of power being abused and hopelessly misunderstood; however, to gain clarity regarding the principle of power — and what it can give us through appropriate use — requires us to develop some worthwhile tools in our lives as we go forward.

As mentioned in Chapter 3: Stage 3 when discussing children's development, and in the section on Discipline in Chapter 5, there are two types of power: *power over* and *power with*. *Power over* is normal, *Power with* is natural; however, because we have become so misguided by our examples of power, to begin developing *power with* will not feel very 'natural'.

To begin developing *power with*, you must first understand *personal power*. If you don't know how to hold power with yourself, it's logical to say that you will find it difficult to have your healthy power respected by anyone else. This is the reason *power over* has become so common.

Let's start by looking at **Boundaries**. The common catch-cry of the late twentieth century and certainly the first decade of the twenty-first century is, *stand up for yourself*. People are entertained, amused, and equally horrified by the attempts they see in those who are attempting to take this phrase and put it into action. Standing up for yourself, however, is the physical result (or expression) of the boundaries you place within yourself rather than your attempts to impose boundaries on another.

Although the external boundaries are important, in order for this process to succeed, you must first place your boundaries internally; from there, you can then affect the external. If you try to enforce a boundary upon another when you don't hold this boundary yourself, it will only reinforce your belief that your personal boundaries are worthless.

For many women involved in violent (physical or emotional) relationships, the boundary that is required here is not the one of stopping the violence — although that is critical — but it is the one that says, she never deserves to be subjected to that kind of treatment. The physical change will occur as a natural byproduct of her sustained personal boundary. In the absence of such boundaries, even when she is removed from the violent offender, the victim will attract another abuser, and reconfirm her belief in herself as the victim. This very negative cycle can be difficult to break; that is not an excuse to condone or perpetuate violence in any form.

Recognising that personal boundaries are often challenging to build, the first step is to define what you will, and will not, continue to accept or believe. You require no one other than yourself for this boundary to be real and effective; it is your personal choice; you hold complete control — and require no one else to change. This can be quite challenging to believe and more so to do, so it helps to understand that part of the difficulty is that your insecure psyche is addicted to perpetual self-doubt. As a master of self-critique, you tend to continue to allow negative self-talk to subtly erode your sense of self-worth.

> **Personal power needs both boundaries and conviction to be present.**

If you can understand this is where a substantial portion of the damage takes place, you have the potential to begin to make changes. Positive affirmations do not work on their own, but they are certainly a step towards reprogramming your self-talk and will help you to move beyond the constant negative chatter that runs in your mind. This form of boundary is the best way to begin to develop your personal power. It's worth repeating here that when you can understand boundaries have little to do with the external lines you draw, and more to do with defining your internal lines, you will begin to feel your inner strength develop.

The time when boundaries really become significant, however, is when they are put to the test. The strength of the positioned boundary is only recognised when an attempt is made to cross or break it. As such, the balancing ingredient required for our boundaries to become powerful is

Conviction. That is to say, it is the strength of your belief or certainty that reinforces the boundary and makes it effective. Boundaries without convictions are like fence posts that mark the ground. The connection to conviction, gives the wire that runs between; it now has direction, delineation, definition, and strength to turn this into purpose. Therefore, the two key ingredients for owning and developing your personal power are *boundaries* and *conviction*.

Once you have your personal power, you still have the choice of how you will use it; will it become *power over* or *power with*? In a nutshell:

- Power Over forces another person to submit to your dominance to achieve your desired outcome.

- Power With works *with* another person's individual power, to achieve the Highest Good for All involved.

> Living with Power With, shifts us into Win with You.

Simplistically speaking, in action this difference displays itself in two ways. The most positive result achievable when using the normal *power over* paradigm, is Win / Win, although more typically it is a Win / Lose outcome. However, using the new way of living with *power with*, shifts this into a *Win with You*.

When we work with power in this manner, we move beyond justifications, excuses, or blame; we focus on where we currently are and what is ahead as we begin to look at the choices, attitudes, and behaviours we have to work with; this constructively shapes our futures.

It is this difference that fuels the further development of our boundaries, beliefs, and conviction, as we give up the need to have our way, and instead, focus on the *Highest Good of All* involved.

It is through the practice of *power with* that we will discover being able to more constantly hold our inner peace and connection; we cease perpetuating suffering or harm. It is through turning our intention towards the betterment of all that we start to live with a deeper connection that becomes contagious to others around us. Through this non-threatening yet extremely powerful approach, we help lead others towards their own personal power, without prolonging the use of normal self-serving *power over* techniques. In this way, we release the attachment to our story and the wounds from our past, and move into the present moment. As we continue to do this, we come to own our attitudes and beliefs, and recognise that we gain more through the unity of *with* than from the division of *over*.

Although you may find yourself in circumstances that have been caused by others, you can recognise that true power resides within your choice of how you are going to respond to these, not the event itself.

Whether you are the Leavee or Leaver, you need to understand and practice appropriate boundaries and conviction; the key here is to continue to grow as a result. When carried out with the unity of *with*, you will be constantly building towards the Highest Good for your family — regardless of its structure.

Principle 4 – Suffering

Whether you are a Leavee or Leaver, it can be said that at some stage, before or after the divorce, you suffered. Most find it too hard to imagine a life beyond the suffering, and therefore believe suffering will always be part of their daily lives. However, suffering is the attitude you hold while you are in pain — physically or emotionally.

Many people can be in pain without suffering. They can do this because they have understood that pain and suffering are two entities:

> ***Pain is an event,***
> ***Suffering is an attitude.***

Understanding this core belief will help you see that you can continue to build your personal power; you will realise it is your attitude towards your pain that causes the ongoing suffering, not the event itself. When you fully understand and live this difference, you can experience life and its pain; you release the ongoing personal suffering, and allow yourself to embrace the learning opportunities within the events.

Within the Complex Family, the art of developing your freedom from suffering will radically alter the way you continue to interact with your Ex, your children, and those you live with on a daily basis.

Principle 5 – Parallel Reaction

Parallel Reaction is where *negative emotions are experienced by both people involved, although uniquely expressed*. While this may not happen in all situations, it has been a particularly strong principle when applied during years of counselling in the Complex Family environment. Let's use an example to help describe this more clearly:

> A woman came to me expressing how she felt intimidated and uneasy in almost every conversation with her Ex. Hoping to avoid this, she took to writing to him instead, thinking it made it easier. The relationship was deteriorating at every turn and needed rapid intervention. As we explored the possibility that he too felt intimidated and uneasy with the interaction, it opened the doorway to resolution.
>
> They met again to try another conversation, during which she expressed her own vulnerability and said that because she had felt intimidated by him she had chosen to write letters to avoid feeling so helpless. As the air between them thawed, he generously explained his own feelings of intimidation when he received the letters and therefore chose to ignore them. For the first time in years, these two former lovers were able to discuss how they no longer trusted each other and how they both felt intimidated.
>
> The Ex husband was 'gob-smacked' that his seemingly together Ex wife had felt intimidated in his presence. Likewise, she had not even considered that a letter might be more threatening to him than her uncomfortable conversation. It allowed them to start to build a foundation for the future, but only because she was willing to consider the possibility of Parallel Reaction being real.

> Negative emotions are experienced by both people involved, although uniquely expressed.

This is one of countless examples where those involved are left speechless at how accurate this principle is. Use it as a reality check in a disagreement; when you feel that something is not fair or someone is being unreasonable, pause and take a step outside your world, and with compassionate eyes, attempt to see how they may be viewing you.

It's not a comfortable principle to apply, because you have to be willing to change perspective mid-flight, but it is a very effective strategy.

Four Tools

The principles above need to be brought into everyday life; we need to show how we practice these and what steps we can take to apply them in all circumstances. Now is the time to take the theory and apply it to the practical, to move from a belief in its power to a place of knowing, as an outcome of gained experience.

The most beautiful and intricate sculpture is a result of someone's desire for exquisiteness. The refinement does not come through the artist deciding to be complacent or disengaged in their task at hand, it is as a result of those who are passionate about working with their medium. The wood sculptor loves the smell, feel, and texture of the wood they work with; they understand the importance of working with the natural beauty of the grain, the knots, and the uniqueness of the wood to reveal more of its beauty. Likewise, you need to be passionate about taking these principles and applying them to your daily life, about using these tools to create your masterpiece. Your family has knots and characteristic grains to work with; these are part of the very structure of your family.

In essence, there are four very simple tools that you can practice in every day life to bring about change in yourself first — and eventually in your circumstances. The application of them does take practice and diligent personal integrity, because only you can know your true intention as you make choices or take action throughout your day. Your personal integrity is the activating ingredient, much like yeast is in bread. It keeps you in check and evaluates your intentions, excuses, justifications, and reasons.

> Personal integrity is the activating ingredient — much like yeast is in bread.

The intention that lies behind your words and actions is very powerful. It is in your intention that your true feelings hide. If you perform a seemingly kind deed, but your intention is to set a trap for the non-suspecting, in reality, this can hardly be considered a kind deed. Universal Law will see that, in due time, you will be the receiver of your ill-intent — even though you may appear to have gotten away with it in the short-term. Likewise, if you have an intention to create a beautiful gift for someone and it goes wrong and causes upset, you are free from the ongoing negativity that ill-intent would have created. Therefore, it is important to understand the principle of being authentic with intention and reveal your true feelings as you work with these four tools. You need to genuinely focus on bringing more harmony, peace, joy, creativity, and love into your own life; it helps no one if you manipulate others and perpetuate pain and misery.

As you begin working with these tools — that are really very simple — you will find that what makes them challenging is your resistance to change, and your emotional reactions to the use of them. Therefore, it's important to use all four tools in the order they are presented, and not give in to the temptation to concluded prematurely. If you only complete the first three, you will have missed the point of transformation. If you ignore the third in favour of the fourth, you will miss the vitality of your feelings, and this process then becomes just another barren head procedure without heart. All four tools need to be used, in order, and in fullness. However, this being said, fullness does not mean it has to be a long drawn out event each time they are used. As you become more practiced, you will be able to meaningfully work through them in a single conscious breath. This is not simply about the mechanics; instead, it means you live these with personal integrity in every moment of every day — this is Being.

Tool 1 – Acknowledge

If you are made uncomfortable by, or react to, someone or some situation, Ex or otherwise, it is because you hold a particular belief about them, their actions, or their words. To be free of these reactions, you will need to cease trying to change them, and instead, deal with your part of this relationship. In reality, this is the only part you have any chance of changing. To work through any frustrations or feelings you hold about this other person, or people, you first need to recognise you hold a belief — and furthermore, a limiting one. By following the five principles outlined above, you can see that it is your perspective that affects you, and therefore, it is within your control to change. Recognition is your focus here, and as simple as this sounds, it is generally recognised that over half of your change process is accomplished in this first step.

While you have reached this halfway milestone, let me put this into perspective. It is not so much that half of your task towards change has been accomplished, it is more the realisation of how critical personal clarity becomes when you have something you want to change.

In modern day society where we hurt and belittle one another in the name of humour, and deem it acceptable to continue this kind of behaviour, to acknowledge that we need to change can be extremely challenging. While the humour may provide temporary relief, it does cause more suffering, and therefore, we ourselves can only be the recipient of further suffering in the course of time. So, acknowledging and recognising we have a limited belief that no longer serves us, that is to say it perpetuates personal suffering, becomes crucial. If it is as simple as saying *we cannot change what we cannot see* — then this step is focused on seeing.

> If we cannot change what we cannot see — then this step is focused on seeing.

As this step is so important, you can expect life to help you and indeed it does. Life has a wonderful way of doing this, especially when you have people in your life to whom you continue to react. In the moment you feel your energy shift into frustration, anger, or some form of negativity, you have the opportunity to recognise you hold another limiting belief. Once you have observed and recognised it, pause and give yourself the breathing space to simply acknowledge it — catch yourself right in it. Even if you are unable to think what it might be or give it a name right now, that's not important; it is the recognition and acknowledgement of its very existence that makes this tool's use complete.

Tool 2 – Validate

Now that you are aware you currently hold a limited belief (albeit nameless), one that is at the root of your negative emotions, you can move on to the next stage: *validation*. To validate what you have acknowledged means you move away from any judgement about feeling this way. If you hold the constant thought that something is wrong, you will find it challenging to accept it — and although you may not want to stay with this negative emotion over the long-term, accepting it now will conclude it sooner.

The paradox is that when we accept we are holding judgement, limitations, or negativity, we move towards transformation; however, if we deny it, or chose not to accept it, we perpetuate its very existence, following the *What we Resist, Persists* principle.

> This paradox was one I struggled to accept. If I felt angry, I believed it was bad because anger is bad, or wrong, so for me to validate my anger took quite a leap. However, getting past my initial judgement was the key — I had to accept the reality that I was angry, and therefore, to make myself feel poorly because I was angry only became a self-defeating spiral.
>
> Eventually, I came to see that by validating my emotions, I was not defining them as right or wrong, I was simply removing the judgement held against myself and replacing it with simple acceptance. When I got this, it was like a key turning in the lock of my prison cell, opening the doorway to freedom beyond bars.

To more quickly reach the point of genuine validation of your recognised limitations, it can be very helpful to say, "It's okay for me to feel this way." Saying this repeatedly helps because it stops the spiraling thoughts inside your head, or the temptation to shut out the initial acknowledgement, or pretend it was not real, and plunge into denial. During the early stages of practicing in validation, it is also very common to experience the recognition and immediately look to an external influence to explain it being as it is. Then, one either passes blame or removes him/herself from the responsibility of their judgement, and invokes further denial. Therefore, we use a simple phrase to keep ourselves focused on validation only:

It's okay for me to feel this way.

You will feel a subtle shift in yourself when you have genuinely reached validation. It is the point of acceptance that allows you to become neutral. Much like a car's engine has a neutral position in its gearbox, where it is neither in forward drive nor reverse, neutral allows for transition into either of these states as another choice. In the same way, you move from where you have been and place yourself into neutral so you can make a better choice.

Tool 3 – Feel the Feelings

The third part of this equation is simply feeling the feelings. The reason this is third and not second will become apparent in the appropriate practice of this tool. If this was second, you would judge the feeling, and remain entrapped; instead, by reaching neutral first, you allow your feelings to continue spinning, but you are disengaged from the momentum the spin would usually create.

How you feel the feelings is most easily described as observing yourself feeling them; it's almost as if you're watching someone else — only it's not, it's you. When you focus on observing your feelings, it is quite different from wallowing or losing yourself within them, as you genuinely feel the hopelessness, emptiness, anger, grief, or even a pang quickly dissipate; you are able to observe yourself as you feel these emotions, and at the same time, see that you are not defined by them.

Here is the word of warning when practicing feeling feelings — stay in the place where you observe yourself throughout. The moment you identify too much with the feelings, you lose your neutral observational stance, and the opportunity to move beyond (or heal) this limitation has passed. All is not lost; life will soon give you another opportunity to continue learning and practicing — and you'll probably do better next time.

Some people become addicted to feeling the feelings and recreate drama in their life so they can continue to experience the feeling; this leads to repetitious cycles of calamity.

The more you practice these tools, the shorter your feeling time becomes as it relates to a particular area. As an example, let's say you have refined your feelings about *anger*, yet you have little or no experience with *grief*. While the time needed to feel the feelings of anger have diminished through your conscientious work, when grief shows up, you may feel out of your depth again, and those feelings will take longer to process in an observant manner.

Although your tools of trade will remain consistent, the portion of the masterpiece you are working on changes; therefore, it may sometimes feel like you are starting at the beginning again. The truth is, the techniques and skill you have already gained through the use of these tools will help you no matter what aspect of yourself you work on.

The step of feeling feelings is frequently either avoided or indulged in; both produce the consequence of perpetuating the initial negative cycle. Remember to keep this simple, and avoid looking for complexity in it. The use of Tool 3 ends with the moment you have that split-second bliss-point that comes after feeling feelings; that is the time to stop the feelings portion of this exercise and move onto Tool 4. If you find yourself having to rework the story in your head to continue feeling something, you have held on too long. If you choose to continue beyond the bliss-point, you will instead become part of an increased drama and thereby defeat the initial intention to gain freedom, or expansion, as you move from the limitation you first acknowledged.

Tool 4 – Choice of Change

If the first three tools are about your immediate past and the present, Tool 4 is focused on your future. This is where the transformation occurs; however, to believe you can skip the first three tools and come straight to this one, is to believe a tree will grow without sun, soil, or water. While a seed holds the potential for greatness, it is only when it is given the right conditions that there can be a realisation of this potential. Likewise, it is only when you come through the first three tools that you are ready to make the changes; the alternative will be many false starts that will ultimately dishearten you.

Once the feelings have been felt, you are ready to move into the change. The pain is healed in the feeling, but the transcendence is in the new choices you will make. When you lean towards your intention to create greater goodness, you make the best choice you can in every moment. Often, it is unnecessary to immediately resolve the issue at hand, and instead of reacting to it, you can choose from a range of new responses. By making a constructive choice you gain healing, and minimise, if not eliminate, the continuation of the discord.

This final step is equally important to the Four Step process; without it, you would be stuck in the spiral of your past, and forever repeat it as you move into your future. It is this final piece that gives you the forward momentum; it transmutes your old patterns and invites freedom and peace into your life. Although hindsight is a wonderful perspective to have, when you use these four tools the moment you experience negative emotions, you gain healing. You will see old habits broken and new patterns formed; this will change your life and begin to affect those around you.

> Tool 4 gives you the forward momentum; stops repeating the past.

Summary

These four tools naturally take practice and also require a commitment towards your own personal development. Although at times you may have someone in your life who can assist you in using them, the bottom-line is you need to own your own feelings, choices, and actions; this means you must be authentic. Being authentic requires you to shift from unconscious to conscious living — from reaction to response — and it gets easier with practice. The only pain you may experience with the use of these tools will be caused by the level of resistance you hold towards this transformational process. The length and bumpiness of the journey will be entirely dependent upon your choices.

Three Attitudes

An attitude is the holding of prolonged thoughts or a settled way of thinking about something or someone. This becomes the automatic filter through which we see the world around us.

Attitudes can either be those we choose or those we absorb from those around us: parents, relatives, friends, co-workers, and the like. But nothing is more certain, attitudes can easily be spotted. It is the attitudes we hold that will make or break our family unit far more than any structure it may hold.

> *"Forgiveness is not an occasional act — it's a permanent attitude."*
> ...... Dr. Martin Luther King

It is hard to find another phrase that describes so beautifully the misconception commonly held around the three key attitudes I believe are vital inside the Complex Family. The misconception I speak of is where we believe we do an act of goodness, (let's say in this case forgiveness) and then delude ourselves that the good act permits all words, thoughts, or deeds before and beyond that moment to now be neutral. As Dr. Martin Luther King so eloquently states within these few words, it is in our attitude that we gain our strength of character; hence, attitudes are what we express in the moment we are presented with each opportunity of choice.

Attitude 1 – Acceptance

The first attitude I speak of is Acceptance. It is an idea, concept, and theme that is discussed throughout almost every chapter of this book due to the effect this developed attitude has on life in the Complex Family. The significance of this as an attitude becomes evident when it is recognised as a transformative tool; it opens the doorway to ultimate personal freedom and peace of mind.

As mentioned earlier, the word *acceptance* does not carry the same meaning as agreement, condone, or resign. It does not mean you become whimsical and complacent, nor does it mean you have no opinion or preferences; it means you understand you can neither attach to nor control the person, event, or situation. It is trusting in the power that comes from an expanded perspective. It is accepting you do not know all the answers to life's curly questions and you embrace this natural law. You become conscientious about feeling your resistance, and are dedicated to maintaining your integrity as you define what you can or cannot change within yourself and other people or circumstances.

Acceptance is when you let go of your attachment to a desired outcome; when you let go of needing to be in control, and instead trust life a little more. It is the process of removing judgement so you become able to see people and circumstances as neutral — as though they hold the opportunity for you to be free to define what these things will mean to you. With acceptance as your chosen attitude, you are released from the treadmill of constant effort in what you are doing, or your never-ending cycles of having, and instead, it lets you genuinely experience Being with a sense of effortlessness.

> Acceptance is when you let go of your attachment to a desired outcome; when you let go of needing to be in control, and trust life a little more.

Acceptance is surrender. Acceptance as an attitude in our life means you diminish resistance, experience effortlessness, and thereby increase your enjoyment and fulfilment in life.

Attitude 2 – Forgiveness

Forgiveness seems to be a word that has lost favour as the ever-increasing focus has turned towards individual rights. Equally so, forgiveness in its authentic meaning has become dimmed with statements such as *'forgive and forget'* becoming the normal code of practice to follow when implementing such a strategy; this all adds to the dismissiveness we feel when confronted with forgiveness. When we strip away the perceived obstacles that may blind us from seeing the truth forgiveness embodies, we see the sense in developing this as an attitude within our daily lives. For without forgiveness, our world perpetuates personal suffering and global wreckage, and moves dangerously close to being beyond our capability to effect positive change.

To *forgive and forget* in its common flippant usage is simply meaningless. Many people become disillusioned because they realise that we do not forget what has occurred, and often we do not want to. However, I would like to emphasise the truth contained in this phrase, and breathe life back into its simplicity.

- The *forgive* portion of this equation describes the action we undertake, while
- The *forget* portion describes the result, and not a second action.

Through forgiving, we remember the event and forget the emotional entanglement of the situation and loose the heaviness that we would otherwise carry. It means to give up the repeated replay of the story inside our heads and replace it with an acceptance of the occurrence. It is the point where what has occurred becomes neutral — devoid of emotion — it just is.

When we take a closer look at forgiveness, we see much of its unpopularity has come from a misunderstanding of its meaning. Some popular comments for turning away from this ancient principle may sound like this; *if I forgive, they'll get away with it;* or *it's not my problem, it's theirs, they did it;* or *I will never forgive, they have hurt me too much;*

and so on. Forgiveness does not give the perpetrator freedom from the consequences of their actions. Forgiveness does not make what occurred right. It does not immediately solve the problem; it simply stops the suffering for you.

When you forgive and adopt an attitude of forgiveness, your judgement and resistance diminishes and you become free. You are able to compassionately see, and while you may live with the pain, you are free from the suffering.

Let's look at forgiveness another way that may help, let's change tack for a moment. To be in a position where we may choose to forgive, we must first have believed someone has wronged us, otherwise there is nothing to forgive. If we believe someone has wronged us, we have judged them and thereby condemn them by our standard of right and wrong — even if there are many others who equally hold this view of right and wrong, in essence, we have still judged. In judging them we have assumed to know all, interpret all appropriately, and still hold a level of contempt for this person that is so severe that it is reasonable to hold judgement and unforgiveness (that slowly poisons us) as an acceptable outcome.

> Forgive & Forget: forgive describes the action we undertake, while forget describes the result.

The alternative view here says that the person who needs to be forgiven is actually the one who judges. Therefore, forgiving another is forgiving ourselves which is why it is known to become such a catalyst for personal transformation.

Many of our great Masters who have walked the planet point towards forgiveness. As Jesus was dying on the cross he said, *"Father forgive them for they do not know what they are doing."* It was not saying that what they were doing was right or okay; what it illustrates is that He clearly saw their lack of clarity. Divine seeing enabled Him to look beyond the events and choose His response instead. Likewise, when we explore other great masters, we see their inclusion of forgiveness (in their alternative wording) as a primary component of personal contentment, attainment of peace, and the expansion of love.

"Unforgiveness is like drinking poison and hoping the other person dies."

Inside the Complex Family, you are granted the opportunity to practice forgiveness daily. The influence, inconvenience, and complications your Ex brings into your day-to-day living, gives you opportunities to make choices that could take you in either direction: *drinking poison or forgiveness*. Your separation or divorce has become the gift — wrapped in the paper of problems — that continues giving, and provides you with the platform from which to develop an attitude of forgiveness, moving beyond judging another and judging yourself.

As you develop this attitude, you expand your own sense of compassion while you recognise the personal bondage of another (even though they may be unaware of it) when they inflict suffering. For someone to harm, withhold, or cause another to suffer, especially children or your child's other parent, is only a reflection of the turmoil in their internal private world; when you truly grasp this, it clearly becomes hypocritical to condemn them.

You will know you have developed an attitude of forgiveness when you are predictably compassionate in your responses. That is to say, you remain compassionate towards the very one who has, or is, causing the pain; when you can see beyond their limitations in belief and character, and instead, look into the part of them where you can recognise a bit of yourself.

Attitude 3 – Gratitude

The third attitude, but by no means the least, can sometimes be confused with being a result rather than an attitude. The reason there is confusion is that spontaneous gratitude flows when acceptance and forgiveness are well developed. This leads us to think of gratitude as a natural consequence, much like compassion is a natural consequence of full forgiveness. However, I believe the cultivation of an *attitude of gratitude* is powerful in itself, and hence deserves separate attention.

As our focus on personal rights develops, with it usually comes an attitude of deserving. Sadly, deserving is an antidote to gratitude; we believe it is expected, therefore, we find ourselves asking, *"What is there to be grateful for?"* The explosion of such expectations has caused toxic levels of apathetic attitudes and numbness in millions. While expectations and rights are important, to continue to expect and always have this delivered upon, results in a 'ho hum' normalcy that is counterproductive to the engine house of abundance — gratitude. If we did not expect and good was delivered, gratitude would come as the natural result.

This is the challenging part of progress — to remain grateful for our achievements when they have become our familiar norm. It only takes a power cut for us to remember how grateful we are for the discovery itself and the adaptations of that power we use in our daily lives. In most countries with a welfare system, basic survival is nearly guaranteed these days; it may be subsistence living, but compared to poverty experienced in countries without welfare, survival is almost guaranteed. Therefore survival is expected as normal, and we have become complacent in our appreciation of it. While I am not suggesting we need to be in raptures over simplistic living at its basic level, we should not ignore being grateful for it either.

> Although gratitude is a result, it is equally a cultivating mechanism for abundance.

The inconsistent part of gratitude is that although it is a result, it is equally a cultivating mechanism for abundance. A genuine attitude of gratitude keeps the most normal of life's routines and repetitive doings as a celebration of abundance, rather than a means to an end while we continue to hanker for more grandeur. It is bizarre that in our world where attainment of more has become our creed, our gratitude has declined, contradicting the very Universal Law that would provide what we are in search of.

Developing gratitude within the Complex Family environment is where we reframe our current perspective regarding loss, and invite that of gain, and gains for our children. We know we have developed the attitude of gratitude when we can be thankful for the challenges in our lives the moment they pop up. When we can be grateful for the event that is providing the platform for us to continue to develop our compassion or acceptance, in that moment, we know we are developing further gratitude.

> *"The depth and willingness with which we serve is a direct reflection of our gratitude."*

As you continue to refine your parenting in a Complex Family, you will come to realise that you are fully *responsible* for your *reactions* or *responses* to life. This does not mean, however, that you are responsible for *life's events*. It is your responses to them that are always your choice — 100 percent of the time.

I have outlined five principles that give greater clarity to your relationships in the Complex Family environment, and four tools to use to effectively change your current mindset from that of reaction to response as it heals much of the pain. Finally, these four tools will assist you to develop the three attitudes that will bring about great transformation in your life.

Going forward from here, the ongoing daily practice of this chapter will enhance the effects of all of the suggestions, advice, theories, and knowledge you have gained from the first eight chapters.

Chapter Ten
Graduation

Moving beyond complex to family.

Continuing to Learn

A most rewarding moment you can have as parents in a Complex Family are when you see your children embrace their family as a whole. Regardless of whether it's traditional or complex in structure, your family has become a whole family extended, and your children are free to discuss and discover the differences between two homes, two, three, or four parents, and two distinct cultures. Your family then lives and breathes as a whole and respects each other's uniqueness, while you continue to develop attitudes of greater harmony, teamwork, and the demonstration of authentic and genuine love for your children. In this way your family graduates and simply becomes *Family*.

Although your structure may once have been the outdated model of a broken home or split family, you now know you have succeeded in transforming it into a Complex Family. Within this environment, you have come to understand the reasons for, and perceived limitations of, what used to be failure and doom; instead, you have brought your children into hope. It enables you to be a stunning family that bears witness to the power of your chosen responses through every moment of every day.

Our Leavee puts away the blanket of blame they previously used to protect and defend their pain, and instead bathes in the beauty of full sunlight that illuminates their path towards fresh hope and new dreams. They will begin to live a life of personal abundance and prosperity, where their children continue to develop into fantastic adults.

Our Leaver gives up the guilt and fear of judgement, the disappointment and frustrations, and instead, embraces an attitude of acceptance; this is so contagious it invites the family to move beyond damaging traditional patterns and become an example of authentic living. They become flag-bearers where love, understanding, and acceptance are normal and their children dare to dream beyond any previously perceived limitations as they become willing to effect change in the world.

> Your family lives and breathes respect for differences ... in this way your Complex Family graduates to simply family.

For all of you, there will still be moments when you fall back into an attitude that manages to persist — even a decade or two after divorce or separation; however, if your constant intention is to become neutral, if it is your intention to accept that you have experienced divorce and it no longer defines you, you and your family will be a living example of what is meant by the *Highest Good of All*, and natural in both essence and function.

Getting it Working Well

Dressed in your black gown with mortarboard in hand, you approach graduation. You can see beyond the wreckage and carnage that was once a broken home or split family; you have begun to have your Complex Family work well. While there may still be times that feel a bit harder than others, maintaining the flow has become your focus.

Graduation does not mean you stop learning — ask any student, even those with a PhD — we all continue to learn throughout life; we do this with each new experience encountered. Your graduation simply means you have moved beyond the emotional complexity of your Complex Family to become family, embracing the larger whole in its entirety, value, and blessing.

Before closing this writing, I want to leave you with a few tips — things that we have continued to do regardless of how many years have passed. For all the strength that we've built, we recognise it is because of love shared for three children that we are connected, and each stage of development has new issues, opinions that conflict, and further complexities to be resolved.

Parenting Team Meetings

We extended the core idea we use with family meetings into Parenting Team Meetings. The intention is to keep these meetings light, although we have certainly experienced a variety of levels in intensity over the years, depending on topics discussed or issues that arise. We keep them going at fairly regular intervals even if there doesn't appear to be much that needs to be discussed. After all, what parent cannot think of things to discuss regarding their children? It is often as simple as having a coffee catch-up and keeping the lines of communication open; this demonstrates that we are always available and willing to be part of the great parenting game.

These Parenting Team Meetings are a great dampener on children (of any age) who feel they have to watch what they say in the presence of the others, or indeed, play one set of parents off against the other. I suppose they give it a go from time to time just to remind themselves of the openness that exists between the Team, but it quickly has them gain the confirmation that their Complex Family operates as a greater whole.

On average most parents find that a catch-up once a term is reasonable during younger children's stages; however, with the complexity of the teen years, this may change. They may become more frequent if intervention is needed, or if the teen years are particularly smooth, they may drop to twice a year, but I do not suggest any less than this. Once at Christmas for the family drink and nibbles together where we show gratitude and genuine appreciation of the year's effort gone into raising great children, and the other mid year, when a little check up and reminder of the basics can help keep things on track.

Another good reason to keep meetings going is to remind yourselves of the differences experienced between the two home environments. You can sometimes forget how much you've changed since your married days, and become complacent about the diversity your children have grown to accept as home. Although they seem to flow effortlessly between the two lifestyles and customs, when you take the time to touch base, you will be reminded of how unique your family culture has become — and a few troubling pieces of the puzzle can fall into place. Sometimes, this get-together even provides answers to questions you didn't know you were waiting to ask.

Short Cuts take a Long Time

In life we sometimes find that by taking what we perceive to be a short cut it winds up to be a long route instead. This also applies to the Complex Family situation, so don't become complacent and think you can start cutting corners. Although the new relationships can become remarkably good, you are nonetheless still dealing with one that is held together through the bonds of love for your children, and is, perhaps not really one of your personal preference; otherwise, you would probably not be divorced. It can be very easy, because of the familiarity, to take certain liberties for granted and forget how little you are involved in the other side of your Parenting Team's daily life. At times you may not even know if they are experiencing a down moment inside life's up and down roller-coaster. To presume or take for granted the status quo, and expect it to be without effort and difficult communication from time to time, is to beg for a moment of hard reality to strike.

> Be wary of what appears to be a short-cut.

Be wary of what appears to be a short-cut. Those moments when you think it's okay not to pass on the message from school, or you give short notice for a family event, will be the ones that come back to bite you. When you become complacent because you've had your way for such a long time that you've come to expect it as normal, there will be the danger of forgetting the delicacy of the relationship, and you can put a little too much pressure on the cord that holds you together. This cord will give you a little ping as a gentle reminder, so take heed and don't wait for it to snap.

The Constant Audience

Being a great parent requires us to be all we can be, do all we can do, and share all we have to share; being a great parent inside a Complex Family, does not limit any of this, but rather enhances our opportunities to thrive with it all. Parenting inside a Complex Family requires us to constantly change tack, yet remain steadfast; to become flexible and yet be rock-solid; be gentle yet firm; the nurturer and provider; the coach and team player; the counsellor and constable; and the entertainer and the oracle. This is why it's such a challenge. And further more, just when we think we have it figured out, our child will develop into the next phase, so we're back to learning all over again.

Inside a Complex Family, unlike the traditional family, there is constant comparison. It highlights the differences in parenting, beliefs, lifestyles, possessions, incomes, education, humour, morals, passion, and so on. It is the constant comparisons the children make, this natural observing that constantly challenges us, inviting us to consciously choose, rather than mindlessly follow along in a reactive pattern.

This constant other sits there reminding us to be careful, thoughtful, and kind, even when we don't feel like it. It encourages us to remain trusting, courageous, and supportive, even when, at times, we doubt our ability to do so.

However, it is only fair to say that the presence of this continual comparing is not always neutral; at times, it can hold more of a subtle feeling of threat. In those times that we fail the children, (and we all do), it hurts more than it otherwise would. Not only because we have screwed up, but more so because our frailty and humanness becomes exposed again to the Ex. The constant feeling of being watched and scrutinised by one we once knew so well leaves us feeling vulnerable because we know the latest calamity, setback, or trip-up will be another story carried forward with great sincerity and innocence by our darlings.

This ongoing presence adds to the constant pressure of parental striving to get it right every time. Any failure or screw up is seldom kept between our four walls, and at best, eight. This means, the times when life is hard, and we are too tired, worn out, or simply cannot be bothered, we know we have to. It is in these times we know that it's not only because of our dedication and commitment to the children that we rise up again and continue on, but also because that if we don't, someone else will. That momentary pause, laziness, or lack, could so easily become a feature of future negotiations, threats, or at the very least, the expected unpleasant conversations. We realise we cannot be lackadaisical in our choices or moods because the consequences will outlast the discomfort of momentary irritation.

Although, at first glance, it might seem fairly straight forward to simply tell the children to keep what happens inside your home to themselves, it is neither healthy nor smart to infer, suggest, or tell them that they must sensor or restrict their talk to us, or their other parent. To do so, is to reinforce the sense of division and throw them into living between two worlds.

Our Complex Family is where we celebrate the diversity, and discover the unity within it, without restricting the differences, or any of the resulting conversation, to appease our own shortfalls. I suggest you seek a balance between appropriateness, responsibility, and general telling of stories, without your children needing to take the parental relationship into account. If you do not want to hear the ins and outs of the latest movie they watched, you can change the subject; however, if it's about the time they shared as a family while watching the movie, it might be best to support the conversation. It may mean you hear continuous stories about their life where you are not a participant, and at times that may even hurt, but as a parent inside a Complex Family, you will do well to accept there is a constant sandpapering, the chipping, and the relentless gnawing of life being a mirror. It is this uncomfortable push out of parenting complacency that drives you to change and grow as a person, becoming a better parent for your children, and ultimately a better person for yourself.

> I could neither influence nor dictate what occurred inside their other home, but I could equip them with the means to handle it — and this became the greatest lesson of all.

> I struggled to find freedom inside comparison. For a while I was trying so hard to be a super parent — doing all the right things, making the best choices, and being the greatest leader of my family I could — I lived fearful of what a slip-up would mean. Only a few houses down the road was the constant reminder of how important it was for me to always be diligent. I knew that if I stopped, there was someone willing to start, and although I could not be replaced as mother, I knew the father was a substitute option on offer.

> Living free from the fear or threat was more of a wishful thought than an accomplishment I set out to achieve. The more pressing feelings of obligations, duty, and commitment, dimmed the watchful eye; however, I became nearly robotic and mechanical in my role as I lacked the spontaneity and joy that the parenting journey naturally provides.

It was when I finally embraced being divorced, and finally came to celebrate the goodness this complexity had brought into my life, that I stepped into freedom. I accepted the constraints of being a Complex Family, and welcomed how it gave greater direction and focus. I thrived with the reminders that every choice I make, does matter, that every moment in parenting does count; I realised how quickly the years roll past, especially when I am a parent only every second weekend and not the other. It came as an immense wakeup call to me. The realisation that although I had previously found divorce a curse, I could now embrace it for all the goodness it brought into my life — and I became better. A better mother, and indeed, a greater person.

Keep it Simple

When all is said and done, inside a Complex Family, it's about keeping things simple. Forget about trying to manipulate or influence the happenings or the lifestyle inside your Ex's home. Give up attempting to control or change the way your Ex wants to parent, and instead focus on who you are being as a parent and the home environment you are creating for your children. Turn your attention towards yourself as you become one of those who has experienced divorce — know that it has added to your life — and does not define you or your family.

Dealing with the Majors

When something of significance occurs inside your family, such as a teen in trouble with the law, drugs, pregnancy, or similar, the true strength of your Parenting Team will be seen. While there maybe individual assistance required, such as with addiction issues, the messages in this book do not alter concerning your parenting style, nor in relationship with your Ex. This is the moment when you all pull together, not apart, as you seek to find solutions, and refuse to look back at what could have, should have, or ought to have been.

This is the moment when you must step up and lead your family, as a parent, while you provide the genuine support this role affords.

Chapter 10 — Graduation

Regardless of all the temptation to behave otherwise, when faced with a major issue inside your Complex Family, strip it back to the bare basics and remember that you all must be guided by the same principles as you build toward the *Highest Good of All*.

A Chinese proverb became a cornerstone of comfort to me through the great distress of my life; it reminded me to live all the good I knew to be.

"The flower that blooms in adversity is the most rare and beautiful of all."

If your family has one of life's majors, bloom in the face of adversity, and take your place as a being both rare and beautiful.

Because They are Children

Over the years, people have asked why I have always been so passionately committed to raising my three children. It is not that I have no life outside my children; I certainly do. However, all schedules, commitments, and activities are arranged with them as top priority. There is little more reason needed for this other than . . . they are children. They do not earn it; they deserve it; just because.

Welcome to Parenting.

While I have given you some ideas, tools, principles, reasons, and suggestions that work — we do not get a handbook when we become parents, and I believe it is purposefully designed this way. I believe it is because parenting is about moving forward in each generation, not standing still. It is about the journey of learning on the job, learning from what has previously been done, building on the strengths of it and overcoming the weaknesses, while expanding into newness previously unknown.

> They are children. They do not earn it; they deserve it; just because.

Each generation has its unique challenges, obstacles, and pressures that its children need to be equipped to handle. History has seen some progressive, some comfortable, and some horrific circumstances that children have been born into. Our children are special. They are the next generation being raised to one day lead our world as they raise their own families, run their businesses, hold positions of political power, confront and solve further environmental issues, perpetuate religious views, become sporting heroes, gain artistic achievements, and educate others with literary brilliance.

Our children will have the opportunity to take the best of what we can offer — and enhance it. They need to continue the effort to overcome the foolish egocentric behaviours that generations — through decades and centuries — have used to cause suffering around the world — and we need to give them the greatest start for this lifelong quest. It only takes a generation or two to stand for change in the world; we have to start by being their parents first.

A New Era
As much as our society has the ability to influence our children's minds at ever earlier ages, we must now move beyond expecting good results from the old strategies of constant forbidding and punishment. Instead, we need to empower our children to grow their inner wisdom.

Our children's lives today are invaded at every moment they associate with the materialistic world; every television, street corner, billboard, movie, magazine, supermarket, gas station, entertainment centre, and so on, transmits messages of what they should want, have, or need — or what they should look like, love like, or experience. To attempt to protect them from all this media madness would be to have them live within a glass bubble; the results would be disempowering and unhealthy.

To raise great children, we need to equip them to handle what life has ahead, not train them to cower from it. They need to be prepared, courageous, and tenacious so they are able to grow with life's new opportunities, and not fearfully hide away from them.

Chapter 10 — Graduation

Your children are part of a new era. For them to move from merely surviving into thriving, they need to develop their own inner discipline because many of the external controls that kept previous generations inline are dissolving — and fast. This new era is stripping away the power that once was held in statements like, "Because I told you so"; parents today are being challenged to step up and give reasons, develop understanding, and be humble enough to say, "I don't know," when you no longer have an answer.

Being *real* is your modern day parenting challenge. Engage in life and be the example your children will model; be a source of inspiration as you motivate them to constantly enquire and as such, ignite their

> Make parenting count; teach your children how to own their values, morals, ethics, and codes by which they live.

passion for continual learning. Make parenting count, and teach your children how to own their values, morals, ethics, and codes by which they live. Let them think; teach them *how* not *what*; encourage them to question the status quo while you continue to support their enquiry. Accept that they will explore, discover and expand as humanity begins to evolve beyond slavery, discrimination, racism, sexism and all forms of prejudice.

> I learned to instill into the children a new way of thinking that did not rely on external controls or manipulation, but instead was birthed from within. I could neither influence nor dictate what occurred inside their other home, but I could equip them with the means to handle it — and this became the greatest lesson of all. Unknown to me at the time, I had been preparing my children for the massive global shift that is occurring, where the external controls we previously relied upon are being eroded, and inner personal discipline and responsibility will need to stand up and be proud.

To prepare your children to continue to evolve beyond the current limitations of the global community, it is going to take courage and conviction. They need to do more than adopt our way of thinking, they need to know what *their* values are, and understand why they believe them. They need to own them for themselves, so when called into question, they have the inner conviction to build or expand upon it. If we can give them this, they will continue to learn, change, and refine as they move through their adulthood.

Parenting Journey

Birthed into our child's spirit is grandeur, but it is only a seed holding potential. It is a seed that needs to be fostered, nurtured, and supported by us as parents, in circumstances where personal challenges are accepted as blessings, not curses. Where overcoming an obstacle becomes the situation they can grow from, not shy away from, as they inspire those around them. Where disagreements are not a reason to fight, but rather another chance to explore, understand, and gain an alternative perspective. Where right and wrong is measured with the intention, not only the outcome; where learning becomes a way of living and being, rather than only an undertaking inside an institution.

> Disagreements are not a reason to fight — rather another chance to explore, understand, and gain an alternative perspective.

When you do this, you will know you have started your child's journey into adulthood with a foundation strong enough to withstand life's trials. For as much as you might like to wish for a life free from hardship for your children, you know you have become the great person you are today because you rose through personal challenges as you learned lessons from a few of life's blows. If you don't already know this, you will come to realise that it was in your time of greatest need that the seed of potential cracked open and you became a better person. Without this, perhaps you would have been content in comfort, unwilling to discover how far you could stretch — thereby your opportunity for growth is lost.

So, although it is normal to want to protect your children from difficulties, or solve their problems for them, parenting is the privileged function of helping them to develop their foundation, so they can grow beyond you. It is the honour of standing aside as you congratulate them when they move forward and gain greater freedom, further clarity, release more judgements and prejudices than you yourself recognised. In much the same way the greatest leaders are not those who lead the most people, but rather those who develop the greatest leaders; great parenting is not the parent who controls or can boast the successful child, but rather the parent who humbly develops the greater parent for the following generation.

> To become a parent, is to invite one of the greatest learning experiences into our lives.

To become a parent, is to invite one of the greatest learning experiences into our lives; it is one journey we cannot undo, nor would most of us ever desire to. Even for those who have run from their responsibilities as a parent, there is still a child who still carries their own "My Mum" or "My Dad" title deep inside their heart. It is a journey for which most of us are nothing short of ill-prepared, and yet ironically, it is one where the consequences of those first two decades are lifelong. It is a journey that is entered into irrespective of any prejudicial delineations we have tried to enforce throughout the millennia, be it religion, wealth, race, creed, and so on; it matters not to the conceiving of a child. Becoming a parent comes from the greatest physical expression of love we can share, yet paradoxically, it does not even require this love to be in existence for its power to lift and place two more people onto the crowded highways of the parenting journey.

Embracing Complex Family Parenting

To wrap this up, let's look over what we have discussed as the major influences that affect our children's lives inside a Complex Family.

- We have the initial event: divorce, separation, or some form of family breakdown that shifts us out of the traditional family structure and creates in its place the Complex Family.

- We have the differences determined by which side of the divorcee coin we occupy: Leavee or Leaver - and the different reactions.

- We have looked into the *How To's* concerning the changes in a Complex Family; discussed Breaking the News, Care, Routines, etc.

- We looked at how we need to change our parenting styles to suit a Complex Family, and how the accent of parenting alters for discipline, sibling rivalry, and more.

- We discussed the inclusion of Stepparents and the challenges and highlights when extending the Parenting Team and establishing new relationship dynamics.

- We have discussed the Law, and matters of Money, and the influence our choices have on the years ahead for a Parenting Team.

- We have learned about five key Principles, four Tools and three Attitudes to develop, to continue our personal development as we live inside a Complex Family.

- And finally, if initially it is only for the sake of our children that we move beyond the disappointment, heartbreak and changes that divorce forces, and start living in a healthy Complex Family — let's do it for them.

Now, armed with knowledge, our next step is to be brave enough to live it. Some are frightened at the thought of stepping out of the normal chaotic zone, and fear they may not be able to do it, but none of us would be brave if we were not scared. Bravery needs scared in order for it to exist. Another may be dismissive of hope, believing this all sounds too good to be true. And more still may announce the impossibility of this working because, "You don't know my Ex." Without invalidating how true that statement is, I can add, every person says the same — and I hear the next line that follows with equal doggedness saying, "No, I know everyone says that, but my Ex really is…" This is normally quickly backed up by the strongest example they can pluck in support of their attitude, as they try to pry from my lips the return comment of, "Oh, I understand now. You're excused."

It is always challenging to change. It is very challenging to change the dynamics inside an environment where a precedent of irreconcilable differences already exists, as demonstrated by the fact we are divorced. The point is, however, if we want our children to no longer have to cope, suffer, or live between two worlds because of our adult decisions, we need to start building a Complex Family. We need to begin by stepping up and becoming great parents; parents who are beyond what we have or do, and become great people. We cannot solve all the problems that are inside our families, but we can stop causing or adding to them.

If we want world peace, we need to begin at home.

Complex Family Foundation

As part of the continuation of my personal passion and gift for developing our next generation for greatness, I have founded the Complex Family Foundation, with a team of like-minded people who share in the core vision. Our organisation provides ongoing support and education for parents, and those who are either part of, or are influenced by, the Complex Family.

To learn more about Complex Family Foundation, please go to www.ComplexFamily.com, where you will find updates on material, programs, speaking engagements, online workshops, forums, podcasts, and more.

Epilogue

Dear Reader; parent, stepparent, guardian, relative or friend,

My greatest achievement in life has not been the accumulation of riches, positions of power, or personal fame, it has been the most humbling of normal undertakings, and yet an immensely rewarding experience — being a great mother. It is a position and function carried out by millions worldwide; each of us brings to it our specialness, combined with the uniqueness of our children, to do the best we know how. Continuing the responsibility of raising my three children, I appreciate that it enables me to learn more than any other path I have walked.

Parenting continues to remind me of my humanness, vulnerability, and personal presence. How nature never fails to teach more wisdom and to show how life is full of perplexing paradoxes that invite us to peel yet another layer as we move towards living as our most authentic self. I have gleaned so much from my years of learning, and yet I see how much more there is to know. Each child is unique and brings fresh issues, new perspectives and further challenges; I am constantly both the teacher and the student in the school of parenting.

When I realised I was staring at the heavy dark doorway of broken homes and split families, I felt compelled to find an alternative route. A way where my efforts to compensate for the breach in my children's upbringing was not a handicap they needed to endure, but would preferably offer a life-giving experience we could all benefit from. Every step of the journey in creating a Complex Family for my three children has been a process of discovery and personal growth. It has been much like the formation of diamonds under extreme pressure that has made my family become as beautiful as it is today. Using the chisel of choice to create our unique and precious Complex cut, our family has been blessed by living in unity while experiencing great diversity.

My heartfelt desire, as more families face the reality of that same choice, is that they will embrace the new parenting model of a Complex Family; one where children are no longer imprisoned by statistical doom, but rather are developed to become great leaders of nations and corporations; and agents of change, where they are prepared to bring greater harmony to the future. Where personal discipline and personal responsibility are not virtues lost in a bygone era, but rather a new code that our young people embrace for themselves, learning and evolving beyond decades of adult and parental foolishness.

With a non-compromising promise to lead my children throughout their developmental years, I dedicated myself to embracing all that was thrown across my path. There have been moments that had I been given a second chance, I would rather redo. This journey has not been without its periods of pain and suffering, and there were times I stumbled; but I can say that I got up at least one more time than I fell. For this, I can be thankful that I have learned how perfection is not the absence of flaws, but rather the perspective through which we view the meaning of perfection itself. It has been through experience that I have developed wisdom, and in so doing I have gained a new freedom in being a parent, partner, daughter, niece, aunt, cousin, and friend. Divorce did not become perfect to me until I embraced the perfection of the gift it handed me to cherish forever.

I will leave you with a poem I have gratefully turned to when I needed perspective in parenting, and one I trust will give you the same encouragement and reminders it has given me.

Jill Darcey.

Parenting

By Kahlil Gibran

Your children are not your children,

They are the sons and daughters of Life's longing for itself.

They come through you, but not from you,

And though they are with you, yet they belong not to you.

You may give them your love, but not your thoughts,

For they have their own thoughts.

You may house their bodies, but not their souls,

For their souls dwell in the house of tomorrow, which you cannot visit, not even in your dreams.

You may strive to be like them, but seek not to make them like you.

For life goes not backward, nor tarries with yesterday.

You are the bows from which your children as living arrows are sent forth.

The archer sees the mark upon the path of the infinite, and he bends you with his might that his arrows may go swift and far.

Let your bending in the archer's hand be for gladness;

For even as he loves the arrow that flies, so he loves the bow that is stable.

www.ComplexFamily.com

Complex Family Foundation's purpose is to deliver world-class programs, inspiring and practical by nature, for the development of Complex Families globally.

We understand the complications, and the uniqueness, of parenting when you no longer live together; we walk beside you through the journey ahead.

To order further copies of *Parenting with the Ex Factor*, please visit www.ComplexFamily.com.

Resources

The following are a very small portion of the texts that have influenced my learnings.

Kids Are Worth It! by Barbara Coloroso

Dreams From My Father by Barack Obama

Eastern Body Western Mind by Anodea Judith

Journey Into A New Consciousness by Christophe Christianson

A New Earth by Eckhart Tolle

The Isaiah Effect by Gregg Braden

The Moon Under Her Feet by Clysta Kinstler

You'll See It When You Believe It by Dr Wayne W. Dyer

Discovering The Inner Self by Dr David A. Phillips

The Invitation by Oriah Mountain Dreamer

Eat Pray Love by Elizabeth Gilbert

Committed by Elizabeth Gilbert

www.ingramcontent.com/pod-product-compliance
Lightning Source LLC
Chambersburg PA
CBHW031248230426
43670CB00005B/92